SOA and WS-BPEL

Composing Service-Oriented Solutions with PHP and ActiveBPEL

Yuli Vasiliev

BIRMINGHAM - MUMBAI

SOA and WS-BPEL

First published: September 2007

Production Reference: 1040907

Published by Packt Publishing Ltd.
32 Lincoln Road
Olton
Birmingham, B27 6PA, UK.

ISBN 978-1-847192-70-7

www.packtpub.com

Cover Image by Vinayak Chittar (vinayak.chittar@gmail.com)

Credits

Author
Yuli Vasiliev

Reviewer
Robert Mark

Acquisition Editor
Priyanka Baruah

Technical Editor
Akshara Aware

Editorial Manager
Dipali Chittar

Project Manager
Patricia Weir

Project Coordinator
Abhijeet Deobhakta

Indexer
Bhushan Pangaonkar

Proofreader
Chris Smith

Production Coordinator
Shantanu Zagade

Cover Designer
Shantanu Zagade

About the Author

Yuli Vasiliev is a software developer, freelance author, and consultant currently specializing in open-source development, Oracle technologies, and service-oriented architecture (SOA). He has over 10 years of software development experience as well as several years of technical writing experience. He wrote a series of technical articles for Oracle Technology Network (OTN) and *Oracle Magazine*.

About the Reviewer

Robert Mark is a Senior Programmer at the McGill University in Montreal, Canada. He completed his B.A. in Environmental Studies specializing in Geographical Information Systems at the University of Winnipeg in 1995. He then went on to complete a Computer Programmer Analyst Diploma at Humber College in Toronto, Canada. He has written articles for Oracle Technical Network and *php | architect* and has been a reviewer of several journals, technical papers, and books.

Table of Contents

Preface

Web services, while representing independent units of application logic, of course, can be used as stand-alone applications fulfilling requests from different service requestors. However, the real power of web services lies in the fact that you can bind them within service compositions, applying the principles and concepts of Service-Oriented Architecture. Ideally, web services should be designed to be loosely coupled so that they can potentially be reused in various SOA solutions and used for a wide range of service requestors.

When utilized within an SOA, services are part of a business process determining the logical order of service activities—logical units of work performed by one or more services. Today, the most popular tool for organizing service activities into business processes is Web Services Business Process Execution Language (WS-BPEL), a language defining an execution format for business processes operating on services. While it is not a trivial task to create a business process definition with WS-BPEL from scratch, using a graphical WS-BPEL tool can significantly simplify this process.

It's fairly obvious that examples and practice are much more valuable than theory when it comes to discussions of how to build applications using specific development tools. Unlike many other books on SOA in the market, *SOA and WS-BPEL: Composing Service-Oriented Solutions with PHP and ActiveBPEL* is not focused on architecture. Instead, with the help of many examples, it discusses practical aspects of SOA and WS-BPEL development, showing you how to apply architecture in practice. The examples in this book are presented in a way that anyone can understand and apply.

As the name implies, the main idea behind this book is to demonstrate how you can implement service-oriented solutions using PHP and ActiveBPEL Designer—free software products allowing you to effectively distribute service processing between the web/PHP server and ActiveBPEL orchestration engine. When it comes to building data-centric services, the book explains how to use MySQL or Oracle Database XE, the most popular free databases.

What This Book Covers

Chapter 1, Web Services, SOA, and WS-BPEL Technologies is an introductory chapter that provides an overview of the service-oriented technologies used throughout the book, explaining how these technologies can be utilized in a complementary way.

Chapter 2, SOAP Servers and Clients with PHP SOAP Extension begins with a simple example on how to use the PHP SOAP Extension to build a service requestor and service provider, using the request-response message exchange pattern. Then, it moves on to a complicated case study showing how the predefined classes of the PHP SOAP Extension can be extended when implementing complex message exchange patterns.

Chapter 3, Designing Data-Centric Web Services explains how to use the two most popular databases today, MySQL and Oracle, when building data-centric Web services, and how to move some part of the web service logic into the database to benefit from distributing the processing between the web/PHP and database servers.

Chapter 4, Building Web Services Applications shows how to combine a set of services into a composition without defining an orchestration process. It also provides an example of how message-level security can be implemented in a Web services application.

Chapter 5, Composing SOA Solutions with WS-BPEL discusses how to leverage the concepts behind service orientation with WS-BPEL, with an emphasis on how to implement service-oriented orchestrations. It shows how you can achieve better reusability by shredding business process logic into a series of primitive activities.

Chapter 6, ActiveBPEL Designer explains in detail how to compose service-oriented solutions with ActiveBPEL Designer—a free, fully-functional, graphical tool for WS-BPEL process design, debugging, and simulation.

Chapter 7, WS-BPEL Process Modeling focuses on how to implement parallel processing of activities within a WS-BPEL process. It also discusses asynchronous communication as an efficient way to call partner services without blocking the execution of the calling WS-BPEL process.

Appendix A, Setting Up Your Working Environment walks through the steps needed to install and configure the software components required to follow the book examples.

Conventions

In this book, you will find a number of styles of text that distinguish between different kinds of information. Here are some examples of these styles, and an explanation of their meaning.

There are three styles for code. Code words in text are shown as follows: "We can include other contexts through the use of the `include` directive."

A block of code will be set as follows:

```
<?php
 //File: SoapClient_typed.php
 require_once "obj2Arr.php";
 $wsdl = "http://localhost/WebServices/wsdl/po_imp.wsdl";
```

When we wish to draw your attention to a particular part of a code block, the relevant lines or items will be made bold:

```
<?php
 //File purchaseOrder_typed.php
 require_once 'obj2Dom.php';
 class purchaseOrder {
   function placeOrder($po) {
```

New terms and **important words** are introduced in a bold-type font. Words that you see on the screen, in menus or dialog boxes for example, appear in our text like this: "clicking the **Next** button moves you to the next screen".

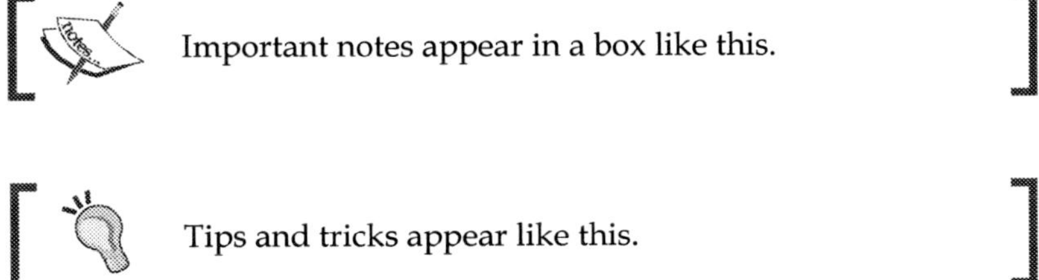

Important notes appear in a box like this.

Tips and tricks appear like this.

Reader Feedback

Feedback from our readers is always welcome. Let us know what you think about this book, what you liked or may have disliked. Reader feedback is important for us to develop titles that you really get the most out of.

To send us general feedback, simply drop an email to `feedback@packtpub.com`, making sure to mention the book title in the subject of your message.

If there is a book that you need and would like to see us publish, please send us a note in the **SUGGEST A TITLE** form on `www.packtpub.com` or email `suggest@packtpub.com`.

If there is a topic that you have expertise in and you are interested in either writing or contributing to a book, see our author guide on `www.packtpub.com/authors`.

Customer Support

Now that you are the proud owner of a Packt book, we have a number of things to help you to get the most from your purchase.

Downloading the Example Code for the Book

Visit `http://www.packtpub.com/support`, and select this book from the list of titles to download any example code or extra resources for this book. The files available for download will then be displayed.

The downloadable files contain instructions on how to use them.

Errata

Although we have taken every care to ensure the accuracy of our contents, mistakes do happen. If you find a mistake in one of our books—maybe a mistake in text or code—we would be grateful if you would report this to us. By doing this you can save other readers from frustration, and help to improve subsequent versions of this book. If you find any errata, report them by visiting `http://www.packtpub.com/support`, selecting your book, clicking on the **Submit Errata** link, and entering the details of your errata. Once your errata are verified, your submission will be accepted and the errata added to the list of existing errata. The existing errata can be viewed by selecting your title from `http://www.packtpub.com/support`.

Questions

You can contact us at `questions@packtpub.com` if you are having a problem with some aspect of the book, and we will do our best to address it.

1
Web Services, SOA, and WS-BPEL Technologies

Service-Oriented Architecture (SOA), as an architectural platform, is adopted today by many businesses as an efficient means for integrating enterprise applications built of Web services—loosely coupled pieces of software that encapsulate their logic within a distinct context and can be easily combined into a composite solution. Although building applications that enable remote access to resources and functionality is not new, doing so according to the principles of service orientation, such as loose coupling, represents a relatively new approach to building composite solutions.

Nowadays, the most common way to build composite applications based on service-oriented principles is to use the Service-Oriented Architecture, Web services, and WS-BPEL (Web Services Business Process Execution Language) technologies together.

While Web Services is a technology that defines a standard mechanism for exposure and consumption of data and application logic over Internet protocols such as HTTP, WS-BPEL is an orchestration language that is used to define business processes describing Web services' interactions, thus providing a foundation for building SOA solutions based on Web services. So, to build an SOA solution utilizing Web services with WS-BPEL, you have to perform the following steps:

- Build and then publish Web services to be utilized within an SOA solution
- Compose the Web services into business flows with WS-BPEL

This chapter gives an overview of the Web services, SOA, and WS-BPEL technologies and how these technologies are interrelated. It also contains references to related documentation and other chapters of this book, which discuss the topics touched upon in this introductory chapter in greater detail. If you already have a basic knowledge of the above technologies, feel free to skip this chapter.

Web Services

The Web Services technology provides an efficient way to share application logic across multiple machines running various operating systems and using different development environments. To achieve this, Web Services utilizes the SOAP, WSDL, XML Schema, and some other XML-based technologies, providing a standards-based approach to overcoming the platform and language differences.

The following sections give you an overview of these technologies, explaining how they fit into the big picture.

Communicating via SOAP

In a nutshell, SOAP is a messaging protocol used to transfer application data in XML format over a transport protocol, such as HTTP. Nowadays, Web service applications employ SOAP as a standard protocol for exchanging information in a decentralized, distributed manner.

For detailed information about SOAP, you can refer the W3C SOAP Recommendation documents. Links to these documents can be found at `http://www.w3.org/TR/soap/`.

SOAP-based interfaces interact with each other by means of SOAP messages that are specially formatted XML documents used to carry data and metadata. The general structure of a SOAP message is shown below:

```
<SOAP-ENV:Envelope ...>
   <SOAP_ENV:Header>
   ...
   ...
   </SOAP_ENV:Header>
   <SOAP_ENV:Body>
   ...
   ...
   </SOAP_ENV:Body>
</SOAP-ENV:Envelope ...>
```

As you can see in the previous code snippet, an XML document representing a SOAP message consists of the following elements:

- An `Envelope` element wrapping the entire message.
- A `Header` element, which is actually optional and may contain subelements carrying metadata associated with the message.

- A `Body` element, which contains the payload of the message. This element may contain an optional fault element, which describes an error if it occurs.

While SOAP messages may be used in various message exchange scenarios, the most popular one is the request/response pattern, which is normally used when calling a remote function exposed by a Web service. Diagrammatically, the request/response scenario might look like the following figure:

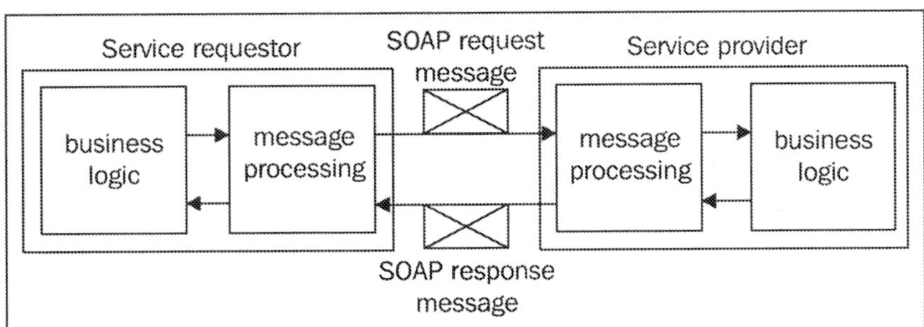

As you can see in the above figure, both the service requestor and service provider include the message processing logic required to send/receive and process SOAP messages involved in the request/response scenario used here. If the service requestor is calling a remote function exposed by the service provider, the request message is supposed to carry the values of the parameters passed to the exposed function. After the request message is received, the service provider processes it, extracting the payload (in this case, the parameters passed to the function) from the envelope. Then, the requested function is invoked, utilizing the parameters specified. Once the function result is ready, the service provider wraps this result in a SOAP envelope and sends it back to the service requestor in the response message. The service requestor in turn extracts the function result from the response message and sends it to the calling code.

[In Chapter 2, you will learn how to implement service providers and service requestors with PHP using the PHP SOAP extension.]

Now that you have a rough idea of how the remote procedure call (RPC) scenario works with SOAP, let's look at an example.

Suppose you have a Web service that exposes the `getOrderStatus` function, taking the number of a purchase order as the parameter and returning the status of that order as the result.

It is important to understand that the `getOrderStatus` function discussed in this example may be implemented in any programming language and run on any platform, provided they allow you to expose this function through SOAP. The fact is that Web services hide the details of underlying logic from their consumers, publicly exposing only their interfaces. In the following chapters, you will see a few examples of implementing service underlying logic with PHP.

The following figure depicts a scenario where a service requestor invokes the `getOrderStatus` function exposed as a Web service:

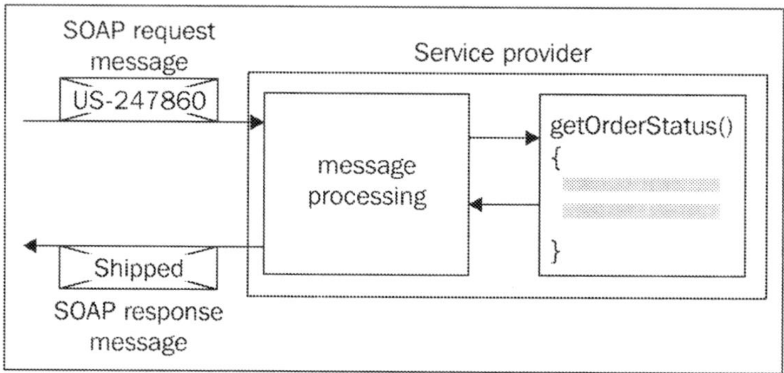

The general steps performed at run time are the following:

1. The service requestor sends a SOAP request message containing the number of a purchase order to the service provider.
2. The service provider processes the request message, extracting the PO number from the SOAP envelope.
3. The service provider invokes the `getOrderStatus` underlying function, passing the extracted PO number as the parameter.
4. The service provider encapsulates the result produced by the `getOrderStatus` function into a SOAP response message.
5. The service provider sends the SOAP response message back to the requestor.

In this example, the SOAP request message sent to the Web service provider might look like the following:

```
<?xml version="1.0" encoding="UTF-8"?>
<SOAP-ENV:Envelope
xmlns:SOAP-ENV="http://schemas.xmlsoap.org/soap/envelope/">
```

```
  <SOAP-ENV:Body>
   <SOAP-ENV:getOrderStatus>
    <body>US-247860</body>
   </SOAP-ENV:getOrderStatus>
  </SOAP-ENV:Body>
</SOAP-ENV:Envelope>
```

As you can see, the body of the above SOAP message contains the purchase order number passed as the parameter to the `getOrderStatus` function. The response to this message might look like the following:

```
<?xml version="1.0" encoding="UTF-8"?>
<SOAP-ENV:Envelope
xmlns:SOAP-ENV="http://schemas.xmlsoap.org/soap/envelope/">
  <SOAP-ENV:Body>
   <SOAP-ENV:getOrderStatusResponse>
    <body>Shipped</body>
   </SOAP-ENV:getOrderStatusResponse>
  </SOAP-ENV:Body>
</SOAP-ENV:Envelope>
```

The `getOrderStatus` function may be designed so that it throws a SOAP exception when something goes wrong. For example, an exception may be thrown upon a failure to connect to the database that contains information about the purchase orders placed. A fault message generated by the Web service exposing the `getOrderStatus` function might look like the following:

```
<?xml version="1.0" encoding="UTF-8"?>
<SOAP-ENV:Envelope
xmlns:SOAP-ENV="http://schemas.xmlsoap.org/soap/envelope/">
  <SOAP-ENV:Body>
   <SOAP-ENV:Fault>
    <faultcode>SOAP-ENV:Server</faultcode>
    <faultstring>Failed to determine the order status</faultstring>
   </SOAP-ENV:Fault>
  </SOAP-ENV:Body>
</SOAP-ENV:Envelope>
```

As you can see, the `fault` section resides within the `body` section of the message, and includes two subelements detailing the fault that occurred, namely: `faultcode` and `faultstring`.

Binding with WSDL

Looking through the SOAP request message discussed in the preceding section, you may notice that it carries only the parameter for the `getOrderStatus` function exposed by the service. The message doesn't actually contain any information about how to get to the service, what remote function is to be invoked, and what that function is to return. Obviously, there must be another document that describes the Web service, providing all this information to consumers of the service.

Web Services Description Language (WSDL) provides a mechanism to describe Web services, making them available for external consumption. A WSDL service description is an XML document that defines how to communicate with the Web service, describing the way in which that Web service has to be consumed.

For detailed information about WSDL, you can refer to the Web Services Description Language (WSDL) W3C Note available at `http://www.w3.org/TR/wsdl`.

Actually, a WSDL service description document consists of two parts: logical and physical. The logical part of a WSDL describes the abstract characteristics of a Web service and includes the following sections:

- **types** is an optional section in which you can define types for the data being carried, normally using the XSD type system.
- **message** contains one or more logical parts representing input and output parameters being used with an operation.
- **operation** describes an action performed by the service, specifying input and output messages being used as parameters of the operation.
- **portType** establishes an abstract set of operations supported by the service.

The physical part of a WSDL describes the concrete characteristics of a Web service and includes the following sections:

- **binding** associates a concrete protocol and message format specifications to operations and messages defined within a particular port type established in the logical part of the document.
- **port** establishes an endpoint by associating a binding with a concrete network address.
- **service** contains one or more port elements representing related endpoints.

Turning back to the example discussed in the preceding section, the WSDL description document that describes the Web service exposing the `getOrderStatus` function might look like the following:

```
<?xml version="1.0" encoding="utf-8"?>
<definitions name ="poService"
             xmlns:http="http://schemas.xmlsoap.org/wsdl/http/"
             xmlns:soap="http://schemas.xmlsoap.org/wsdl/soap/"
             xmlns:xsd="http://www.w3.org/2001/XMLSchema"
             xmlns="http://schemas.xmlsoap.org/wsdl/"
        targetNamespace="http://localhost/WebServices/ch1/poService">
    <message name="getOrderStatusInput">
        <part name="body" element="xsd:string"/>
    </message>
    <message name="getOrderStatusOutput">
        <part name="body" element="xsd:string"/>
    </message>
    <portType name="poServicePortType">
        <operation name="getOrderStatus">
           <input message="tns:getOrderStatusInput"/>
           <output message="tns:getOrderStatusOutput"/>
        </operation>
    </portType>
    <binding name="poServiceBinding" type="tns:poServicePortType">
        <soap:binding style="rpc"
              transport="http://schemas.xmlsoap.org/soap/http"/>
        <operation name="getOrderStatus">
           <soap:operation
              soapAction=
                "http://localhost/WebServices/ch1/getOrderStatus"/>
           <input>
               <soap:body use="literal"/>
           </input>
           <output>
               <soap:body use="literal"/>
           </output>
        </operation>
    </binding>
    <service name="poService">
        <port name="poServicePort" binding="tns:poServiceBinding">
           <soap:address
              location=
                "http://localhost/WebServices/ch1/SOAPserver.php"/>
        </port>
    </service>
</definitions>
```

Let's go through this document in detail to understand the format of a WSDL description document.

The `definitions` element is the root in every WSDL document, wrapping all the WSDL definitions used in the document. Also, it houses the namespaces used within the document:

```
<definitions name ="poService"
           xmlns:http="http://schemas.xmlsoap.org/wsdl/http/"
           xmlns:soap="http://schemas.xmlsoap.org/wsdl/soap/"
           xmlns:xsd="http://www.w3.org/2001/XMLSchema"
           xmlns="http://schemas.xmlsoap.org/wsdl/"
              targetNamespace=
                  "http://localhost/WebServices/ch1/poService">
```

Next, you define the abstract definitions for the messages to be used for exchanging data. Here is the abstract definition for the message that will be used for carrying the input parameter for the `getOrderStatus` function:

```
<message name="getOrderStatusInput">
    <part name="body" element="xsd:string"/>
</message>
```

Here is the abstract definition for the message to be used for sending back the result of the `getOrderStatus` function:

```
<message name="getOrderStatusOutput">
    <part name="body" element="xsd:string"/>
</message>
```

Once you have messages defined, you can group them into operations, which in turn are grouped into a service interface. Here is the `portType` section representing an abstract view of the service interface, which, in this example, supports only one operation:

```
<portType name="poServicePortType">
    <operation name="getOrderStatus">
       <input message="tns:getOrderStatusInput"/>
       <output message="tns:getOrderStatusOutput"/>
    </operation>
</portType>
```

Now that you have an abstract service interface defined, you can go ahead and specify physical details of the data exchange. In a `binding` section, you map the abstract service interface defined within a `portType` section earlier into a concrete format, specifying the concrete protocol for data transmission and message format specifications. In this example, the binding section is used to deploy the `getOrderStatus` operation—the only operation supported by the service:

```
<binding name="poServiceBinding" type="tns:poServicePortType">
    <soap:binding style="rpc"
      transport="http://schemas.xmlsoap.org/soap/http"/>
    <operation name="getOrderStatus">
       <soap:operation soapAction=
          "http://localhost/WebServices/ch1/getOrderStatus"/>
       <input>
           <soap:body use="literal"/>
       </input>
       <output>
           <soap:body use="literal"/>
       </output>
    </operation>
</binding>
```

In the above snippet, you define a SOAP binding of the request-response RPC operation over HTTP and specify the concrete URI indicating the purpose of the SOAP HTTP request.

Finally, you use the service element hosting the port element to specify the physical address of the service.

```
<service name="poService">
    <port name="poServicePort" binding="tns:poServiceBinding">
       <soap:address location=
           "http://localhost/WebServices/ch1/SOAPServer.php"/>
    </port>
</service>
```

In the above example, the `getOrderStatus` function exposed as a Web service takes only one input parameter. But what if you need to pass more than one parameter to a Web service? Suppose you modify the `getOrderStatus` function so that it takes one more parameter, say, `poDate` specifying the date an order was placed. If so, you have to include a new `part` element to the message construct describing the logical abstract content of an input message in the WSDL document:

```
<definitions name ="poService"
            xmlns:http="http://schemas.xmlsoap.org/wsdl/http/"
            xmlns:soap="http://schemas.xmlsoap.org/wsdl/soap/"
            xmlns:xsd="http://www.w3.org/2001/XMLSchema"
            xmlns="http://schemas.xmlsoap.org/wsdl/"
            targetNamespace=
                         "http://localhost/WebServices/ch1/poService">
```

```
<message name="getOrderStatusInput">
      <part name="poNumber" element="xsd:string"/>
      <part name="poDate" element="xsd:string"/>
  </message>
  <message name="getOrderStatusOutput">
      <part name="body" element="xsd:string"/>
  </message>
...
</definitions>
```

Now, a SOAP message issued by a service requestor when calling the `getOrderStatus` remote function would look as follows:

```
<?xml version="1.0" encoding="UTF-8"?>
<SOAP-ENV:Envelope
xmlns:SOAP-ENV="http://schemas.xmlsoap.org/soap/envelope/">
 <SOAP-ENV:Body>
  <SOAP-ENV:getOrderStatus>
   <poNumber>US-247860</poNumber>
   <poDate>21-jan-07</poDate>
  </SOAP-ENV:getOrderStatus>
 </SOAP-ENV:Body>
</SOAP-ENV:Envelope>
```

Using XML Schema Types within WSDL Definitions

As you might notice, the WSDL document discussed in the preceding section doesn't contain the `types` construct. It is OK in this particular example because you don't actually need any custom XML Schema Definition (XSD) types when defining message parts in the WSDL document. Instead, you use the native XSD schema type `string`.

However, in some situations you may find it useful to utilize custom XML Schema types within a WSDL document. You can define custom XSD types within the `types` construct of a WSDL document and then reference them within message elements. For example, you might define a complex XSD type in the `types` section of the WSDL document discussed in the previous section and then reference this XSD type when creating the abstract definition of the output message:

```
<?xml version="1.0" encoding="utf-8"?>
<definitions name ="poService"
             xmlns:http="http://schemas.xmlsoap.org/wsdl/http/"
```

```
              xmlns:soap="http://schemas.xmlsoap.org/wsdl/soap/"
              xmlns:xsd1="http://localhost/WebServices/schema/"
              xmlns="http://schemas.xmlsoap.org/wsdl/"
              xmlns:xsd="http://www.w3.org/2001/XMLSchema"
              targetNamespace=
                           "http://localhost/WebServices/ch1/po.wsdl">
   <types>
    <xsd:schema
      targetNamespace="http://localhost/WebServices/schema/">
     <xsd:element name="poInfo">
        <xsd:complexType>
         <xsd:sequence>
           <xsd:element name="pono" type="xsd:string" />
           <xsd:element name="shippingDate" type="xsd:string" />
           <xsd:element name="status" type="xsd:string" />
         </xsd:sequence>
        </xsd:complexType>
     </xsd:element>
    </xsd:schema>
   </types>
  <message name="getOrderStatusInput">
        <part name="poNumber" element="xsd:string"/>
        <part name="poDate" element="xsd:string"/>
    </message>
    <message name="getOrderStatusOutput">
        <part name="poStatus" element="xsd1:poInfo"/>
    </message>

...

</definitions>
```

In this example, a response message sent by the service to a service requestor might look as follows:

```
<SOAP-ENV:Envelope
xmlns:SOAP-ENV="http://schemas.xmlsoap.org/soap/envelope/">
 <SOAP-ENV:Body>
  <SOAP-ENV:getOrderStatusResponse>
   <poStatus>
    <pono>US-247860</pono>
    <shippingDate>21-jan-07</shippingDate>
    <status>Shipped</status>
   </poStatus>
```

```
    </SOAP-ENV:getOrderStatusResponse>
  </SOAP-ENV:Body>
</SOAP-ENV:Envelope>
```

While this example shows how to define custom XML Schema types within the `types` construct of a WSDL document, you can achieve better reusability by putting XSD type definitions in a single XSD document.

Continuing with this example, you might remove the contents of the `types` construct into a separate file so that it's available, say, at `http://localhost/WebServices/schema/po.xsd`. The contents of this file should look as follows:

```
<?xml version="1.0"?>
 <schema targetNamespace="http://localhost/WebServices/schema/"
                          xmlns="http://www.w3.org/2001/XMLSchema">
   <element name="poInfo">
      <complexType>
       <sequence>
         <element name="pono" type="string" />
         <element name="shippingDate" type="string" />
         <element name="status" type="string" />
       </sequence>
      </complexType>
     </element>
 </schema>
</schema>
```

With that done, you can make use of the `import` statement in the WSDL document in order to associate the namespace representing the custom XSD schema with the location of the above document, thus making the contents of the schema available within the WSDL document:

```
<?xml version="1.0" encoding="utf-8"?>
<definitions name ="poService"
             xmlns:http="http://schemas.xmlsoap.org/wsdl/http/"
             xmlns:soap="http://schemas.xmlsoap.org/wsdl/soap/"
             xmlns:xsd1="http://localhost/WebServices/schema/"
             xmlns="http://schemas.xmlsoap.org/wsdl/"
             xmlns:xsd="http://www.w3.org/2001/XMLSchema"
             targetNamespace=
                          "http://localhost/WebServices/ch1/po.wsdl">
   <import namespace="http://localhost/WebServices/schema/"
           location="http://localhost/WebServices/schema/po.xsd"/>
  <message name="getOrderStatusInput">
        <part name="poNumber" element="xsd:string"/>
```

```
        <part name="poDate" element="xsd:string"/>
    </message>
    <message name="getOrderStatusOutput">
        <part name="poStatus" element="xsd1:poInfo"/>
    </message>
...
</definitions>
```

As you no doubt have realized, having XSD type definitions in separate files allows you to build more flexible, reusable, and modular solutions. In Chapter 3, you will see how the XSD documents referenced in WSDL can be then reused by an Oracle database holding and processing SOAP messages data.

Service-Oriented Architecture

While using Web services allows you to achieve interoperability across applications built on different platforms with different languages, applying service-oriented concepts and principles when building applications based on using Web services can help you create robust, standards-based, interoperable SOA solutions.

It is interesting to note that Service-Oriented Architecture, while providing architectural foundation for building service-oriented solutions, is not tied to a concrete technology or technology set. In contrast, it may be implemented with various technologies, such as DCOM, CORBA, or Web Services. However, only the Web Services technology set is currently the primary way to put SOA into practice.

Basic Principles of Service Orientation

As mentioned, to build an SOA solution based on Web services, you need to follow the service-orientation principles when pulling the services together into an application. Here are some of the key principles of service-orientation you need to keep in mind when designing SOA solutions:

- **Loose coupling** represents a relationship that allows the underlying logic of a service to change with minimal or no impact on the other services utilized within the same SOA. Loose coupling is the key principle of service orientation. Implementing services as loosely coupled pieces of software allows you to keep up with the other key principles of service orientation, such as service reusability, service autonomy, and service statelessness.

- **Service contract** represents service descriptions and other documents describing how a service can be programmatically accessed. In the *Binding with WSDL* section earlier in this chapter, you saw an example of a WSDL service description document that describes a service, defining the contract for that service.
- **Abstraction of underlying logic** means that a service publicly exposes only logic described in the service contract, hiding the implementation details from service consumers. This means that services interact with each other only via their public interfaces. As you learned in the preceding example, the WSDL descriptor describing a service actually provides the interface for service consumers.
- **Autonomy** means that services control only the logic they encapsulate. Dividing application logic into a set of autonomous services allows you to build flexible SOA solutions, achieving loose coupling, reusability, and composability.
- **Reusability** in service-orientation is achieved by distributing application logic among services so that each service can be potentially used by more than one service requestor. Building reusable services supports the principle of composability.
- **Composability** represents the ability of services to be grouped into composite services that coordinate an exchange of data between services being aggregated. For example, using an orchestration language, such as WS-BPEL, allows you to compose fine-grained services into more coarse-grained ones. WS-BPEL is discussed in the *WS-BPEL* section later in this chapter.
- **Statelessness** means that services don't maintain their state specific to an activity. Building stateless services encourage loose coupling, reusability, and composability.
- **Interoperability** between services is easily achieved as long as the services interact with each other through interfaces that are platform- and implementation-independent.
- **Discoverability** refers to standard mechanisms that make it possible for service descriptions describing services to be discovered by service requestors. Universal Description, Discovery, and Integration (UDDI) specification provides such a mechanism, which allows for publishing service descriptions documents in an XML-based registry, thus making them available for public use.

As you can see, most of these principles are tightly related. For example, if you bear the autonomy principle in mind when dividing application logic into services to be utilized within an SOA, you will have reusable, composable, and loosely coupled pieces of software that can be reused in future projects.

On the other hand, ignoring at least one principle of service-orientation makes it very hard to keep up with the others. For example, if you ignore the principle of statelessness when designing services, you will end up with less reusable and less composable building blocks for your SOA solutions.

Applying SOA Principles

Now that you know the key principles of service orientation, it's time to look at how these principles can be applied when designing SOA solutions. This section briefly discusses process of designing a service-oriented application, applying the service-orientation principles outlined in the preceding section.

The service-oriented analysis phase is the first one in the process of designing a service-oriented application. Regardless of whether you are going to build an SOA solution upon the existing application logic or build it from scratch, you have to consider the following questions:

- Which services are required to satisfy business requirements?
- How should application logic be divided between services?
- How should services be composed to implement the required SOA solution?

The easiest way to understand what has to be done at this stage is by taking up an example.

Imagine you run an online magazine that specializes in publishing technical articles submitted by technical people working on a contract basis. When a potential author submits an article proposal, you look through it and then either accept it or reject it, depending on your current editorial needs and some other things. Here are the general steps you perform upon accepting a proposal:

1. Save the proposal in the database.
2. Save information about the author (for new authors only).
3. Notify the author about accepting the proposal.
4. Issue a PO.
5. Send the PO to the author.

Now, suppose you want to design an SOA solution automating this process.

As mentioned earlier, the first thing you have to determine is which services have to be built. Keeping in mind the service-orientation principles outlined in the preceding section, you might create the following services to be then used as building blocks in the SOA solution being designed:

- Proposal service
- Author service
- Purchase order service
- Notification service

As you can see, the first three services in the above list are entity-centric, representing corresponding business entities.

> There are two main approaches for designing services representing business logic: entity-centric and task-centric. While a task-centric service is tightly bound to a specific task and so has a poor chance of reuse, an entity-centric service represents a specific business entity, standing a good chance of being reused in solutions dealing with the same business entity. Both the approaches are discussed in more detail later in Chapter 7, which focuses on issues related to service-oriented business modeling.

An entity-centric service usually provides a full set of operations required to manipulate an instance of a specific business entity. For example, the Proposal service might support the following set of operations to fulfill processing requirements:

- `saveProposal`
- `getProposalById`
- `getProposalByTitle`
- `getProposalsByAuthor`
- `getProposalsByTopic`

Assuming that submitted proposal documents have a certain structure (say, each proposal includes the `Topic` and `Outline` sections), the above list of operations supported by the `Proposal` service might need to be expanded to include some operations responsible for retrieving specific parts of a proposal.

However, it is important to realize that including new operations impacts on the service interface, making you edit the WSDL document describing the service each time you add a new operation. One way to work around this issue is to use parameter-driven operations that invoke the required piece of underlying logic depending on the arguments passed in. In this case, the function encapsulating the underlying logic of a parameter-driven operation delegates the work to some other function where the real work is done.

For example, you might expose a single operation for getting the contents of a proposal, passing parameters identifying whether to find the proposal document by ID or title and which part of the proposal must be returned. In this case, a request message issued by a requestor to invoke the `getProposal` operation might look as follows:

```
<SOAP-ENV:Envelope
xmlns:SOAP-ENV="http://schemas.xmlsoap.org/soap/envelope/">
 <SOAP-ENV:Body>
  <SOAP-ENV:getProposal>
    <IdType>title</IdType>
    <IdValue>Building services with PHP and Oracle XML DB</IdValue>
    <DocPart>all</DocPart>
  </SOAP-ENV:getProposal>
 </SOAP-ENV:Body>
</SOAP-ENV:Envelope>
```

As you no doubt have guessed, the parameters used in this example tell the service provider to return the entire document representing the proposal whose title is "Building services with PHP and Oracle XML DB". If you recall from the example discussed in the *Binding with WSDL* section, the message construct describing the logical abstract content of an input or output message that will be used with an RPC operation contains `part` elements to define parameters belonging to the operation. So, the message construct describing the above input message in the WSDL document might look as follows:

```
<definitions ...>

...

  <message name="getProposalInput">
        <part name="IdType" element="xsd:string"/>
        <part name="IdValue" element="xsd:string"/>
        <part name="DocPart" element="xsd:string"/>
    </message>

...

</definitions>
```

When the `getProposal` operation is executed, the input parameters arriving with the request message are passed to the underlying controller method, which in turn invokes an appropriate `getProposal*` underlying method, depending on the values of parameters passed in.

This approach allows you to cut down the number of operations exposed by a service while still providing the required functionality. Now, you may add a new method to the underlying layer of the service (normally, this layer is represented by a class) and make that method available for the service requestors without having to edit the WSDL document defining the service interface.

In Chapter 2, you will learn how to implement this approach when encapsulating the underlying logic of a service in a PHP class. When continuing with this discussion in Chapter 3, you will see an example of how you can improve the extensibility of parameter-driven service operations by passing operation parameters as XML. Then, Chapter 4 explains in detail how to build services providing generic, parameter-driven operations upon more fine-grained services, rather than directly upon classes or individual functions encapsulating entity-specific logic. With this approach, you actually employ two service layers to implement application logic manipulating business entities. The first layer includes the services that provide nothing but contact points to the specific operations supported by the services belonging to the second, underlying layer, allowing you to achieve a high level of loose coupling, composability, and reusability.

Now, assuming that you apply the above approach to all the business services mentioned earlier in this section, you might significantly cut down on the number of operations exposed by these services, publicly exposing only generic operations as shown in the following figure:

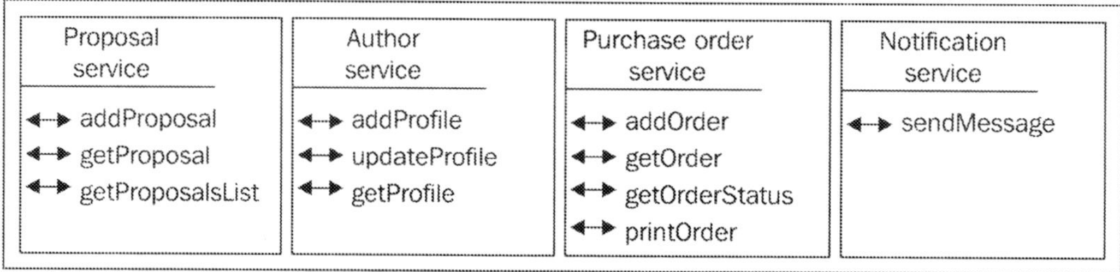

As you can see, each service depicted in the figure, except for the **Notification service**, supports more than one operation. This means that unlike the WSDL document discussed in the *Binding with WSDL* section, the WSDL documents describing the services discussed here will contain multi-operation `portType` and `binding` sections.

For example, the WSDL document describing the Proposal service might look like the following:

```
<?xml version="1.0" encoding="utf-8"?>
<definitions name ="proposalService"
       xmlns:http="http://schemas.xmlsoap.org/wsdl/http/"
       xmlns:soap="http://schemas.xmlsoap.org/wsdl/soap/"
       xmlns:xsd1="http://localhost/WebServices/schema/"
       xmlns:xsd="http://www.w3.org/2001/XMLSchema"
       xmlns="http://schemas.xmlsoap.org/wsdl/"
  targetNamespace="http://localhost/WebServices/ch1/proposal.wsdl">
   <import namespace="http://localhost/WebServices/schema/"
         location="http://localhost/WebServices/schema/proposal.xsd"/>
    <message name="addProposalInput">
        <part name="body" element="xsd1:proposalEntireDoc"/>
    </message>
    <message name="addProposalOutput">
        <part name="body" element="xsd:string"/>
    </message>
    <message name="getProposalInput">
        <part name="body" element="xsd1:proposalDetails"/>
    </message>
    <message name="getProposalOutput">
        <part name="body" element="xsd1:proposalDoc"/>
    </message>
    <message name="getProposalsListInput">
        <part name="body" element="xsd1:proposalsDetails"/>
    </message>
    <message name="getProposalsListOutput">
        <part name="body" element="xsd1:proposalsList"/>
    </message>
    <portType name="proposalServicePortType">
        <operation name="addProposal">
           <input message="tns:addProposalInput"/>
           <output message="tns:addProposalOutput"/>
        </operation>
        <operation name="getProposal">
           <input message="tns:getProposalInput"/>
           <output message="tns:getProposalOutput"/>
        </operation>
        <operation name="getOrderStatus">
           <input message="tns:getProposalListInput"/>
           <output message="tns:getProposalListOutput"/>
```

```
        </operation>
    </portType>
    <binding name="proposalServiceBinding"
      type="tns:proposalServicePortType">
        <soap:binding style="document"
           transport="http://schemas.xmlsoap.org/soap/http"/>
        <operation name="addProposal">
           <soap:operation
          soapAction="http://localhost/WebServices/ch1/addProposal"/>
           <input>
               <soap:body use="literal"/>
           </input>
           <output>
               <soap:body use="literal"/>
           </output>
        </operation>
        <operation name="getProposal">
           <soap:operation
          soapAction="http://localhost/WebServices/ch1/getProposal"/>
           <input>
               <soap:body use="literal"/>
           </input>
           <output>
               <soap:body use="literal"/>
           </output>
        </operation>
        <operation name="getProposalLists">
           <soap:operation
     soapAction="http://localhost/WebServices/ch1/getProposalLists"/>
           <input>
               <soap:body use="literal"/>
           </input>
           <output>
               <soap:body use="literal"/>
           </output>
        </operation>
    </binding>
    <service name="proposalService">
        <port name="proposalServicePort"
          binding="tns:proposalServiceBinding">
           <soap:address
         location="http://localhost/WebServices/ch1/SOAPServer.php"/>
        </port>
    </service>
</definitions>
```

Note that this WSDL document assumes that the data type definitions used when defining the messages involved are described in a separate XSD document located at `http://localhost/WebServices/schema/proposal.xsd`.

As you can see, in this WSDL document the `portType` construct contains three `operation` elements, each of which represents an abstract definition of an operation supported by the Proposal service. The binding information for each of these operations is then specified with a corresponding `operation` element defined within the `binding` construct.

SOA Compositions

Once you have created all the services needed to automate the process of submitting proposals, it's time to think about how to put them into action.

Actually, there are several ways in which services can be organized to compose an SOA solution. For example, you might create a composite service as a PHP script exposed as a Web service, and which programmatically invokes other services as necessary. However, the most common way to build an SOA composition is by using WS-BPEL, an orchestration language that allows you to create orchestrations—composite, controller services defining how the services being consumed will interoperate to get the job done.

Orchestration

An orchestration assembles services into an executable business process that is to be executed by an orchestration engine. Schematically, an orchestration might look like the following figure:

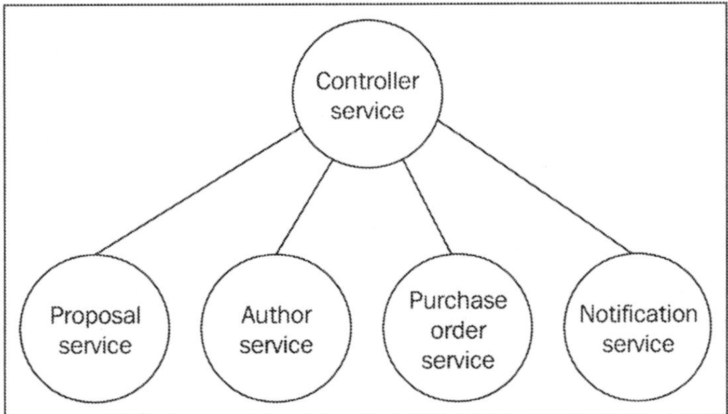

As you can see, the previous figure illustrates an assembly of services coordinated by the logic encapsulated in the controller service. This controller service may be a WS-BPEL business process, which when executed against the orchestration engine completes a certain business task. In this particular example, the controller service may be organized so that it completes the steps outlined at the beginning of the preceding section *Applying SOA Principles*.

Built with WS-BPEL orchestration language, a controller service, like any other service, should have a corresponding WSDL document describing the service to its consumers. Building WSDL definitions for composite services built with WS-BPEL is discussed in the *WSDL Definitions for Composite Services* section later in this chapter.

You can create an orchestration to be used as a service within another, larger orchestration. For example, the orchestration depicted in the previous figure might be a part of an WS-BPEL orchestration automating the entire editorial process—from accepting the proposal to publishing the article.

Choreography

The Web Services Choreography specification along with its corresponding Web Services Choreography Description Language (WS-CDL) provides another way to building SOA compositions. While WS-BPEL is used to orchestrate services into composite solutions usually expressing organization-specific business process flows, WS-CDL allows you to describe peer-to-peer relationships between Web services and/or other participants within or across trust boundaries.

Unlike an orchestration, choreography does not imply a centralized control mechanism, assuming control is shared between the interacting participants. What this means is that an orchestration represents an executable process to be executed by an orchestration engine in one place, whereas choreography in essence represents a description of how to distribute control between the collaborating participants, using no single engine to get the job done.

To define choreography, you create a WS-CDL choreography description document that will serve as the contract between the interacting participants. Specifically, a WS-CDL document describes the message exchanges between the collaborating participants, defining how these participants must be used together to achieve a common business goal. For example, there may be a choreography enabling collaboration between an orchestration, a controller service representing a WS-BPEL process, and a client service interacting with that controller service.

Schematically, this might look like the following figure:

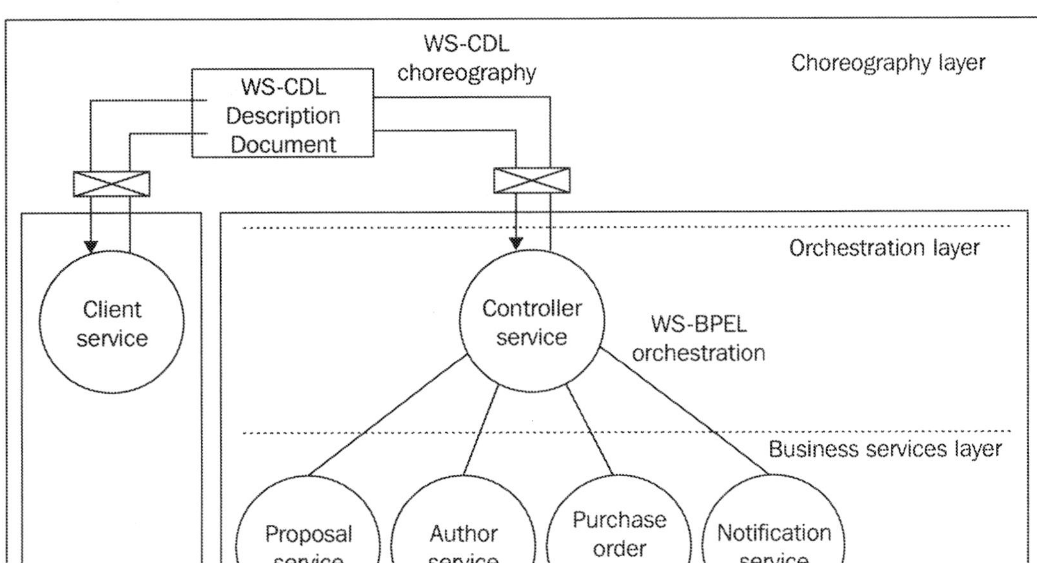

In the scenario depicted in the figure, the choreography layer is used to specify the peer-to-peer collaborations of two services. In particular, the WS-CDL choreography document describes message exchanges between the composite service discussed in the preceding section and one of its consumers.

> A full discussion of the Choreography specification and its corresponding WS-CDL language is outside the scope of this book. To learn more about these subjects, you can refer to the W3C document on WS-CDL, which can be found at `http://www.w3.org/TR/ws-cdl-10/`.

WS-BPEL

As mentioned earlier, WS-BPEL is an orchestration language used to describe execution logic of Web services applications by defining their control flows and providing a way for partner services to share a common context. To clarify, partner services are those that interact with the WS-BPEL process.

It is interesting to note that although WS-BPEL is currently the most popular executable business process language, it is not the only way to define execution logic of an application based on Web services. There are some other specifications, such as XLANG, WSFL, XPDL, and BPML, each of which might be used as an alternative to WS-BPEL.

WS-BPEL is based on several specifications, such as SOAP, WSDL, and XML Schema, where WSDL perhaps is the most important one. WSDL is what makes a service usable within composite services based on WS-BPEL. WS-BPEL allows you to define business processes interacting with cooperating services through WSDL descriptions. This will be explained in detail in the *WSDL Definitions for Composite Services* sub-section later in this section.

WS-BPEL Processes

With WS-BPEL, you build a business process by integrating a collection of Web services into a business process flow. A WS-BPEL business process specifies how to coordinate the interactions between an instance of that process and its partner services.

The following figure illustrates an example of a workflow diagram representing a WS-BPEL business process:

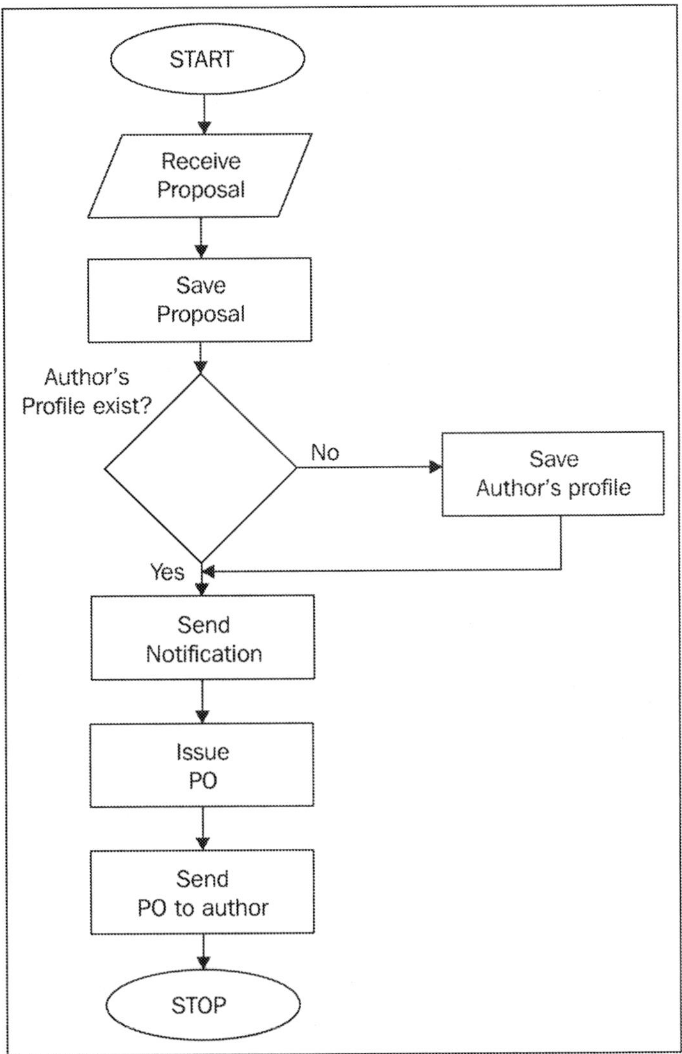

As you can see, the WS-BPEL process depicted in the figure integrates the services required to complete the steps performed after accepting a proposal into an end-to-end process, as outlined at the beginning of the *Applying SOA Principles* section earlier. In this particular example, the process integrates four Web services, as depicted in the figure shown in the *Orchestration* section earlier. As you will see in the next section, a WS-BPEL process connects to a Web service through a partner link defined in the WSDL document.

Apart from the ability to invoke multiple services, a WS-BPEL process may manipulate XML data and perform parallel execution, conditional branching, and looping to control the flow of the process. For example, in this process you use a switch activity, setting up the two branches. If the proposal being processed has been submitted by a new author, the process will call the Author service's operation responsible for saving the information about the author in the database. Otherwise, this step is omitted.

For simplicity's sake, this section illustrates only a workflow diagram of the WS-BPEL process, rather than executable BPEL code of that process. You will have plenty of opportunities to get your hands dirty with WS-BPEL code in Chapter 5. Then, in Chapter 6 you will learn how to design WS-BPEL processes with ActiveBPEL Designer.

WSDL Definitions for Composite Services

In the *Binding with WSDL* section earlier in this chapter, you learned how to use WSDL, providing a way for a service consumer to get knowledge of a service provider. Actually, WSDL plays a major role in SOA development. As mentioned, even a WS-BPEL orchestration can be associated with WSDL definitions, thus making it possible to treat that orchestration as a service itself that can be invoked by another service or can be a part of another orchestration or choreography.

Being a service itself, a WS-BPEL process should have a corresponding WSDL document, making it possible for client services to invoke the process. For example, the WS-BPEL process depicted in the previous figure might be associated with the following WSDL definition:

```
<?xml version="1.0" encoding="utf-8"?>
<definitions name="proposalProcessingService"
      xmlns="http://schemas.xmlsoap.org/wsdl/"
      xmlns:wsdl="http://schemas.xmlsoap.org/wsdl/"
      xmlns:soap="http://schemas.xmlsoap.org/wsdl/soap/"
      xmlns:xsd="http://www.w3.org/2001/XMLSchema"
      xmlns:xsd1="http://localhost/WebServices/schema/"
```

```
    xmlns:plink=
             "http://schemas.xmlsoap.org/ws/2004/03/partner-link/"
    targetNamespace=
            "http://localhost/WebServices/ch1/proposalProcessing/">
  <types>
   <xsd:schema targetNamespace=
        "http://localhost/WebServices/ch1/proposalProcessing.wsdl">
   <xsd:import namespace="http://localhost/WebServices/schema/"
     schemaLocation="http://localhost/WebServices/schema/
                                            propProc.xsd"/>
   </xsd:schema>
  </types>
  <message name="receiveProposalInput">
       <part name="body" element="xsd1:proposalDocType"/>
  </message>
  <message name="receiveProposalOutput">
       <part name="body" element="xsd:string"/>
  </message>
  <portType name="proposalProcessingServicePortType">
      <operation name="receiveProposal">
         <input message="tns:receiveProposalInput"/>
         <output message="tns:receiveProposalOutput"/>
      </operation>
  </portType>
  <plink:partnerLinkType name="proposalProcessingService">
        <plink:role name="proposalProcessingServiceRole">
          <portType="tns:proposalProcessingServicePortType"/>
       </plink:role>
  </plink:partnerLinkType>
</definitions>
```

As you can see, this WSDL document doesn't contain binding or service elements. The fact is that a WSDL document of a WS-BPEL process service contains only the abstract definition of the service and `partnerLinkType` sections that represent the interaction between the process service and its client services. In this particular example, the WSDL definition contains only one `partnerLinkType` section, supporting one operation used by a client to initiate the process.

> A `partnerLinkType` section defines up to two roles, each of which in turn is associated with a `portType` defined within the WSDL document earlier. WS-BPEL uses the partner links mechanism to define a relationship between a WS-BPEL process and the involved parties. As you will learn later in this section, a WS-BPEL process definition contains `partnerLink` elements to specify the interactions between a WS-BPEL process and its clients and partners. Each `partnerLink` in a WS-BPEL process definition document is associated with a `partnerLinkType` defined in a corresponding WSDL document. Schematically, this looks like the following figure (shown overleaf).

Once you have created the WSDL definition for a process service, make sure to modify WSDL documents of the services that will be invoked during the process execution as partner services. To enable a service to be part of a WS-BPEL orchestration, you might want to add a `partnerLinkType` element to the corresponding WSDL document. For example, to enable the **Notification service** to participate in the orchestration depicted in the previous figure, you would need to create the following WSDL document:

```
<?xml version="1.0" encoding="utf-8"?>
<definitions name="notificationService"
     xmlns="http://schemas.xmlsoap.org/wsdl/"
     xmlns:wsdl="http://schemas.xmlsoap.org/wsdl/"
     xmlns:soap="http://schemas.xmlsoap.org/wsdl/soap/"
     xmlns:xsd="http://www.w3.org/2001/XMLSchema"
     xmlns:plink=
    "http://schemas.xmlsoap.org/ws/2004/03/partner-link/"
     targetNamespace="http://localhost/WebServices/ch1/notification/">
   <message name="sendMessageInput">
        <part name="body" element="xsd:string"/>
   </message>
   <message name="sendMessageOutput">
        <part name="body" element="xsd:string"/>
   </message>
   <portType name="notificationServicePortType">
       <operation name="sendMessage">
          <input message="tns:sendMessageInput"/>
          <output message="tns:sendMessageOutput"/>
       </operation>
   </portType>
   <binding name="notificationServiceBinding"
                  type="tns:notificationServicePortType">
       <soap:binding style="document"
                transport="http://schemas.xmlsoap.org/soap/http"/>
```

```
        <operation name="sendMessage">
            <soap:operation soapAction=
                    "http://localhost/WebServices/ch1/sendMessage"/>
              <input>
                  <soap:body use="literal"/>
              </input>
              <output>
                  <soap:body use="literal"/>
              </output>
         </operation>
    </binding>
    <service name="notificationService">
         <port name="notificationServicePort"
                   binding="tns:notificationServiceBinding">
              <soap:address
          location="http://localhost/WebServices/ch1/SOAPserver.php"/>
         </port>
    </service>
    <plink:partnerLinkType name="notificationService">
          <plink:role name="notificationServiceRole">
            <portType="tns:notificationServicePortType"/>
         </plink:role>
    </plink:partnerLinkType>
 </definitions>
```

Note the `partnerLinkType` block, which is highlighted. By including this section at the end of the WSDL document describing the service, you enable that service as a partner link, making it possible for it to be part of an orchestration.

As mentioned, WS-BPEL uses the partner links mechanism to model the services interacting within the business process. Here is a fragment of the definition of the WS-BPEL business process depicted in the previous figure and representing the `proposalProcessingService` process service, showing the use of partner links:

```
<process name="BusinessTravelProcess"
   targetNamespace="http://localhost/WebServices/ch1/
proposalProcessing/"
      xmlns="http://schemas.xmlsoap.org/ws/2003/03/business-process/"
         xmlns:prc="http://localhost/WebServices/ch1/
proposalProcessing/"
         xmlns:ntf="http://localhost/WebServices/ch1/notification/"

   <partnerLinks>
      <partnerLink name="client"
                   partnerLinkType="prc:proposalProcessingService"
                   myRole="proposalProcessingServiceRole"/>
```

```
        <partnerLink name="sendingNotification"
                     partnerLinkType="ntf:notificationService"
                     partnerRole="notificationServiceRole"/>
    ...
      </partnerLinks>
    ...
    </process>
```

To save space, the above snippet shows only two `partnerLink` sections in the process definition. The first `partnerLink` section specifies the interaction between the WS-BPEL process and its clients, and the other `partnerLink` specifies the interaction between the WS-BPEL process and the Notification service that acts as a partner service here.

The following figure may help you gain a better understanding of how the partner links mechanism used in WS-BPEL work.

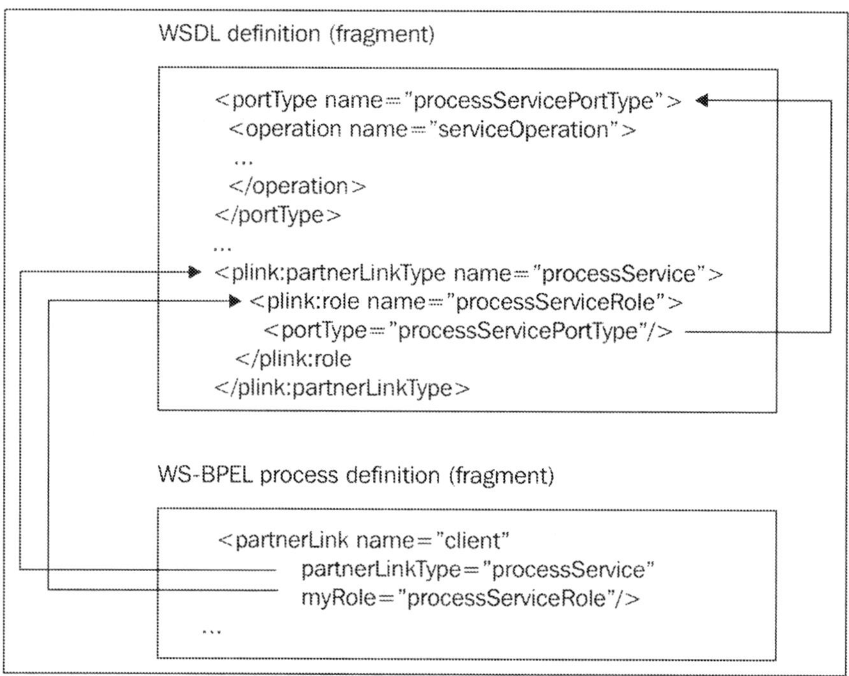

The example depicted in the figure represents the relationship between a `partnerLinkType` defined in the WSDL document describing a WS-BPEL process service and a `partnerLink` specified in the process definition. When defining the `partnerLinkType`, you use the `myRole` attribute to specify the role of the WS-BPEL process. In contrast, to specify the role of a partner, you would use the `partnerRole` attribute, as shown in the process definition document discussed above.

Looking through the `partnerLink` sections in the process definition document discussed here, you may notice that they do not actually provide any information about the location of the WSDL documents containing the corresponding partner link types. This information is stored in the process deployment descriptor file. The format of this document varies depending on the WS-BPEL tool you are using. For example, if you are designing your SOA solution with Oracle BPEL Process Manager, the process deployment descriptor file is called `bpel.xml` and might look as follows:

```
<?xml version="1.0" encoding="UTF-8"?>
<BPELSuitcase>
  <BPELProcess src="proposalProcess.bpel" id="proposalProcess">
    <partnerLinkBindings>
      <partnerLinkBinding name="client">
        <property name="wsdlLocation">proposalProcess.wsdl</property>
      </partnerLinkBinding>
      <partnerLinkBinding name="sendingNotification">
        <property name="wsdlLocation">
        http://localhost/WebServices/ch1/notification?wsdl</property>
      </partnerLinkBinding>
...
    </partnerLinkBindings>
  </BPELProcess>
</BPELSuitcase
```

In ActiveBPEL Designer, a process deployment descriptor file has the `pdd` extension. This description document contains the information required for the ActiveBPEL server to execute the corresponding WS-BPEL process. A `pdd` description specifies the location of the WSDL documents describing parties involved in the references section, as shown in the following snippet:

```
<?xml version="1.0" encoding="UTF-8"?>
<process ...>
 ...
   <references>
      <wsdl location="project:/proposalProcess/WSDL/
                                   proposalProcess.wsdl"
   namespace="http://localhost/WebServices/ch1/proposalProcessing/"/>
      <wsdl location="project:/proposalProcess/WSDL/notification.wsdl"
   namespace="http://localhost/WebServices/ch1/notification/"/>
   </references>
</process>
```

Tools for Designing, Deploying, and Testing Solutions Based on WS-BPEL

Currently, the list of WS-BPEL engines and WS-BPEL modeling tools contains more than 20 items (`http://en.wikipedia.org/wiki/List_of_BPEL_engines`), including open-source and commercial implementations. The most significant commercial implementations of WS-BPEL engine and WS-BPEL business process management software include: Oracle BPEL Process Manager, IBM WebSphere Process Server, and Microsoft BizTalk Server.

The most popular open-source implementation of WS-BPEL engine is ActiveBPEL Engine. According to the FAQ on the Active Endpoints Website (`http://www.active-endpoints.com/open-source-faq.htm`), ActiveBPEL Engine is used by more organizations than any other WS-BPEL implementation. ActiveBPEL Designer is a visual tool for creating and testing WS-BPEL-based solutions to be executed against an ActiveBPEL engine.

As mentioned, Chapter 6 discusses how to compose SOAs with ActiveBPEL Designer, a tool whose 3.X version fully supports WS-BPEL 2.0.

Perhaps the most powerful WS-BPEL tool available on a commercial basis is Oracle BPEL Process Manager, which can be used as a standalone application or as part of Oracle SOA Suite—a set of designing, deploying, and monitoring tools enabling you to build service-oriented solutions and then deploy them to Oracle BPEL Server.

A discussion of Oracle BPEL Process Manager is outside the scope of this book. To learn how to build WS-BPEL based solutions with this powerful tool from Oracle, you can refer to the vendor documentation. To start with, you might visit the Oracle BPEL Process Manager page on the Oracle Technology Network Website at `http://www.oracle.com/technology/products/ias/bpel/` and the Service-Oriented Architecture page at `http://www.oracle.com/technology/soa`.

Summary

This introductory chapter gave you the basics on what you must know to get started while designing your own service-oriented applications.

In particular, you learned about Web Services technology, which has great potential as a robust means of building platform-neutral applications. Then, you looked at the common service-orientation principles and how they can be applied when designing applications based on Web services. You also learned about Orchestration and Choreography, which represent two basic approaches to composing SOA solutions. You should now have a sufficient grasp of the ideas behind WS-BPEL, an orchestration language that provides a way of defining an orchestration level when building SOA solutions.

In the next chapter, you will learn how to create building blocks for SOA applications, services, using PHP as the underlying technology. These services will then be used as partner services when building WS-BPEL-based SOA solutions, as discussed in the following chapters.

2

SOAP Servers and Clients with PHP SOAP Extension

The PHP 5's SOAP extension is implemented as a set of predefined PHP classes that allow the developer to build SOAP servers and clients. In this chapter, you will learn how to use the PHP SOAP extension when building Web services that might then be utilized within SOA applications. In particular you will learn how to:

- Expose application logic as a Web service
- Build Web service providers and requestors
- Encapsulate the underlying logic of a Web service in a PHP class
- Use the XML Schemas specification with WSDL
- Transmit XML documents containing attributes
- Extend predefined classes of the PHP SOAP Extension
- Build Web services supporting parameter-driven operations

Building Service Providers and Service Requestors

Depending on the interaction scenario in which a Web service is involved, it can either act as a service provider or a service requestor. In the following sections, you will see how to build a Web service provider and a requestor that will consume the service provider.

To start with, let's look at a simple example. Suppose that you need to implement an application based on Web services that performs the following sequence of steps:

1. Receives a purchase order (PO) document in XML format
2. Validates a PO against the appropriate XML schema
3. Stores a PO in the database
4. Sends a response message to the requestor

In a real-world situation, to build such an application, you would have to design more than one service and pull these services together into a composite solution. However, for simplicity's sake, the example discussed here uses the only service to handle all of the above tasks.

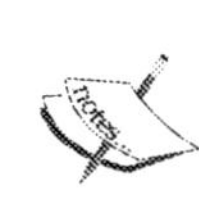

Of course, the above service would be only a part of an entire real-world solution. A service requestor sending a PO document for processing to this service would act as a service provider itself towards another requestor, or would be part of a composite service built, for example, with WS-BPEL.

Diagrammatically, the scenario involving the PO Web service that performs the tasks described above might look like the following figure:

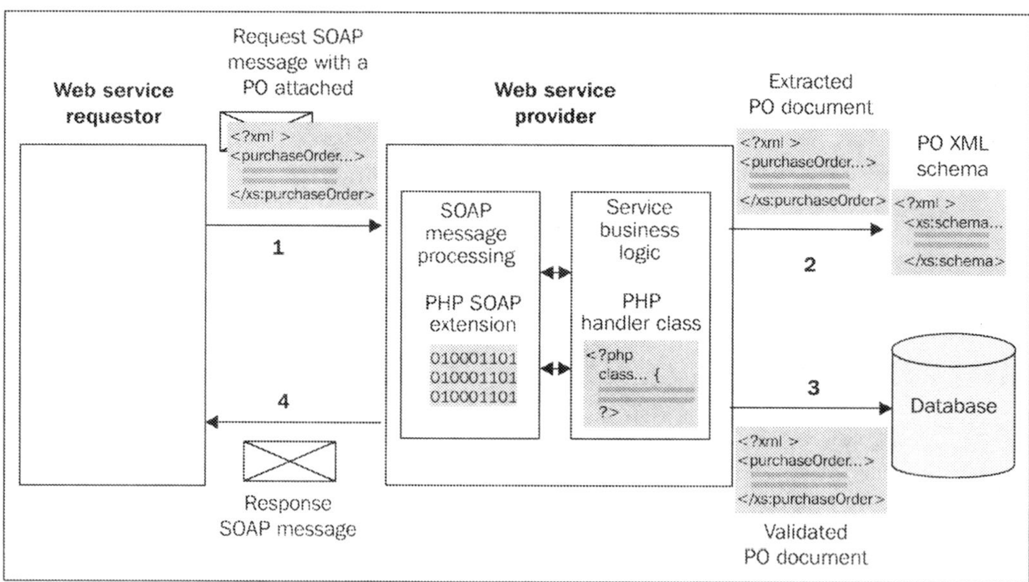

Here is the detailed explanation of the steps in the figure:

- Step 1: The service requestor sends a PO XML document wrapped in a SOAP envelope to the service provider.

- Step 2: The service provider extracts the PO document received from the SOAP envelope and validates the extracted PO against the appropriate XML schema.
- Step 3: The service provider stores the validated PO document in the database.
- Step 4: The service provider sends the response message to the service requestor, informing it if the operations being performed have completed successfully or not.

To build the PO Web service depicted in the previous figure, you need to accomplish the following five general steps:

1. Set up a database to store incoming PO documents
2. Develop a PHP handler class implementing the PO Web service logic
3. Design an XML schema to validate incoming PO documents
4. Design a WSDL document describing the PO Web service to its requestors
5. Build a SOAP server to handle incoming messages carrying POs

The following sections take you through each of the above steps. First, you will see how to create a simple PO Web service that actually performs no validation. Then, you will learn how the XML Schema feature can be used with WSDL to define types in messages being transmitted, making sure that transmitted data is valid with respect to a specific XML schema.

Setting Up the Database

Before we go any further, let's take a moment to set up the database required for this example. This example assumes that you are using Oracle Database Express Edition (XE)—a free edition of Oracle Database, or any other edition of Oracle database.

You can download a copy of Oracle Database from the Download page of the Oracle Technology Network (OTN) Website at `http://www.oracle.com/technology/software/index.html`. In Chapter 3, you will also see an example of using MySQL as the backend database in a Web services application. As for this particular example, Oracle is used because it provides native support for XML, which makes it easier for you to get the job done, allowing you to concentrate on using the PHP SOAP extension while building the application.

To keep things simple, this section actually discusses how to create a minimal set of the database objects required only to store incoming PO documents. When continuing with this example in Chapter 3, you will learn how to leverage the Oracle XML Schema, an Oracle XML feature, to validate incoming POs inside the database.

The Oracle XML Schema is part of the Oracle XML DB, which is a set of Oracle XML features available in any edition of Oracle Database by default. The Oracle XML DB is discussed in extensive detail in Chapter 3.

With Oracle database, you have several options when it comes to creating, accessing and manipulating the database objects. You can use both the graphical and command-line tools shipped with Oracle Database. As for Oracle Database XE, you might use the Oracle Database XE graphical user interface, a browser-based tool that allows you to administer the database.

However, to create the database objects required for this example, it is assumed that you will make use of Oracle SQL*Plus, a command-line SQL tool, which is installed by default with every Oracle database installation.

For information on Oracle database installation, see Appendix A, section *Installing Oracle Database Express Edition (XE).*

With SQL*Plus, you interact with the database server by entering appropriate SQL statements at the `SQL>` prompt.

Assuming that you have an Oracle database server installed and running, launch SQL*Plus and then follow these steps:

Set up a database account that will be used as a container for the database objects by issuing the following SQL statements:

```
//connect to the database as sysdba to be able to create a new
account
CONN /as sysdba

//create a user identified as xmlusr with the same password
CREATE USER xmlusr IDENTIFIED BY xmlusr;

//grant privileges required to connect and create resources
GRANT connect, resource TO xmlusr;
```

Issue the following SQL statements to create a table that will be used to store PO XML documents:

```
//connect to the database using the newly created account
CONN xmlusr/xmlusr;
//create a purchaseOrders table to be used for storing POs
CREATE TABLE purchaseOrders(
    doc VARCHAR2(4000)
);
```

As you can see, the `purchaseOrders` table created by the above statement contains only one column, namely `doc` of `VARCHAR2`. Using the `VARCHAR2` Oracle data type is the simplest option when it comes to storing XML documents in an Oracle database. In fact, Oracle provides much more powerful options for storing XML data in the database. These options will be discussed in detail in Chapter 3.

Developing the PHP Handler Class

Now that you have set up the database to store the incoming PO documents, it's time to create the PHP code that will perform just that operation: storing incoming POs into the database. Consider the `purchaseOrder` PHP class containing the PO Web service underlying logic. It is assumed that you will save this class in the `purchaseOrder.php` file in the `WebServices\ch2` directory within the document directory of your Web server, so that it will be available at `http://localhost/WebServices/ch2/purchaseOrder.php`.

```
<?php
 //File purchaseOrder.php
 class purchaseOrder {
   function placeOrder($po) {
    if(!$conn = oci_connect('xmlusr', 'xmlusr', '//localhost/xe')){
        throw new SoapFault("Server","Failed to connect to
                                                  database");
    };
    $sql = "INSERT INTO purchaseOrders VALUES(:po)";
    $query = oci_parse($conn, $sql);
    oci_bind_by_name($query, ':po', $po);
    if (!oci_execute($query)) {
        throw new SoapFault("Server","Failed to insert PO");
    };
    $msg='<rsltMsg>PO inserted!</rsltMsg>';
    return $msg;
   }
 }
?>
```

Looking through the code, you may notice that the `purchaseOrder` class actually contains the only method, namely `placeOrder`. As its name implies, the `placeOrder` method is responsible for placing an incoming PO document. What this method actually does is take a PO XML document as the parameter and then store it in the `purchaseOrders` table created in the preceding section. Upon failure to connect to the database or execute the `INSERT` statement, the `placeOrder` method stops execution and throws a SOAP exception.

For now, you should not necessarily have to understand in detail how the database-related code in the `placeOrder` method works. This will be discussed in greater detail in Chapter 3.

Another important point to note here is that the `placeOrder` method doesn't contain any code required to validate an incoming PO document. For simplicity, this example assumes no validation for the moment. However, when continuing with the example in the next sections of this chapter, you will see how XML schema-based validation can be used with WSDL, defining types for parts of the messages described in WSDL definitions. Then, in Chapter 3, you will learn how the incoming PO documents can be automatically validated against a PO XML schema within the database, upon inserting them into the `purchaseOrders` table. As the *Using XML Schemas with Oracle XML DB* section in Chapter 3 will explain, to reach this goal, you need to create and register a PO XML schema against the database and then create an `INSERT` trigger on the `purchaseOrders` table.

Designing the WSDL Document

To expose the functionality of the `purchaseOrder` PHP class discussed in the preceding section as a Web service, you first need to create a WSDL document that will describe that Web service. Here is the WSDL that might serve this purpose. It is assumed that you will save this document as `po.wsdl` in the `WebServices/wsdl` directory within the document directory of your Web server.

```
<?xml version="1.0" encoding="utf-8"?>
<definitions name ="poService"
             xmlns:http="http://schemas.xmlsoap.org/wsdl/http/"
             xmlns:soap="http://schemas.xmlsoap.org/wsdl/soap/"
             xmlns:xsd="http://www.w3.org/2001/XMLSchema"
             xmlns="http://schemas.xmlsoap.org/wsdl/"
             targetNamespace=
                          "http://localhost/WebServices/wsdl/po.wsdl">
    <message name="getPlaceOrderInput">
        <part name="body" element="xsd:string"/>
    </message>
```

```
    <message name="getPlaceOrderOutput">
        <part name="body" element="xsd:string"/>
    </message>
    <portType name="poServicePortType">
        <operation name="placeOrder">
           <input message="tns:getPlaceOrderInput"/>
           <output message="tns:getPlaceOrderOutput"/>
        </operation>
    </portType>
    <binding name="poServiceBinding" type="tns:poServicePortType">
        <soap:binding style="document" transport=
                             "http://schemas.xmlsoap.org/soap/http"/>
        <operation name="placeOrder">
           <soap:operation
           soapAction="http://localhost/WebServices/ch2/placeOrder"/>
           <input>
               <soap:body use="literal"/>
           </input>
           <output>
               <soap:body use="literal"/>
           </output>
        </operation>
    </binding>
    <service name="poService">
        <port name="poServicePort" binding="tns:poServiceBinding">
           <soap:address
         location="http://localhost/WebServices/ch2/SOAPserver.php"/>
        </port>
    </service>
</definitions>
```

As you may notice, the `getPlaceOrderInput` message described in this document consists of a single part called `body`, which represents an element of `xsd:string`. Actually, the `body` part used here represents the parameter being passed to the `placeOrder` method of the `purchaseOrder` class discussed in the preceding section. So, this WSDL document implies that an incoming PO XML document will be passed from a service consumer to the PO Web service as a string.

As you no doubt have realized, the `string` XSD type is used in this example for simplicity's sake. In the *Using XML Schemas with WSDL* section later in this chapter, you will see an example of using the user-defined XSD types when it comes to describing XML documents being transmitted between a service provider and service requestor.

Building the SOAP Server

Now that you have created the WSDL definition document describing the PO Web service, the next step is to create a SOAP server that will be responsible for handling and transmitting SOAP messages via HTTP. Save the following PHP script as `SoapServer.php` in the `WebServices/ch2` directory within the document directory of your Web server.

```
<?php
 //File: SoapServer.php
 require_once "purchaseOrder.php";
 $wsdl= "http://localhost/WebServices/wsdl/po.wsdl";
 $srv= new SoapServer($wsdl);
 $srv->setClass("purchaseOrder");
 $srv->handle();
?>
```

At the beginning of this script you add the contents of the `purchaseOrder.php` script discussed in the *Developing the PHP Handler Class* section earlier in this chapter. Then, you create an instance of the `SoapServer` class.

The `SoapServer` class, as well as `SoapClient` and `SoapFault` classes discussed in the next section, belongs to the PHP's SOAP extension library, which is not enabled by default. To enable the SOAP extension on a Unix-like platform, you need to recompile your PHP installation with the configure option `--enable-soap`. If you are a Windows user, you need to append the extension =`php_soap.dll` to the list of extensions in the `php.ini` configuration file.

Once you have created an instance of `SoapServer`, you can export the methods of the PHP handler class stored in the `purchaseOrder.php` script. This is done with the help of the `setClass` method of the `SoapServer` instance.

Finally, you call the `handle` method of `SoapServer`, which is responsible for handling and processing SOAP requests, calling methods of the handler class, and sending responses back to service consumers.

Building the Service Requestor

Before you can test the PO Web service built as discussed in the preceding sections, you need to build a service requestor that will interact with the service. Here is a simple client to test the PO Web service. You may save this script in any directory. However, for simplicity's sake you might save it in the same directory as all the other scripts discussed previously.

```
<?php
 //File: SoapClient.php
 $wsdl = "http://localhost/WebServices/wsdl/po.wsdl";
 $handle = fopen("purchaseOrder.xml", "r");
 $po= fread($handle, filesize("purchaseOrder.xml"));
 fclose($handle);
 $client = new SoapClient($wsdl);
 try {
  print $result=$client->placeOrder($po);
 }
 catch (SoapFault $exp) {
  print $exp->getMessage();
 }
?>
```

As you can see, this script loads a PO document from the `purchaseOrder.xml` file, which is supposed to be in the same directory as the script. Then, it creates an instance of the `SoapClient` class, passing a URI of the WSDL document to be used, as the parameter. Note that you use the same WSDL document you used for the server discussed in the preceding section. Finally, the script calls the `placeOrder` remote function as a method of the newly created `SoapClient` instance, surrounding that call in a `try` block. If something goes wrong during the `placeOrder` execution and a `SoapFault` exception is thrown, the `catch` block catches it.

A simplified version of a PO document stored in the `purchaseOrder.xml` file being used in this example might look as follows:

```
<purchaseOrder >
    <pono>108128476</pono>
    <billTo>
     <name>Tony Jamison</name>
     <street>24 Johnson Road</street>
     <city>Big Valley</city>
     <state>VA</state>
     <zip>23032</zip>
     <country>US</country>
    </billTo>
    <shipTo>
     <name>Janet Thomson</name>
     <street>11 Maple Street</street>
     <city>Small Valley</city>
     <state>VA</state>
     <zip>23037</zip>
     <country>US</country>
   </shipTo>
```

```
    <items>
       <item>
        <partId>743</partId>
        <quantity>4</quantity>
        <price>15.50</price>
       </item>
       <item>
         <partId>235</partId>
        <quantity>7</quantity>
        <price>15.75</price>
       </item>
    </items>
</purchaseOrder>
```

In a real-world situation, a PO XML document might be derived from different sources, not necessarily from a file. For example, it might be created on the fly (dynamically) by a PHP script, with the help of the DOM API that is part of the PHP core.

You will see an example of building an XML document with the help of the PHP DOM extension in the *Converting SOAP Messages' Payloads to XML* section later in this chapter.

Testing the Service

Now you are ready to test the PO Web service. To do this, you simply need to point your browser at the service requestor discussed in the preceding section. If you saved the `SoapClient.php` script in the `WebServices/ch2` directory within the document directory of your Web server, enter the following URL in the address box of your browser: `http://localhost/WebServices/ch2/SoapClient.php`.

If everything goes as planned, you will see a **PO inserted!** message in your browser. Otherwise, a SOAP fault message appears. For example, if the `placeOrder` method of the `purchaseOrder` class fails to connect to the database, you will see an error message that will look as follows:

Failed to connect to database

Turning back to the `placeOrder` method of the `purchaseOrder` class discussed in the *Developing the PHP Handler Class* section earlier, you may notice that it also throws a SOAP exception upon failure to insert the received PO into the database.

If the request was successful, the purchaseOrders table was created as discussed in the *Setting Up the Database* section earlier should contain one more row. To make sure it does so, you can issue the following query from Oracle SQL*Plus or any other command-line tool you use to communicate with the database:

```
CONN xmlusr/xmlusr

SELECT * FROM purchaseOrders;
```

When executed, the above SELECT statement should output the string representing the same PO XML document as the one shown in the *Building the Service Requestor* section earlier. If so, this means the PO Web service has worked successfully.

Using XML Schemas with WSDL

The PO Web service discussed above represents a simplified example of a Web service provider. As mentioned, it receives a PO XML document as a simple string and saves it as it is in the database. In practice, of course, it is rarely as simple as this. When receiving an XML document of a specific structure from a consumer, a Web service wants to make sure that the received document has an appropriate structure, that is, the document conforms to a specific schema.

To solve this problem, WSDL allows you to include XML Schema definitions describing the data structures being transmitted between the service provider and its consumers. In WSDL, you can either enclose XML Schema data type definitions within the types element or import an XML schema stored in a separate file using the import statement. In the following sections, you will look at both these approaches.

Including XML Schema Data Type Definitions in WSDL

In the PO Web service, you might want to modify its WSDL document so that it includes an XSD data type definition for the PO XML document received with the input message. Assuming that the PO Web service expects to receive a PO XML document having the same structure as the one shown in the *Building the Service Requestor* section earlier, the WSDL document describing the PO Web service might look now as follows. It is assumed that you save this document as po_typed.wsdl in the WebServices/wsdl directory in which you saved po.wsdl document discussed in the *Designing the WSDL Document* section previously.

```
<?xml version="1.0" encoding="utf-8"?>
<definitions name ="poService"
```

```
            targetNamespace="http://localhost/WebServices/wsdl/po/"
            xmlns:tns="http://localhost/WebServices/wsdl/po/"
            xmlns:http="http://schemas.xmlsoap.org/wsdl/http/"
            xmlns:soap="http://schemas.xmlsoap.org/wsdl/soap/"
            xmlns:xsd="http://www.w3.org/2001/XMLSchema"
            xmlns:xsd1="http://localhost/WebServices/schema/"
            xmlns="http://schemas.xmlsoap.org/wsdl/">
  <types>
   <schema targetNamespace="http://localhost/WebServices/schema/"
      xmlns="http://www.w3.org/2001/XMLSchema">
     <element name="purchaseOrder">
      <complexType>
       <sequence>
        <element name="pono" type="xsd:string" />
        <element name="shipTo" type="xsd1:AddressType" />
        <element name="billTo" type="xsd1:AddressType"/>
        <element name="items" type="xsd1:LineItemsType"/>
       </sequence>
      </complexType>
     </element>
     <complexType name="AddressType">
      <sequence>
       <element name="name" type="xsd:string"/>
       <element name="street" type="xsd:string"/>
       <element name="city" type="xsd:string"/>
       <element name="state" type="xsd:string"/>
       <element name="zip" type="xsd:int"/>
       <element name="country" type="xsd:NMTOKEN" />
      </sequence>
     </complexType>
     <complexType name="LineItemsType">
      <sequence>
       <element minOccurs="1" maxOccurs="unbounded" name="item"
                                    type="xsd1:LineItemType" />
      </sequence>
     </complexType>
     <complexType name="LineItemType">
      <sequence>
       <element name="partId" type="xsd:int"/>
       <element name="quantity" type="xsd:decimal"/>
       <element name="price" type="xsd:decimal"/>
```

```
            </sequence>
          </complexType>
        </schema >
      </types>
      <message name="getPlaceOrderInput">
          <part name="body" element="xsd1:purchaseOrder"/>
      </message>
      <message name="getPlaceOrderOutput">
          <part name="body" element="xsd:string"/>
      </message>
      <portType name="poServicePortType">
          <operation name="placeOrder">
             <input message="tns:getPlaceOrderInput"/>
             <output message="tns:getPlaceOrderOutput"/>
          </operation>
      </portType>
      <binding name="poServiceBinding" type="tns:poServicePortType">
          <soap:binding style="document"
              transport="http://schemas.xmlsoap.org/soap/http"/>
          <operation name="placeOrder">
             <soap:operation
             soapAction="http://localhost/WebServices/ch2/placeOrder"/>
             <input>
                 <soap:body use="literal" />
             </input>
             <output>
                 <soap:body use="literal" />
             </output>
          </operation>
      </binding>
      <service name="poService">
          <port name="poServicePort" binding="tns:poServiceBinding">
             <soap:address
     location="http://localhost/WebServices/ch2/SOAPServer_typed.php"/>
          </port>
      </service>
  </definitions>
```

As you can see, the `getPlaceOrderInput` message described in this document includes a `body` part representing an element of a complex XSD type, namely `xsd1:purchaseOrder`. This type is described in the XML schema defined within the `types` construct of the WSDL document. What this means is that a PO XML document passed to the `placeOrder` method as the input argument must now conform to the `xsd1:purchaseOrder` type definition.

Importing XML Schemas into WSDL Documents

In the preceding section you saw how an XML schema containing data type definitions used for typing messages' contents can be added to a WSDL document. However, to achieve better reusability you might save that XML schema in a single file and then import it into the WSDL document. In this case, you won't have to modify your WSDL document when you modify a type definition in the imported XML schema. Instead, you will modify the document containing the schema, while leaving the WSDL document representing the contract between the service provider and its consumers untouched.

Returning to the WSDL document discussed in the preceding section, you first need to separate the XML schema enclosed within the `types` element. It is assumed that you save the following schema document as `po.xsd` in the `WebServices/schema` directory within the document directory of your Web server.

```
<?xml version='1.0'?>
<schema targetNamespace="http://localhost/WebServices/schema/po/"
        xmlns="http://www.w3.org/2001/XMLSchema"
        xmlns:types1="http://localhost/WebServices/schema/po/">
  <element name="purchaseOrder">
   <complexType>
     <sequence>
       <element name="pono" type="string" />
       <element name="shipTo" type="types1:AddressType" />
       <element name="billTo" type="types1:AddressType"/>
       <element name="items" type="types1:LineItemsType"/>
     </sequence>
   </complexType>
  </element>
  <complexType name="AddressType">
   <sequence>
    <element name="name" type="string"/>
    <element name="street" type="string"/>
    <element name="city" type="string"/>
    <element name="state" type="string"/>
    <element name="zip" type="int"/>
    <element name="country" type="NMTOKEN" />
   </sequence>
  </complexType>
  <complexType name="LineItemsType">
   <sequence>
    <element minOccurs="0" maxOccurs="unbounded" name="item"
```

```
                                         type="types1:LineItemType" />
      </sequence>
    </complexType>
    <complexType name="LineItemType">
      <sequence>
        <element name="partId" type="int"/>
        <element name="quantity" type="decimal"/>
        <element name="price" type="decimal"/>
      </sequence>
    </complexType>
  </schema >
```

Now you can import the entire XML schema shown above into the WSDL document describing the PO Web service, rather than enclosing that schema in the `types` element in the WSDL document. To achieve this, you use the `import` WSDL element, modifying the `po_types.wsdl` document discussed in the previous section as shown below. It is assumed that you save this document as `po_imp.wsdl` in the `WebServices/wsdl` directory.

```
<?xml version="1.0" encoding="utf-8"?>
<definitions name ="poService"
             targetNamespace="http://localhost/WebServices/wsdl/po/"
             xmlns:tns="http://localhost/WebServices/wsdl/po/"
             xmlns:http="http://schemas.xmlsoap.org/wsdl/http/"
             xmlns:soap="http://schemas.xmlsoap.org/wsdl/soap/"
             xmlns:xsd="http://www.w3.org/2001/XMLSchema"
             xmlns:xsd1="http://localhost/WebServices/schema/po/"
             xmlns="http://schemas.xmlsoap.org/wsdl/">
    <import namespace="http://localhost/WebServices/schema/po/"
              location="http://localhost/WebServices/schema/po.xsd" />
...
</definitions>
```

In this example, you associate the `xsd1` namespace defined in the WSDL document with the PO XML schema stored in a separate file, using the `namespace` and `location` attributes of the `import` statement.

> Looking through the XML schema and WSDL documents discussed here, you may notice that each of these documents uses a different prefix for the namespace whose URI is `http://localhost/WebServices/schema/po/`. In fact, you might use the same prefix here. However, it doesn't matter as long as the URI is the same.

Getting Data Types Defined in the XML Schema

With a great number of XSD data types defined in the XML schema document or documents used by the WSDL definition, there is often a need to be able to look into those types from within the client code at run time.

> In the design stage, the above is not a problem. Regardless of whether the WSDL document describing the service incorporates the XML schema in the way you saw in the *Including XML Schema Data Type Definitions in WSDL* section or imports one or more XML schemas as discussed in the *Importing XML Schemas into WSDL Documents* section, you can examine the XSD types used by looking either through the `types` section of the WSDL document or the imported XML schema documents. This is possible because service providers share their WSDL definitions with their consumers.

To meet this challenge, the PHP SOAP extension introduces the `__getTypes` method of the `SoapClient` class. To simply output the information about actual XSD data types, you might use `__getTypes` as follows:

```
<?php
 ...
 $wsdl= "http://localhost/WebServices/wsdl/po_imp.wsdl";
 $client = new SoapClient($wsdl);
 print_r($client->__getTypes());
 ...
?>
```

The highlighted line in the above code will output the following array of structures that are representations of the XSD types defined in the `po.xsd` XML schema document imported into the `po_imp.wsdl` WSDL definition document:

```
Array
(
    [0] => struct purchaseOrder {
 string pono;
 AddressType shipTo;
 AddressType billTo;
 LineItemsType items;
}
    [1] => struct AddressType {
 string name;
 string street;
 string city;
```

```
    string state;
    int zip;
    NMTOKEN country;
   }
       [2] => struct LineItemsType {
    LineItemType item;
   }
       [3] => struct LineItemType {
    int partId;
    decimal quantity;
    decimal price;
   }
   )
```

While the above example simply outputs the array of structures returned by the __getTypes method, in a real-world application you might make practical use of this information. For example, you might dynamically build an input form based on these structures, so that a user could manually input data to be sent to the service. While constructing such a form, you might use information about the types of the fields of the returned structures when defining validation rules.

To quickly build such a form, you might take advantage of the PEAR::HTML_QuickForm package. The discussion of this package, though, is outside the scope of this book. To find out more about PEAR::HTML_QuickForm, you can visit http://pear.php.net/HTML_QuickForm.

Transmitting Complex Type Data

In the preceding example, you simply send a string representing a PO XML document as the input argument of the placeOrder method exposed by the PO Web service. Now that you have modified the WSDL document describing the PO Web service so that the PO Web service receives a PO XML document conforming to a specific structure, you cannot send that document as a simple string any more.

The following sections explain in detail how the complex type data structures are transmitted between SOAP nodes built with the PHP SOAP extension.

Exchanging Complex Data Structures with PHP SOAP Extension

Like any other SOAP-based interfaces, service providers and service consumers built with the PHP SOAP extension use XML format when it comes to exchanging structured and typed data. However, in the case of the PHP SOAP extension you are not supposed to provide an XML document ready for transmitting. Instead, you provide an array having an appropriate structure and containing all the data to be sent. The SOAP software transforms this array to an XML document conforming to the specified type definition defined in the XML schema employed, and then sends that XML document wrapped in a SOAP envelope to the receiver. The receiver extracts the document from the SOAP envelope assuming that the receiver uses the PHP SOAP extension and converts it to an instance of the `stdClass` built-in PHP class.

In practice, a service requestor built with the PHP SOAP extension may send requests to a service provider built with other software, and also a PHP SOAP extension-based service provider may be consumed by a requestor built with a non-PHP tool. In either case, the requestor and provider will exchange the data organized as specified in the corresponding WSDL and XML schema documents. The details of manipulating the data structures being exchanged, though, will vary depending on the SOAP software specifics. In Chapter 5, for example, you will learn how a WS-BPEL process service handles complex type data arriving with request messages sent by consumers of that service. You also will learn how a WS-BPEL process handles complex data being sent to its partners.

Diagrammatically, the process of transmitting a complex data structure between two SOAP nodes built with the PHP SOAP extension might look like the following figure:

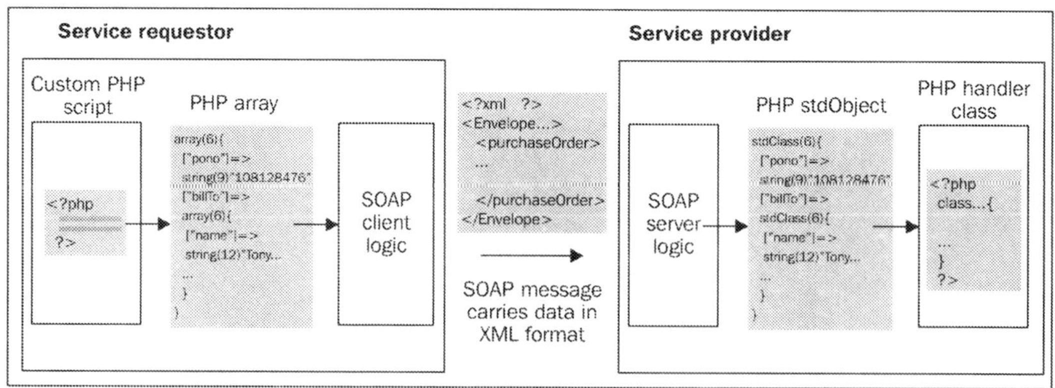

Generally, when you call a function exposed by the service, in the way you did in the `SoapClient.php` script discussed in the *Building the Service Requestor* section earlier, the instance of the `SoapClient` class assumes that you pass arrays as the arguments of that function.

However, in the case of the `SoapClient.php` mentioned here you don't have to worry about this, since you send a simple string as the parameter of the exposed function.

For example, the following PHP array might be used as the argument of the `placeOrder` function exposed by the PO Web server described by the `po_imp.wsdl` document shown in the *Importing XML Schemas into WSDL Documents* section earlier:

```
array(4) {
  ["pono"]=>        string(9) "108128476"
  ["billTo"]=>      array(6) {
    ["name"]=>        string(12) "Tony Jamison"
    ["street"]=>      string(15) "24 Johnson Road"
    ["city"]=>        string(10) "Big Valley"
    ["state"]=>       string(2) "VA"
    ["zip"]=>         string(5) "23032"
    ["country"]=>     string(2) "US"
  }
  ["shipTo"]=>      array(6) {
    ["name"]=>        string(13) "Janet Thomson"
    ["street"]=>      string(15) "11 Maple Street"
    ["city"]=>        string(12) "Small Valley"
    ["state"]=>       string(2) "VA"
    ["zip"]=>         string(5) "23037"
    ["country"]=>     string(2) "US"
  }
  ["items"]=>       array(1) {
    ["item"]=>        array(2) {
      [0]=>             array(3) {
        ["partId"]=>      string(3) "743"
        ["quantity"]=>    string(1) "4"
        ["price"]=>       string(7) "10.5"
      }
      [1]=>          array(3) {
        ["partId"]=>      string(3) "235"
        ["quantity"]=>    string(1) "7"
        ["price"]=>       string(2) "15.75"
      }
    }
  }
}
```

We could pass the variable containing this array to the `placeOrder` function as the parameter like the following:

```
<?php
 ...
 $wsdl= "http://localhost/WebServices/wsdl/po_imp.wsdl";
 $client = new SoapClient($wsdl);
 ...
 $result=$client->placeOrder($poarray);
 ...
?>
```

The SOAP software operating on the client side will transform this array into an XML document conforming to the `purchaseOrder` data type definition described in the `po.xsd` XML schema document shown in the *Importing XML Schemas into WSDL Documents* section, thus generating a PO XML document like that you saw in the *Building the Service Requestor* section earlier. This XML document is then wrapped in an SOAP envelope and sent to the server.

On the server side, the posted document is extracted from the SOAP envelope and by default is transformed to an instance of the `stdClass` built-in PHP class. You may look into that instance with the help of the `var_dump` standard PHP function and output the instance structure and data to a file as shown:

```
<?php
 class purchaseOrder {
   function placeOrder($po) {
     ...
     ob_start();
     var_dump($po);
     $buffer = ob_get_flush();
     file_put_contents('buffer.txt', $buffer);
     ob_end_clean();
     ...
   }
 }
?>
```

On inspecting the `buffer.txt` file you see that the instance of `stdClass` containing the data received by the server is similar in structure to the array processed and posted by the client, and contains the same actual data as that array. In this particular example, the instance of `stdClass` would look as follows:

```
object(stdClass)#2 (4) {
  ["pono"]=>      string(9) "108128476"
  ["shipTo"]=>    object(stdClass)#3 (6) {
    ["name"]=>      string(13) "Janet Thomson"
```

```
      ["street"]=>   string(15) "11 Maple Street"
      ["city"]=>     string(12) "Small Valley"
      ["state"]=>    string(2) "VA"
      ["zip"]=>      int(23037)
      ["country"]=>  string(2) "US"
    }
    ["billTo"]=>   object(stdClass)#4 (6) {
      ["name"]=>     string(12) "Tony Jamison"
      ["street"]=>   string(15) "24 Johnson Road"
      ["city"]=>     string(10) "Big Valley"
      ["state"]=>    string(2) "VA"
      ["zip"]=>      int(23032)
      ["country"]=>  string(2) "US"
    }
    ["items"]=>    object(stdClass)#5 (1) {
      ["item"]=>     array(2) {
        [0]=>          object(stdClass)#6 (3) {
          ["partId"]=>   int(743)
          ["quantity"]=> string(1) "4"
          ["price"]=>    string(7) "10.5"
        }
        [1]=>          object(stdClass)#7 (3) {
          ["partId"]=>   int(235)
          ["quantity"]=> string(1) "7"
          ["price"]=>    string(2) "15.75"
        }
      }
    }
  }
```

Examining the difference between the array and `stdClass` object discussed here, you may notice that the latter contains fields in an order that is different from that used in the former. Specifically, the first upper element called `pono` is followed by the `shipTo` element in the `stdClass` object but by the `billTo` element in the array. To understand why the order of the elements has changed, you need to come back to the `po.xsd` XML schema discussed in the *Importing XML Schemas into WSDL Documents* section. Looking through the schema, you may notice that the `purchaseOrder` XSD type assumes that the order of the upper-level elements in its type representations must be as follows:

1. `pono`
2. `shipTo`
3. `billTo`
4. `items`

As you no doubt have guessed, the SOAP client, while processing the input array containing the data being sent, applied the required changes to the input structure, changing the order of the elements so that the XML document being transmitted conforms to the `purchaseOrder` XSD type definition described in the `po.xsd` XML schema document.

It's interesting to note that if the input array discussed here contained some extra fields that did not have corresponding elements defined within the `purchaseOrder` XSD type, the `stdClass` object on the server side actually would not change. The fact is that the SOAP client not only makes sure that the elements in the XML document being sent are in the correct order, but also prevent unnecessary elements presented in the input array from being included in that document.

Structuring Complex Data for Sending

Now that you know the basics of how the service requestors and services providers based on the PHP SOAP extension handle the data being exchanged, it's a good time to see how all this works in practice.

In this section, you will see an example of how you can prepare a complex type data structure being sent as the argument of the function exposed by a Web service. In the following section, you will see how to handle the received data on the service provider side.

Suppose you are building a service requestor that will take the information to be sent from a file holding the data in XML format. In this case, you need to create the code that will first read an XML document from the file, and then convert the uploaded XML document to a PHP array being specified as the argument of the function exposed by the service provider. To read a well-formed XML document from a file into a PHP structure that might be easily converted to an array, you might take advantage of the `simplexml_load_file` PHP function that reads the XML document from the file specified as the argument to an object of the `SimpleXMLElement` class. Once you have the XML document as an instance of `SimpleXMLElement`, you can convert it to an array with the help of the function as follows:

```
<?php
 //File: obj2Arr.php
 function obj2Arr($obj)
 {
  $result = NULL;
  if(!is_array($obj))
  {
   if($var = get_object_vars($obj))
```

```
      {
       foreach($var as $key => $value)
        $result[$key] = obj2Arr($value);
      }
      else
      return $obj;
    }
    else
    {
     foreach($obj as $key => $value)
      $result[$key] = obj2Arr($value);
    }
    return $result;
  }
?>
```

As you can see, the obj2Arr custom function takes the object to be converted as the argument, and may perform a number of recursive calls (calling itself), depending on the complexity of the structure being converted.

> Please note that the obj2Arr function shown above assumes that the SimpleXMLElement object passed in as the argument represents an XML document containing no attributes. Processing XML documents containing attributes will be discussed in the *Dealing with Attributes* section later.

With the simplexml_load_file and obj2Arr functions, the client script calling the placeOrder function might now look as follows. It is assumed that you save this script as SoapClient_typed.php in the WebServices/ch2 directory.

```
<?php
 //File: SoapClient_typed.php
 require_once "obj2Arr.php";
 $wsdl = "http://localhost/WebServices/wsdl/po_imp.wsdl";
 $xmldoc = simplexml_load_file('purchaseOrder.xml');
 $xmlarr = obj2Arr($xmldoc);
 $client = new SoapClient($wsdl);
 try {
  print $result=$client->placeOrder($xmlarr);
 }
 catch (SoapFault $exp) {
  print $exp->getMessage();
 }
?>
```

However, before you can test this client code you need to create the SOAP server and the PHP handler class to handle requests coming from the client. Both are discussed in the next section.

Converting SOAP Messages' Payloads to XML

As discussed previously, on the server side, assuming that the server is built with the PHP SOAP extension, the exposed methods of the PHP handler class receive their arguments carrying complex type data as instances of the `stdClass` class. So, in this particular example, the `placeOrder` method of the `purchaseOrder` PHP handler class will receive its argument as a `stdClass` object.

Suppose you want to convert the `stdClass` object received by the `placeOrder` method back to XML. To handle this task, you might want to create a custom class. Here is the code for the `obj2Dom` class that takes care of converting a `stdClass` to XML:

```
<?php
class obj2Dom {
 private $dom;
 private $rootNode;
 private $arrayName;

 public function __construct($rootElmName='root')
 {
  $this->dom = new DomDocument('1.0');
  $root = $this->dom->createElement($rootElmName);
  $this->rootNode = $this->dom->appendChild($root);
 }

 private function buildDom($result, $node) {
  $attrFlag=0;
  foreach($result as $key => $value) {
   if (!is_int($key)){
      $nodeName=$key;
   }
   else {
     $nodeName=$this->arrayName;
   }
   if (!is_object($value)){
      if (is_array($value)) {
          $this->arrayName=$key;
          $this->buildDom($value,$node);
      }
```

```
        else {
            $elm = $this->dom->createElement($nodeName);
            $elm = $node->appendChild($elm);
            $txt = $this->dom->createTextNode($value);
            $txt = $elm->appendChild($txt);
        }
    }
    else {
          $elm = $this->dom->createElement($nodeName);
          $elm = $node->appendChild($elm);
          $this->buildDom($value,$elm);
         }
    }
  }
  public function trans2Dom($result)
  {
   $this->buildDom($result, $this->rootNode);
  }
  public function printDomTree()
  {
   return $this->dom->saveXML();
  }
 }
 ?>
```

> Like the obj2Arr function discussed in the preceding section, the obj2Dom class shown here assumes that the stdClass objects being converted represent XML documents that do not contain attributes. In the *Dealing with Attributes* section, though, you will see a modified version of obj2Dom that can handle XML documents containing attributes.

Once you have created the obj2Dom class, you can include the file containing it in the PHP handler script, and then use this class as follows. It is assumed that you save the following PHP handler class in the puchaseOrder_typed.php file.

```
<?php
 //File purchaseOrder_typed.php
 require_once 'obj2Dom.php';
 class purchaseOrder {
   function placeOrder($po) {
    $obj = new obj2Dom('purchaseOrder');
    $obj->trans2Dom($po);
    $po=$obj->printDomTree();
    if(!$conn = oci_connect('xmlusr', 'xmlusr', '//localhost/XE')){
       throw new SoapFault("Server","Failed to connect to database");
```

```
        };
        $sql = "INSERT INTO purchaseOrders VALUES(:po)";
        $query = oci_parse($conn, $sql);
        oci_bind_by_name($query, ':po', $po);
        if (!oci_execute($query)) {
            throw new SoapFault("Server","Failed to insert PO");
        };
        $msg='<rsltMsg>PO inserted!</rsltMsg>';
        return $msg;
      }
   }
?>
```

In the `placeOrder` method shown above, you first create an instance of the `obj2Dom` custom class, passing `'purhaseOrder'` as the argument in order to explicitly set up the name of the root element in the XML document being built. Then, you call the `trans2Dom` method of the newly created instance, passing in the value of the argument received by the `placeOrder` method. As discussed previously, `placeOrder` is supposed to receive the `stdClass` object representing the PO document posted by a service consumer. The `trans2Dom` method will translate the `stdClass` object received as the argument into an instance of the `DomDocument` class. By calling the `printDomTree` method of the `obj2Dom` class in the next step, you obtain the generated XML document as a string, which then is inserted into `purchaseOrders` table in the database.

Now that you have created the PHP handler class that will translate an incoming structure representing a PO XML document back into XML format, you have to build a SOAP server that will receive and process requests coming from the client. It is assumed that you save the following server as `SoapServer_typed.php` in the `WebServices/ch2` directory.

```
<?php
 //File: SoapServer_typed.php
 require_once "purchaseOrder_typed.php";
 $wsdl= "http://localhost/WebServices/wsdl/po_imp.wsdl";
 $srv= new SoapServer($wsdl);
 $srv->setClass("purchaseOrder");
 $srv->handle();
?>
```

Now you can test the client shown in the preceding section. To do this, you need to point your browser at `http://localhost/WebServices/ch2/SoapClient_typed.php`. If everything goes as planned, you will see a **PO inserted!** message in your browser. Otherwise, a SOAP fault message appears.

Using PHP SOAP Extension Tracing Capabilities

In the development and testing stage, there's often a need to look at the incoming and outgoing SOAP messages. To look through the headers of the last SOAP request and response, you can use the `__getLastRequestHeaders` and `__getLastResponseHeaders` methods of a `SoapClient` instance respectively. To look through the entire messages representing the last SOAP request and response, you can use the `__getLastRequest` and `__getLastResponse` methods respectively, as shown in the following example:

```
<?php
 //File: SoapClient_trace.php
 require_once 'obj2Arr.php';
 $wsdl = "http://localhost/WebServices/wsdl/po_imp.wsdl";
 $xml = simplexml_load_file('purchaseOrder.xml');
 $arr = obj2Arr($xml);
 $client = new SoapClient($wsdl, array('trace' => 1));
 try {
  print "RESULT:\n".$result=$client->placeOrder($arr)."\n";
 }
 catch (SoapFault $exp) {
  print $exp->getMessage();
 }
 print "REQUEST:\n".htmlspecialchars
                        ($client->__getLastRequest())."\n";
 print "RESPONSE:\n" .htmlspecialchars
                        ($client->__getLastResponse())."\n";
?>
```

To test the above script, you don't have to write another SOAP server or PHP handler class—those discussed in the preceding sections will do. So, you specify the same WSDL document as you did in the `SoapClient_typed.php` script discussed in the *Structuring Complex Data for Sending* section earlier.

If you recall, the physical part of the WSDL document describes the concrete characteristics of the Web service, including information about the concrete network address of the service provider.

If you execute the `SoapClient_trace.php` script as shown previously, it should return the following output (the output has been formatted for clarity and the PO XML document in the request has been cut down to save space):

```
RESULT:
PO inserted!

REQUEST:
<?xml version="1.0" encoding="UTF-8"?>
 <SOAP-ENV:Envelope xmlns:
   SOAP-ENV="http://schemas.xmlsoap.org/soap/envelope/"
                    xmlns:ns1=
                             "http://localhost/WebServices/schema/po/">
 <SOAP-ENV:Body>
   <ns1:purchaseOrder>
    <pono>108128476</pono>

    ...

   </ns1:purchaseOrder>
  </SOAP-ENV:Body>
 </SOAP-ENV:Envelope>

RESPONSE:
<?xml version="1.0" encoding="UTF-8"?>
 <SOAP-ENV:Envelope xmlns:
     SOAP-ENV="http://schemas.xmlsoap.org/soap/envelope/">
  <SOAP-ENV:Body>
   <body><rsltMsg>PO inserted!</rsltMsg></body>
  </SOAP-ENV:Body>
 </SOAP-ENV:Envelope>
```

Dealing with Attributes

In the preceding sections, you learned how an XML document can be transmitted via SOAP as a complex data structure, and then converted back to an XML format on the receiver side. It was assumed, though, that the document being transmitted contains no attributes. This section discusses how to deal with documents containing attributes.

On the client side, perhaps the safest way to go when it comes to dealing with an XML document containing attributes is to first convert the attributes to elements and then transform the document into an array, as discussed in the *Structuring Complex Data for Sending* section earlier. The SOAP software converting this array to XML to be transmitted as the payload of a SOAP message will generate an XML document conforming to a certain XSD type, as defined in the WSDL definition for this particular part of the message.

Turning back to the po.xsd XML schema document discussed in the *Importing XML Schemas into WSDL Documents* section, you might now use it as the basis for another XML schema document, changing it a bit by adding the id attribute to the item element. The highlighted line in the po_attr.xsd XML schema document shown below is the only difference between this document and the po.xsd document discussed previously (the po_attr.xsd document shown here has been cut down to save space):

```
<?xml version='1.0'?>
<schema targetNamespace="http://localhost/WebServices/schema/po/"
        xmlns="http://www.w3.org/2001/XMLSchema"
        xmlns:types1="http://localhost/WebServices/schema/po/">
  <element name="purchaseOrder">

  ...

  <complexType name="LineItemType">
    <sequence>
      <element name="partId" type="int"/>
      <element name="quantity" type="decimal"/>
      <element name="price" type="decimal"/>
    </sequence>
    <attribute name="id" type="int"/>
  </complexType>
</schema >
```

The full versions of the PHP scripts, WSDL definitions, XML schemas, and other documents discussed here can be found in the downloadable archive on the book's Web page.

Now you can call the placeOrder SOAP function, passing as the argument the following array, which is the same as the one shown in the *Exchanging Complex Data Structures with PHP SOAP Extension* section, except for the id fields added:

```
array(4) {
  ["pono"]=>      string(9) "108128476"

  ...

  ["items"]=>     array(1) {
    ["item"]=>      array(2) {
      [0]=>           array(3) {
        ["id"]=>        string(2) "24"
        ["partId"]=>    string(3) "743"
```

```
        ["quantity"]=>  string(1) "4"
        ["price"]=>     string(7) "10.5"
      }
      [1]=>        array(3) {
        ["id"]=>        string(2) "25"
        ["partId"]=>    string(3) "235"
        ["quantity"]=>  string(1) "7"
        ["price"]=>     string(2) "15.75"
      }
    }
  }
}
```

The following section explains how to convert attributes to elements in the XML documents to be transmitted, so that you can generate an array, like the one shown above, with the help of the `obj2Arr` function discussed in the *Structuring Complex Data* for sending section previously.

When generating the payload of the message to be sent, the SOAP software will automatically recognize the attributes in the input array and produce the appropriate XML document. In this particular example, you will have the following document as the payload (it has been cut down to save space):

```
<ns1:purchaseOrder>

...

  <items>
   <item id="24">
    <partId>743</partId>
    <quantity>4</quantity>
    <price>15.5</price>
   </item>
   <item id="25">
    <partId>235</partId>
    <quantity>7</quantity>
    <price>15.75</price>
   </item>
  </items>
 </ns1:purchaseOrder>
```

As you can see, the SOAP software correctly generated `item` elements, according to the `LineItemType` complex type definition described in the XML schema document.

However, the most interesting thing about documents containing attributes is how these documents are handled on the receiver side, assuming the receiver of the message is built with the PHP SOAP extension.

When the message carrying this payload reaches the receiver (in this example, it's the PO Web service provider), the SOAP software operating on the receiver side will convert the payload to the following `stdClass` object before sending it to the `placeOrder` method of the `purchaseOrder` PHP handler class (the object has been cut down to save space):

```
object(stdClass)#2 (4) {
  ["pono"]=>   string(9) "108128476"

  ...

  ["items"]=>
  object(stdClass)#5 (1) {
    ["item"]=>
    array(2) {
      [0]=>
      object(stdClass)#6 (4) {
        ["partId"]=>       int(743)
        ["quantity"]=>     string(1) "4"
        ["price"]=>        string(7) "15.5"
        ["id"]=>           int(24)
      }
      [1]=>
      object(stdClass)#7 (4) {
        ["partId"]=>       int(235)
        ["quantity"]=>     string(1) "7"
        ["price"]=>        string(2) "15.75"
        ["id"]=>           int(25)
      }
    }
  }
}
```

As you can see, the SOAP software operating on the SOAP server side treats attributes like elements when processing a payload representing an XML document. Obviously, if you now try to transform the above `stdClass` object back to XML, using methods of the `obj2Dom` class as discussed in the *Converting SOAP Messages' Payloads to XML* section earlier, you will have an XML document in which all attributes have been converted to elements.

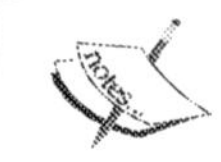

In the following section, you will learn how to handle this problem by applying XSLT transformations to the XML documents derived from `stdClass` objects.

It's important to note that the above example shows only the case when the element containing the attributes also contains nested elements. But, what if the element containing the attributes represents a text node? For example, you might use the currency name as the attribute of the `price` element in the `purchaseOrder` document discussed here, as shown below:

```
<purchaseOrder>

...

  <items>
    <item id="24">
      <partId>743</partId>
      <quantity>4</quantity>
      <price currency = "USD">15.5</price>
    </item>
    <item id="25">
      <partId>235</partId>
      <quantity>7</quantity>
      <price currency = "USD">15.75</price>
    </item>
  </items>
</purchaseOrder>
```

The `price` element in the above snippet might be described by the highlighted type definition in the `po_attr_price.xsd` XML schema document shown below. It is assumed that you save this document in the `WebServices/schema` directory.

```
<?xml version='1.0'?>
<schema targetNamespace="http://localhost/WebServices/schema/po/"
        xmlns="http://www.w3.org/2001/XMLSchema"
        xmlns:types1="http://localhost/WebServices/schema/po/">
  <element name="purchaseOrder">
  <element name="purchaseOrder">
   <complexType>
     <sequence>
       <element name="pono" type="string" />
       <element name="shipTo" type="types1:AddressType" />
       <element name="billTo" type="types1:AddressType"/>
       <element name="items" type="types1:LineItemsType"/>
```

```
      </sequence>
    </complexType>
   </element>
   <complexType name="AddressType">
    <sequence>
     <element name="name" type="string"/>
     <element name="street" type="string"/>
     <element name="city" type="string"/>
     <element name="state" type="string"/>
     <element name="zip" type="int"/>
     <element name="country" type="NMTOKEN" />
    </sequence>
   </complexType>
   <complexType name="LineItemsType">
    <sequence>
     <element minOccurs="0" maxOccurs="unbounded" name="item"
       type="types1:LineItemType" />
    </sequence>
   </complexType>
   <complexType name="LineItemType">
     <sequence>
       <element name="partId" type="int"/>
       <element name="quantity" type="decimal"/>
       <element name="price">
         <complexType>
            <simpleContent>
              <extension base="decimal">
                <attribute name="currency" type="string"/>
              </extension>
            </simpleContent>
          </complexType>
        </element>
     </sequence>
     <attribute name="id" type="int"/>
   </complexType>
 </schema >
```

As you can see, the above document is the same as the `po_attr.xsd` discussed previously, except for the highlighted definition describing the `price` element.

Now, if you call the `placeOrder` function to transmit the `purchaseOrder` document shown prior to the above XML schema document, you should pass the following array as the argument (it has been cut down to save space):

```
object(stdClass)#2 (4) {
  ["pono"]=>   string(9) "108128476"

  ...

  ["items"]=>
  array(1) {
    ["item"]=>
    array(2) {
      [0]=>
      array(4) {
        ["id"]=>           string(2) "24"
        ["partId"]=>       string(3) "743"
        ["quantity"]=>     string(1) "4"
        ["price"]=>
        array(2) {
          ["_"]=>            string(4) "15.5"
          ["currency"]=>     string(3) "USD"
        }
      }
      [1]=>
      array(4) {
        ["id"]=>           string(2) "25"
        ["partId"]=>       string(3) "235"
        ["quantity"]=>     string(1) "7"
        ["price"]=>
        array(2) {
          ["_"]=>            string(5) "15.75"
          ["currency"]=>     string(3) "USD"
        }
      }
    }
  }
}
```

Note that each `price` element is represented as a two-field array in which the value of the `price` element is mapped to an _ (underscore) field, and the `currency` attribute is mapped to the `currency` field.

In this example, the `stdClass` object generated by the SOAP server and then sent to the `placeOrder` method of the `purchaseOrder` PHP handler class as the argument is as follows (again, fields of the object that are unimportant to this discussion have been omitted to save space):

```
object(stdClass)#2 (4) {
  ["pono"]=>   string(9) "108128476"

  ...

  ["items"]=>
  object(stdClass)#5 (1) {
    ["item"]=>
    array(2) {
      [0]=>
      object(stdClass)#6 (4) {
        ["partId"]=>        int(743)
        ["quantity"]=>      string(1) "4"
        ["price"]=>
        object(stdClass)#7 (2) {
          ["_"]=>             string(4) "15.5"
          ["currency"]=>      string(3) "USD"
        }
        ["id"]=>            int(24)
      }
      [1]=>
      object(stdClass)#8 (4) {
        ["partId"]=>        int(235)
        ["quantity"]=>      string(1) "7"
        ["price"]=>
        object(stdClass)#9 (2) {
          ["_"]=>             string(5) "15.75"
          ["currency"]=>      string(3) "USD"
        }
        ["id"]=>            int(25)
      }
    }
  }
}
```

You might want to convert the above `stdClass` object back to XML. To do this, you might make use of the `obj2Dom` class discussed in the *Converting SOAP Messages' Payloads to XML* section. However, before you can do that you should modify the `buildDom` method of `obj2Dom` by adding some lines of code as shown below (the added code is highlighted):

```
private function buildDom($result, $node) {
  $attrFlag=0;
  foreach($result as $key => $value) {
```

```
        if (!is_int($key)){
          $nodeName=$key;
        }
        else {
          $nodeName=$this->arrayName;
        }
        if ($attrFlag==1) {
          $node->setAttribute($nodeName,$value);
          continue;
        }
        if ($nodeName=='_') {
          $txt = $this->dom->createTextNode($value);
          $txt = $node->appendChild($txt);
          $attrFlag = 1;
          continue;
        }
        if (!is_object($value)){
              if (is_array($value)) {
                $this->arrayName=$key;
                $this->buildDom($value,$node);
              }
              else {
                $elm = $this->dom->createElement($nodeName);
                $elm = $node->appendChild($elm);
                $txt = $this->dom->createTextNode($value);
                $txt = $elm->appendChild($txt);
              }
            }
         else {
            $elm = $this->dom->createElement($nodeName);
            $elm = $node->appendChild($elm);
            $this->buildDom($value,$elm);
          }
        }
    }
```

Now, when invoked, the `buildDom` method shown above will correctly handle the _ fields in the input `stdClass` object, creating attributes in the appropriate text-node elements of the resultant DOM document.

However, note that the updated `obj2Dom` class still doesn't provide you a mechanism to create attributes in the resultant document when it comes to dealing with attributes of elements containing nested elements. To handle this problem, you might add the following method to the `obj2Dom` class:

```
public function elmToAttr($nodeName)
{
   $items = $this->dom->getElementsByTagName($nodeName);
   $count= $items->length;
   for ($i = 0; $i < $count; $i++) {
      $node = $items->item(0);
      $parent = $node->parentNode;
      $parent->setAttribute($node->nodeName, $node->nodeValue);
      $parent->removeChild(
                 $parent->getElementsByTagName($nodeName)->item(0));
  }
}
```

The above method takes the name of the element to be processed as the parameter. If the DOM tree contains more than one element with the name specified, this method will process each of these elements, converting such an element to an attribute of its parent element. You will see this method in action in the following section, when converting `id` elements in the `item` constructs to `id` attributes.

Transforming XML Documents with XSLT

As you learned in the preceding section, if you need to send an XML document containing attributes from a SOAP node built with the PHP SOAP extension, then you first have to convert that document into an array in which both the attributes and elements of the document are represented as fields. To build such an array on an attribute-containing XML document, you might find it useful first to transform that document into the one containing no attributes but only elements. This is where XSLT (eXtensible Stylesheet Language Transformations) may come in very handy.

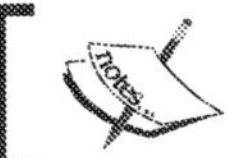

> To learn more about XSLT, you can visit the following resource: `http://www.w3.org/TR/xslt`.

Suppose you need to transform the following PO XML document, say, saved as `po.xml`, so that the result document can be easily translated into an array to be passed as the argument to the `placeOrder` function exposed by the PO Web service.

```
<?xml version="1.0" ?>
<purchaseOrder>
  <pono>108128476</pono>
 ...
  <items>
   <item id="24">
```

```
        <partId>743</partId>
        <quantity>4</quantity>
        <price currency="USD">15.5</price>
      </item>
      <item id="25">
        <partId>235</partId>
        <quantity>7</quantity>
        <price currency="USD">15.75</price>
      </item>
      </items>
    </purchaseOrder>
```

Now, to transform this document into another one that in turn can be easily converted into an array to be passed to the `placeOrder` function as the argument, you can create an XSL stylesheet that might look as follows. It is assumed that you save this XSL stylesheet as `AttrsToElms.xsl` in the `WebServices/ch2` directory.

```
<?xml version='1.0' encoding='utf-8' ?>
<xsl:stylesheet xmlns:xsl="http://www.w3.org/1999/XSL/Transform"
version="1.0">
  <xsl:output method="xml"/>
   <xsl:template match="purchaseOrder">
    <purchaseOrder>
      <xsl:apply-templates/>
    </purchaseOrder>
   </xsl:template>
   <xsl:template match="@*|*|text()">
    <xsl:copy>
     <xsl:apply-templates select="@*|*|text()"/>
    </xsl:copy>
   </xsl:template>
   <xsl:template match="items">
    <items>
     <xsl:for-each select="item">
      <xsl:element name="{name()}">
        <xsl:for-each select="@*">
          <xsl:element name="{name()}">
            <xsl:value-of select="."/>
          </xsl:element>
        </xsl:for-each>
        <xsl:for-each select="*">
          <xsl:choose>
           <xsl:when test="name()='price'">
            <price>
```

```
                <_>
                 <xsl:value-of select="."/>
                </_>
                <xsl:for-each select="@*">
                 <xsl:element name="{name()}">
                  <xsl:value-of select="."/>
                 </xsl:element>
                </xsl:for-each>
               </price>
              </xsl:when>
              <xsl:otherwise>
               <xsl:element name="{name()}">
                <xsl:value-of select="."/>
               </xsl:element>
              </xsl:otherwise>
             </xsl:choose>
            </xsl:for-each>
           </xsl:element>
        </xsl:for-each>
       </items>
      </xsl:template>
   </xsl:stylesheet>
```

In the first highlighted block you transform all the attributes of the `item` element being processed into nested elements of this `item` element.

In the second highlighted block you process the elements nested in the `item` elements, performing conditional processing with the `xsl:choose` construct. Specifically, when the nested element being processed is `price`, all its attributes are transformed into elements nested in `price`, and its value is wrapped in the _ element. Otherwise, the `item`'s nested element being processed remains the same as before.

To test the XSL stylesheet, create the following script:

```
<?php
 //File: XSLTest.php
 $xml = new DOMDocument();
 $xml->load('po.xml');
 $xsl = new DOMDocument();
 $xsl->load('AttrsToElms.xsl');
 $proc = new XSLTProcessor;
 $proc->importStyleSheet($xsl);
 print $proc->transformToXML($xml);
?>
```

If you execute this script, it should produce the following document:

```
<?xml version="1.0" ?>
<purchaseOrder>
  <pono>108128476</pono>

 ...

  <items>
   <item>
    <id>24</id>
    <partId>743</partId>
    <quantity>4</quantity>
    <price>
       <_>15.5</_>
       <currency>USD</currency>
    </price>
   </item>
   <item>
    <id>25</id>
    <partId>235</partId>
    <quantity>7</quantity>
    <price>
       <_>15.75</_>
       <currency>USD</currency>
    </price>
   </item>
   </items>
  </purchaseOrder>
```

If you see the above document in your browser, it means the XSL transformation performed within the `XSLtest.php` script has been successfully applied, and everything works as expected. If so, you can move on and use this mechanism in a SOAP client script to transform the `po.xml` document shown at the beginning of this section to the above XML document, the one that is then translated into the array to be passed to the `placeOrder` function as the argument.

For example, you might create the following script and save it as `SoapClient_attr_price.php` in the `WebServices/ch2` directory.

```
<?php
 //File: SoapClient_attr_price.php
 require_once "obj2Arr.php";
 $wsdl = "http://localhost/WebServices/wsdl/po_attr_price.wsdl";
```

```
$xml = new DOMDocument();
$xml->load('po.xml');
$xsl = new DOMDocument();
$xsl->load('AttrsToElms.xsl');
$proc = new XSLTProcessor;
$proc->importStyleSheet($xsl);
$poxml = $proc->transformToXML($xml);
$xmldoc = simplexml_load_string($poxml);
$xmlarr = obj2Arr($xmldoc);
$client = new SoapClient($wsdl);
try {
 print $result=$client->placeOrder($xmlarr);
}
catch (SoapFault $exp) {
 print $exp->getMessage();
}
?>
```

As you can see, the above script starts by performing the XSL transformation, the same as the one you saw in the `XSLTest.php` script earlier. Next, it loads the resultant document into a SimpleXML object, which is then transformed into an array being passed to the `placeOrder` function as the argument.

However, before you can execute the above SOAP client script you need to create a SOAP server and PHP handle class to handler responses from the client.

When creating the `SoapServer_attr_price.php` SOAP server script, you can use the `SoapServer.php` script discussed in the *Building the SOAP Server* section as the basis, changing the included PHP handler class to `purchaseOrder_attr_price.php` and the WSDL document location to `http://localhost/WebServices/wsdl/po_attr_price.wsdl`.

If you don't have the `po_attr_price.wsdl` created, you should build it now. As the base, you can use the `po_imp.wsdl` document discussed in the *Importing XML Schemas into WSDL Documents* section, importing the `po_attr_price.xsd` XML schema discussed in the *Dealing with Attributes* section and pointing the `soap:address location` attribute to `http://localhost/WebServices/ch2/SOAPServer_attr_price.php`.

The purchaseOrder_attr_price.php script containing the handler class should look as follows:

```
<?php
 //File purchaseOrder_attr_price.php
 require_once 'obj2Dom.php';
 class purchaseOrder {
   function placeOrder($po) {
    $obj = new obj2Dom('purchaseOrder');
    $obj->trans2Dom($po);
    $obj->elmToAttr('id');
    $po=$obj->printDomTree();
    if(!$conn = oci_connect('xmlusr', 'xmlusr', '//localhost/XE')){
       throw new SoapFault("Server","Failed to connect to database");
    };
    $sql = "INSERT INTO purchaseOrders VALUES(:po)";
    $query = oci_parse($conn, $sql);
    oci_bind_by_name($query, ':po', $po);
    if (!oci_execute($query)) {
        throw new SoapFault("Server","Failed to insert PO");
    };
    $msg='<rsltMsg>PO inserted!</rsltMsg>';
    return $msg;
   }
 }
?>
```

As you can see, the placeOrder function is similar to the one in the purchaseOrder_typed.php script discussed in the *Converting SOAP Messages' Payloads to XML* section earlier. The only difference is that you utilize the elmToAttr method of the obj2Dom instance here, passing 'id' as the argument.

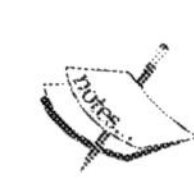

As an alternative to the elmToAttr method here, you might apply an XSL transformation to the resultant XML document returned by the printDomTree method, converting id elements into attributes, as they were in the original document.

Now, if you execute the SoapClient_attr_price.php script, the placeOrder function should insert into the purchaseOrders table the po.xml document shown at the beginning of this section.

Extending PHP SOAP Extension Predefined Classes

You can extend predefined classes of the PHP SOAP extension as needed. Here is an example of how you might extend the `SoapServer` class. It is assumed that you save this script as `SoapServer_ext.php` in the in the `WebServices\ch2`:

```
<?php
 //File: SoapServer_ext.php
 require_once "purchaseOrder.php";
 class MySoapServer extends SoapServer {
  var $client;
  function __construct($wsdl1, $wsdl2) {
   parent::__construct($wsdl1);
   $this->client = new SoapClient($wsdl2);
  }
  function handle() {
   ob_start();
   parent::handle();
   $buf=ob_get_contents();
   ob_get_flush();
   $buf=html_entity_decode($buf);
   $env = simplexml_load_string($buf);
   $rslt= $env->xpath('//rsltMsg');
   if ($rslt==null) {
    $rslt= $env->xpath('//faultstring');
   }
   $this->client->regOrder(htmlentities((string) $rslt[0]));
  }
 }
 $wsdl1= "http://localhost/WebServices/wsdl/po_ext.wsdl";
 $wsdl2= "http://localhost/WebServices/wsdl/reg.wsdl";
 $srv= new MySoapServer($wsdl1, $wsdl2);
 $srv->setClass("purchaseOrder");
 $srv->handle();
?>
```

The `MySoapServer` class extending the `SoapServer` predefined class overrides the constructor and the `handle` method of the parent class. The overridden constructor takes links to the two WSDL documents as the parameters, and creates a `SoapClient` instance that is then used in the overridden `handle` method to invoke the `regOrder` SOAP function.

Before you put this SOAP server script into action, you have to create a few other scripts and documents. First of all, make sure to create the `po_ext.wsdl` and `reg.wsdl` documents used here.

To create the `po_ext.wsdl` document, you can use the `po.wsdl` file discussed in the *Designing the WSDL Document* section as the base. The only thing you have to change is the value of the `location` attribute in the `soap:address` element within the `service` definition of the document. In particular, you should specify the following URL: `http://localhost/WebServices/ch2/SOAPServer_ext.php`. In the case of `reg.wsdl`, you should specify the following value for the `soap:address location` attribute: `http://localhost/WebServices/ch2/SOAPServer_reg.php`.

The next step is to create the `SOAPServer_reg.php` SOAP server script that will be automatically invoked each time the overridden `handle` method of `MySoapServer` is called. The `SOAPServer_reg.php` should look like the following:

```
<?php
 //File: SoapServer_reg.php
 $wsdl= "http://localhost/WebServices/wsdl/reg.wsdl";
 require_once "reg.php";
 $srv = new SoapServer($wsdl);
 $srv->setClass("reg");
 $srv->handle();
?>
```

As you can see, the above SOAP server exposes methods of the `reg` custom class. So, make sure to create the `reg` class. It might look like the following:

```
<?php
 //File reg.php
 class reg {
   function regOrder($reginfo) {
    if(!$conn = oci_connect('xmlusr', 'xmlusr', '//localhost/XE')){
        throw new SoapFault("Server","Failed to connect to
                                                        database");
    };
    $sql="INSERT INTO regDocs VALUES(SYSDATE, :reginfo)";
    $query = oci_parse($conn, $sql);
    oci_bind_by_name($query, ':reginfo', $reginfo);
    if (!oci_execute($query)) {
        throw new SoapFault("Server","Failed to execute query");
    };
    $msg='Ok!';
    return $msg;
   }
 }
?>
```

Looking through this code, you may notice that the `regOrder` method takes one parameter and inserts it into the `regDocs` database table. So you need to create the `regDocs` table before you can use `regOrder`. This can be done from SQL*Plus by issuing the following statements:

```
CONN xmlusr/xmlusr;

CREATE TABLE regDocs(
    dateTime DATE,
    msg VARCHAR2(100)
);
```

Finally, you have to create the `SoapClient_ext.php` script that will call the `placeOrder` method of the `purchaseOrder` class exposed by the `SoapServer_ext.php` SOAP server script. The `SoapClient_ext.php` is almost the same as the `SoapClient.php` script discussed in the *Building the Service Requestor* section, except for the WSDL document specified. In the case of `SoapClient_ext.php`, you should specify `http://localhost/WebServices/wsdl/reg.wsdl` as the WSDL document.

Now, if you execute the `SoapClient_ext.php` script, you should see a **PO inserted!** message. Then, you can check out the `regDocs` table by issuing the following statements from SQL*Plus:

```
CONN xmlusr/xmlusr;

SELECT * FROM regDocs;
```

The above should return output that might look as follows:

```
DATETIME    MSG
---------------------------
02-APR-07   PO inserted!
```

Defining Parameter-Driven Operations

As mentioned in Chapter 1, using parameter-driven service operations allows you to invoke the required piece of underlying logic depending on the arguments passed in. So, you can expose a single operation—passing parameters identifying what actually has to be done. This section shows a simple example of using this technique. You'll build a Web service that exposes a single function, namely `getOrder`. This function takes two parameters: the ID of a `purchaseOrder` and the parameter identifying what you want to receive: the document itself or its status.

To start with, you need to create a database table to store the orders' status information. Here are the statements you should issue from SQL*Plus:

```
CONN xmlusr/xmlusr;

CREATE TABLE poStatusInfo(
    pono VARCHAR2(9),
    status VARCHAR2(15)
);


INSERT INTO poStatusInfo VALUES(

    '108128476',

    'shipped'

);


COMMIT;
```

The next step is to create the underlying service logic. To achieve this, create the following class and save it in the `orderInfo.php` file:

```
<?php
 //File orderInfo.php
 class orderInfo {
   function getOrder($pono, $par) {
    if(!$conn = oci_connect('xmlusr', 'xmlusr', '//localhost/XE')){
        throw new SoapFault("Server","Failed to connect to
                                          database");
    };
    switch ($par) {
     case 'doc':
      $sql="SELECT doc FROM purchaseOrders WHERE
         extractValue(XMLType(doc), '/purchaseOrder/pono')=:pono
         AND rownum=1";
      break;
     case 'status':
      $sql="SELECT status FROM poStatusInfo WHERE pono=:pono";
      break;
    }
    $query = oci_parse($conn, $sql);
    oci_bind_by_name($query, ':pono', $pono);
```

```
        if (!oci_execute($query)) {
            throw new SoapFault("Server","Failed to execute query");
        };
        oci_fetch($query);
        $rslt = oci_result($query, strtoupper($par));
        return $rslt;
      }
   }
?>
```

As you can see, `orderInfo` uses a different SQL statement querying the database, depending on the value passed in with the second parameter.

Next, you need to create the WSDL document describing the Web service discussed here. Here is the WSDL document being used in this example. It is assumed that you save it as `po_params.wsdl` in the `WebServices/wsdl` directory:

```
<?xml version="1.0" encoding="utf-8"?>
<definitions name ="poInfoService"
             xmlns:http="http://schemas.xmlsoap.org/wsdl/http/"
             xmlns:soap="http://schemas.xmlsoap.org/wsdl/soap/"
             xmlns:xsd="http://www.w3.org/2001/XMLSchema"
             xmlns="http://schemas.xmlsoap.org/wsdl/"
             targetNamespace=
                          "http://localhost/WebServices/wsdl/poInfo">
    <message name="getOrderInfoInput">
        <part name="pono" element="xsd:string"/>
        <part name="par" element="xsd:string"/>
    </message>
    <message name="getOrderInfoOutput">
        <part name="body" element="xsd:string"/>
    </message>
    <portType name="poInfoServicePortType">
        <operation name="getOrder">
           <input message="tns:getOrderInfoInput"/>
           <output message="tns:getOrderInfoOutput"/>
        </operation>
    </portType>
    <binding name="poInfoServiceBinding"
             type="tns:poInfoServicePortType">
        <soap:binding style="rpc"
             transport="http://schemas.xmlsoap.org/soap/http"/>
        <operation name="getOrder">
           <soap:operation
             soapAction="http://localhost/WebServices/ch2/getOrder"/>
```

```
            <input>
                <soap:body use="literal"/>
            </input>
            <output>
                <soap:body use="literal"/>
            </output>
        </operation>
    </binding>
    <service name="poInfoService">
        <port name="poInfoServicePort"
             binding="tns:poInfoServiceBinding">
            <soap:address
  location="http://localhost/WebServices/ch2/SOAPServer_params.php"/>
        </port>
    </service>
</definitions>
```

Note that the `getOrderInfoInput` message in the above document consists of two parts that represent parameters of the `getOrder` operation described in the document.

To expose the `getOrder` method of the `orderInfo` class, you use the following SOAP server script, saved as `SOAPServer_params.php`:

```
<?php
//File: SoapServer_params.php
require_once "orderInfo.php";
$wsdl= "http://localhost/WebServices/wsdl/po_params.wsdl";
$srv= new SoapServer($wsdl);
$srv->setClass("orderInfo");
$srv->handle();
?>
```

Once you've done all that, you can test the Web service. To do this, you might build and then execute the following SOAP client.

```
<?php
 //File: SoapClient_params.php
 $wsdl = "http://localhost/WebServices/wsdl/po_params.wsdl";
 $client = new SoapClient($wsdl);
 $pono='108128476';
 $par-'doc';
 try {
  print $result=$client->getOrder($pono, $par);
 }
 catch (SoapFault $exp) {
  print $exp->getMessage();
 }
?>
```

When executed, this script should output the entire PO XML document whose `pono` is `108128476`. However, if you specify `$par='status'` in the above code, you will get only the message saying `shipped`.

Summary

As you have learned in this chapter, creating service providers and service requestors with the PHP SOAP extension is quite easy in most cases—you simply manipulate predefined SOAP classes. Things become a bit more complicated when it comes to transmitting complex type data—especially if you are dealing with XML documents whose elements contain attributes. This is where intermediate transformations are required. We looked at how to employ a custom PHP class to perform such transformations and how to use standard XSLT mechanism.

In this chapter, you also learned how to extend predefined classes of the PHP SOAP extension and how standard methods of these classes can be overridden to suit the needs of your application. The chapter wrapped up by explaining how to build Web services supporting parameter-driven operations.

3

Designing Data-Centric Web Services

The PO Web service discussed in the preceding chapter used a database to store the incoming PO XML documents. Another common usage of a database by a Web service is to retrieve from the database data required to satisfy the request of a consumer. It is worth noting that a service consumer may also interact with a database to store or retrieve data being received from or sent to the service provider. However, in a real-world situation, a service or service consumer may use a database not only to store or retrieve data, but also to perform some processing on that data, thus putting some data processing logic inside the database.

This chapter contains several examples on using the two most popular databases today—MySQL and Oracle—when building data-centric Web services. The examples provided here will help you understand the differences between these two databases and help you choose the most appropriate one when planning your solution. In this chapter, you will learn the following:

- Factors to consider when choosing a database for your data-centric service
- Building services interacting with MySQL
- Using relational tables to store XML data processed by a service
- Creating services interacting with Oracle
- Effectively distributing data processing between the Web/PHP server and database server
- Utilizing Oracle's XML features when building the underlying logic of a service
- Moving the conditional logic of a parameter-driven operation into the database

Which Database to Choose

It's important to realize, when designing a data-centric service, the database is just a part of the solution—some underlying logic is still implemented outside the database. Which part of the underlying logic may be implemented inside the database depends on the database used. You should keep in mind that databases are different—many of them allow you not only to store data, but also to process it, thus moving data processing into the database. So, knowing your database, its capabilities and features, is the only way you'll be able to come up with effective data-centric Web services. This section focuses on the two most popular databases today: MySQL and Oracle.

Before moving on to the discussion of issues related to a specific database, though, let's look at the general structure of a data-centric service. The following figure gives a conceptual depiction of a data-centric service.

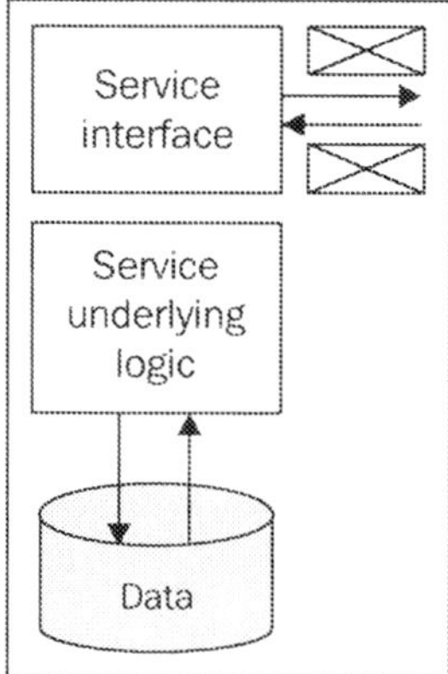

As you can see in the figure, a data-centric Web service, like any other Web service, uses its service interface to communicate with the outside world by means of SOAP messages. The service underlying logic is responsible for interacting with the database.

What the above figure doesn't tell you is that how underlying logic of a data-centric service is distributed between the Web/PHP server and database server. Actually, there may be several different variations. As stated earlier, the most important factor that influences the underlying logic implementation is the database you use. For example, if you are using Oracle, in most cases you can implement the underlying logic of a service entirely within the database. In contrast, when using MySQL, you probably will have to implement most of this logic in PHP.

Going back to the examples you saw in the preceding chapter, you will remember that a SOAP message payload is usually an XML document of a certain XSD type. When the message arrives, though, the payload is by default transformed into an `stdClass` object.

> However, sometimes you may need to pass over this transformation and utilize the XML document in the form in which it arrives.

On the other hand, databases usually deal with relational data. So, when developing data-centric services using PHP SOAP extension, you often need to implement some transformation logic responsible for transforming PHP structures or XML into relational data and vice versa. The following figure shows an example in which all the data processing is implemented in PHP, using the database only as a repository for storing data. This particular example assumes that the data arriving with incoming messages is not translated into PHP structures such as `stdClass` objects, and is processed as XML.

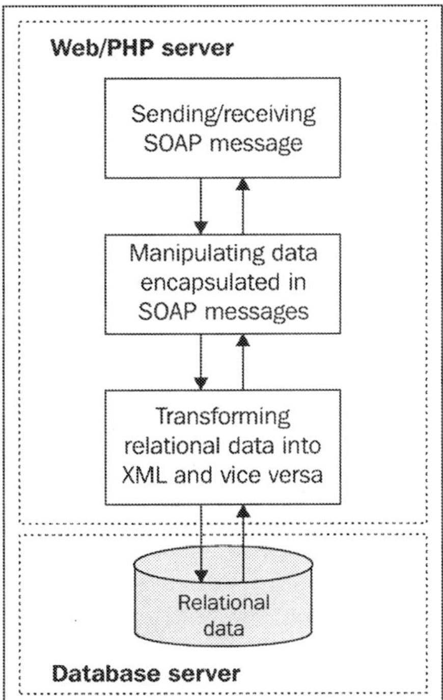

You may use the approach depicted in the figure when your database doesn't provide the native XML support. This approach can also be employed when using PHP in conjunction with Oracle; however, in the case of Oracle you have several options when it comes to dealing with XML content based on relational data. For example, you might move transformation logic into the database, or even implement logic for manipulating data encapsulated in SOAP messages inside the database. These two options are depicted in the following figure:

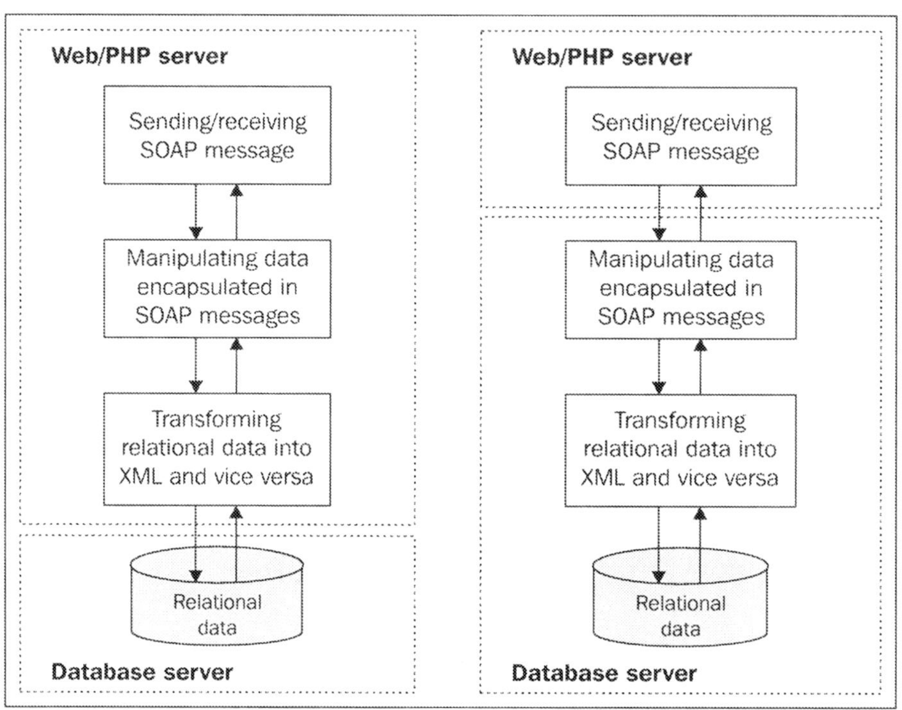

As you can see in the figure, Oracle allows you to perform data processing inside the database, rather than operating on the Web/PHP server side. By moving the key business logic of your service into the database, you will have more reusable solutions, since the implementation details of the service's underlying logic are removed from the PHP handler class, thus making it easier to reuse either the PHP class or the underlying logic implemented inside the database in another project. Moreover, this approach of moving underlying logic of a service inside the database makes it possible to take advantage of the Oracle XML features, including XML-specific memory optimizations, thus increasing performance of the service.

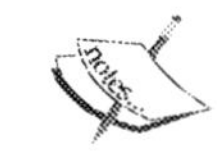

In the *Moving Conditional Logic into the Database* section later in this chapter, you will see an example of moving underlying logic of a service inside an Oracle database.

While the previous figure illustrates how the processing logic of a data-centric service operating on relational data might be moved into the database, Oracle, however, provides a better option. With Oracle, you can store and retrieve the data you are working with in an XML format, thus avoiding the need to transform your data from XML to a relational set and vice versa. The following figure gives a graphical depiction of this design.

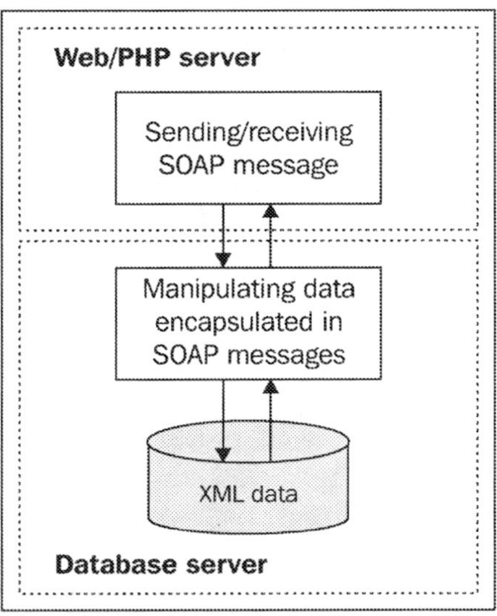

To handle XML data in the database natively, Oracle introduced the `XMLType` datatype. With the help of `XMLType`, you can handle XML documents via SQL and PL/SQL interfaces much as you do when it comes to working with relational data.

In fact, Oracle provides a set of XML features to assist native handling of XML data. Use of Oracle's XML features is discussed in greater detail in the *Using Oracle Database XE* section later in this chapter. For more details, you can refer to Oracle Documentation: *Oracle XML DB Developer's Guide*.

Using MySQL

MySQL remains the most popular open-source database today. Although MySQL lacks native XML support, it can still be efficiently used as the database back end in data-centric Web services.

As of PHP 5, MySQL support is not enabled by default. On Linux systems, you have to compile your PHP installation using the `--with-mysql` configure option to enable the MySQL extension. If you are a Windows user, you need to uncomment the `extension=php_mysql.dll` line in the `php.ini` configuration file and restart the Web server.

In the following sections, you will see some examples showing how you might organize your data-centric services to interact with MySQL.

Building a Service Interacting with MySQL

Coming back to the example discussed in the *Building Service Providers and Service Requestors* section in Chapter 2, you might want to rebuild it to interact with MySQL instead of Oracle.

To start with, you need to create a new database and then define a user to connect to the newly created database, granting the required privileges to that user. Next, you need to shift to this database and create the `purchaseOrder` table to be used to store PO XML documents. To handle this task, you can issue the following SQL statements from the MySQL Command Line Client:

```
CREATE DATABASE my_db;

GRANT CREATE, DROP, SELECT, INSERT, UPDATE, DELETE
ON my_db.*
TO 'usr'@'localhost'
IDENTIFIED BY 'pswd';

USE my_db

CREATE TABLE purchaseOrders(
 id INTEGER AUTO_INCREMENT PRIMARY KEY,
 doc VARCHAR(2000)
);
```

Once you're done, you have the database with the `purchaseOrders` table required to store the incoming purchase orders. Now you can move on to the next subject: the PHP handler class.

In the case of MySQL, the `purchaseOrder` class discussed in the *Developing the PHP Handler Class* section in Chapter 2 might look like the following:

```
<?php
 //File purchaseOrder.php
 class purchaseOrder {
   function placeOrder($po) {
    if(!$conn = mysql_connect('localhost', 'usr', 'pswd')){
```

```
            throw new SoapFault("Server","Failed to connect to
                                                database");
        };
        if(!mysql_select_db('my_db')){
            throw new SoapFault("Server","Failed to select database");
        };
        $sql = "INSERT INTO purchaseOrders SET doc='".$po."'";
        if (!$result = mysql_query($sql)) {
            throw new SoapFault("Server","Failed to insert PO");
        };
        mysql_close($conn);
        $msg='<rsltMsg>PO inserted!</rsltMsg>';
        return $msg;
      }
  }
?>
```

The above example uses the PHP MySQL extension functions to interact with the database. If you're using MySQL 4.1.3 or newer, you can take advantage of the MySQL Improved extension. In that case, the `purchaseOrder` class shown above might be rewritten as follows:

```
<?php
 //File purchaseOrder_mysqli.php
 class purchaseOrder {
   function placeOrder($po) {
     if(!$conn = new mysqli('localhost', 'usr', 'pswd', 'my_db')){
         throw new SoapFault("Server","Failed to connect to
                                                database");
     };
     $sql = "INSERT INTO purchaseOrders(doc) VALUES (?)";
     $stmt = $conn->prepare($sql);
     $stmt->bind_param('s', $po);
     if (!$result = $stmt->execute()) {
         throw new SoapFault("Server","Failed to insert PO");
     };
     $stmt->close();
     $conn->close();
     $msg='<rsltMsg>PO inserted!</rsltMsg>';
     return $msg;
   }
 }
?>
```

While this script looks a bit better than the previous one, from the user's standpoint, though, they both come to the same result.

> The PHP MySQL Improved extension is a new feature bundled with PHP 5. To enable it on a Linux system, you need to have your PHP installation compiled using the `--with-mysqli=mysql_config_path/mysql_config` configure option, specifying the actual path to the `mysql_config` program shipped with MySQL, in place of `mysql_config_path`. If you are a Windows user, you need to have the `extension=php_mysqli.dll` line uncommented in the `php.ini` configuration file.

It is important to note that moving towards MySQL in the `purchaseOrder.php` PHP handler class as shown in the above examples doesn't require any changes in the `SoapClient.php` and `SoapServer.php` scripts discussed in Chapter 2 in the *Building the Service Requestor* and *Building the SOAP Server* sections respectively.

To be able to test the example discussed here, you will need to copy the `SoapClient.php` and `SoapServer.php` scripts, as well as the `purchaseOrder.xml` document, from the `/WebServices/ch2` directory to `/WebServices/ch3` and then modify these scripts so that they employ the `po_mysql.wsdl` WSDL document rather than the `po.wsdl` document used in those scripts in Chapter 2. So, the updated `SoapClient.php` should look as follows:

```
<?php
 //File: SoapClient.php
 $wsdl = "http://localhost/WebServices/wsdl/po_mysql.wsdl";
 $handle = fopen("purchaseOrder.xml", "r");
 $po= fread($handle, filesize("purchaseOrder.xml"));
 fclose($handle);
 $client = new SoapClient($wsdl);
 try {
  print $result=$client->placeOrder($po);
 }
 catch (SoapFault $exp) {
  print $exp->getMessage();
 }
?>
```

This means you will also need to create `po_mysql.wsdl` in the `/WebServices/wsdl` directory. The only difference between the `po.wsdl` WSDL document discussed in Chapter 2 and `po_mysql.wsdl` used here is that the latter, using the `location` attribute of the `soap:address` element, references the `SOAPServer.php` script stored in the `/WebServices/ch3` directory, while the former references `/WebServices/ch2/SOAPServer.php` script.

Once you've done all that, you can execute the /WebServices/ch3/SoapClient.php script. As a result, you should see a **PO inserted!** message in your browser.

To make sure a PO document has been inserted, you can execute the following simple script that selects the data stored in the doc column of the purchaseOrders MySQL table and outputs it to the browser:

```
<?php
    //getOrders.php
    $conn = mysql_connect('localhost', 'usr', 'pswd')
        or die("Failed to connect to database: ".mysql_error());
    mysql_select_db('my_db')
        or die("Failed to select database");
    $sql = "SELECT doc FROM purchaseOrders";
    $result = mysql_query($sql)
        or die("Failed to select data: ".mysql_error());
    while ($line = mysql_fetch_array($result, MYSQL_ASSOC)) {
    foreach ($line as $col_value) {
       echo $col_value;
     }
    }
    mysql_free_result($result);
    mysql_close($conn);
?>
```

As a result, you should see the same PO XML document as the one passed to the placeOrder method as the parameter in the SoapClient.php script discussed earlier in this section.

Storing XML Data in Relational Tables

As you saw in the preceding section, storing an XML document as a string in MySQL is as easy as in Oracle. But what if you want to shred an incoming XML document into relational data and then store it in a set of related tables?

To handle this task, you first need to examine the structure of the XML documents being stored. Schematically, the PO XML document discussed here looks as follows:

```
<purchaseOrder>
 <pono>...</pono>
 <shipTo>
  ...
 </shipTo>
 <billTo>
  ...
```

```
  </billTo>
  <items>
    <item>
     ...
    </item>
    ...
  </items>
</purchaseOrder>
```

Looking through the above structure, you might divide it into the following four logical blocks:

- Upper-level elements containing no nested elements. In this particular example, there is only one such element, namely `pono`. A real-world PO would contain more such elements; for example, `shipDate` and `customerId`.
- Elements within the `shipTo` construct.
- Elements within the `billTo` construct.
- `item` elements within the `items` construct.

What this means in practice is that you need to create four tables to store the shredded PO XML documents. For the purpose of this example, you might create the tables as shown below, using the MySQL Command Line Tool—a simple SQL shell that comes with MySQL.

```
CREATE TABLE orders (
    pono VARCHAR(9) PRIMARY KEY
) ENGINE= InnoDB;
CREATE TABLE shipTo (
    pono VARCHAR(9) PRIMARY KEY,
    name VARCHAR(30),
    street VARCHAR(50),
    city VARCHAR(50),
    state VARCHAR(2),
    zip INTEGER,
    country VARCHAR(3),
    FOREIGN KEY (pono) REFERENCES orders (pono)
) ENGINE= InnoDB;
CREATE TABLE billTo (
    pono VARCHAR(9) PRIMARY KEY,
    name VARCHAR(30),
    street VARCHAR(50),
    city VARCHAR(50),
    state VARCHAR(2),
```

```
        zip INTEGER,
        country VARCHAR(3),
        FOREIGN KEY (pono) REFERENCES orders (pono)
    ) ENGINE= InnoDB;
    CREATE TABLE items (
        id INTEGER AUTO_INCREMENT PRIMARY KEY,
        pono VARCHAR(9),
        partId INTEGER,
        quantity DECIMAL(20,4),
        price DECIMAL(12,2),
        FOREIGN KEY (pono) REFERENCES orders (pono)
    ) ENGINE= InnoDB;
```

As you can see, in this particular example the `orders` table contains a single field, namely `pono`. You declare this field as the primary key because you don't want the `orders` table to contain two or more rows representing the same PO document.

Each of the other tables created here also contains a `pono` field, which is used in these case as a foreign key to the `orders` table. The foreign key constraints used here guarantee that the `billTo`, `shipTo`, and `items` tables will contain only those rows that have a matching row in the `orders` table. The difference between these tables is that the `billTo` and `shipTo` tables use the `pono` field as a foreign key and primary key simultaneously, while the `items` table uses that field only as a foreign key. There is a simple explanation: this is because a PO XML document may contain only one shipping address and one billing address, while still containing more than one purchased item.

To learn more about using foreign key constraints in MySQL, you can refer to MySQL documentation at `www.mysql.com/doc/en/index.html`.

Now that you have created the database tables to store incoming PO XML documents, you can move on and create the PHP handler class that will shred those documents into appropriate pieces and then store them into the database. The `purchaseOrder_relational.php` script containing the `purchaseOrder` PHP handler class is as follows:

```
<?php
 //File purchaseOrder_relational.php
 class purchaseOrder {
   function placeOrder($po) {
    if(!$conn = new mysqli('localhost', 'usr', 'pswd', 'my_db')){
        throw new SoapFault("Server","Failed to connect to
                                                   database");
```

```
};
$conn->autocommit(FALSE);
//Into orders table you insert only upper-level PO XML
//doc elements containing no nested elements
$sql="INSERT INTO orders SET ";
foreach($po as $key => $value){
 if(!is_object($value))
 {
  $sql=$sql.$key."='".$value."',";
 }
};
$sql = substr($sql, 0, strlen($sql)-1);
$stmt = $conn->prepare($sql);
if (!$stmt->execute()) {
    throw new SoapFault("Server","Failed to insert PO");
};
//Then, you insert billTo and shipTo elements into
//appropriate tables
foreach($po as $key => $value){
 if(is_object($value) AND $key!='items')
 {
   $sql="INSERT INTO ".$key." SET pono ='".$po->pono."',";
   foreach($value as $elmname => $elmvalue){
      $sql=$sql.$elmname."='".$elmvalue."',";
   }
   $sql = substr($sql, 0, strlen($sql)-1);
   $stmt = $conn->prepare($sql);
   if (!$stmt->execute()) {
     throw new SoapFault("Server","Failed to insert PO");
   }
  }
};
//Finally, you fill up the items table
foreach($po->items->item as $key => $value){
   $sql="INSERT INTO items SET pono ='".$po->pono."',";
   foreach($value as $elmname => $elmvalue){
      $sql=$sql.$elmname."='".$elmvalue."',";
   }
   print $sql = substr($sql, 0, strlen($sql)-1);
   $stmt = $conn->prepare($sql);
   if (!$stmt->execute()) {
```

```
            throw new SoapFault("Server","Failed to insert PO");
          }
        }
        $conn->commit();
        $stmt->close();
        $conn->close();
        $msg='<rsltMsg>PO inserted!</rsltMsg>';
        return $msg;
      }
    }
  ?>
```

Despite the fact that an incoming PO XML document is supposed to be shredded into four parts and saved in four different database tables, the above implementation of the `purchaseOrder` class contains three separate processing blocks implementing this shredding logic. Each of these blocks is highlighted in bold in the above listing.

The `foreach` construct in the first highlighted block iterates over each upper-level element in the `stdClass` structure representing the incoming PO document, but only those iterated elements that contain no nested elements are selected here to be inserted into the `orders` table as a single row. In this particular example, the document contains the only such element, namely `pono`.

The `foreach` construct in the second highlighted block iterates the same `stdClass` structure as in the preceding block. However, this time only the complex upper-level elements are processed, excluding the `items` element. In this particular example, this block will process the `billTo` and `shipTo` elements of the document.

In the third highlighted block, the outer `foreach` construct iterates over each item in the `items` construct of the document, inserting each iterated item into the `items` table as a single row.

> In the *Using XML Schemas with Oracle XML DB* section later in this chapter, you will see how the example discussed here might be implemented when using Oracle as the back-end database for the service. In particular, you will learn how to use the XML schema Oracle XML DB feature to make the database implicitly perform the shredding logic implemented here in PHP.

Another important thing to note about the above code is that it is transactional. You turn off the auto-commit mode with the following line:

```
$conn->autocommit(FALSE);
```

By doing so, you explicitly control transactional behavior of the `placeOrder` method, ensuring that an unfinished transaction will not be committed to the database. In this particular example, if at least one `INSERT` operation performed within this method fails, the entire transaction will be automatically rolled back. Only if each `INSERT` operation has been completed successfully, will the transaction be committed to the database, making the changes made permanent. However, this is not going to happen by default; you explicitly commit the transaction after performing all the `INSERT` operations, using the `commit` method of the `mysqli` object as follows:

```
$conn->commit();
```

To put the `purchaseOrder` class shown above into action, you need to create the `SoapServer_relational.php` and `SoapClient_relational.php` scripts in the `WebServices/ch3` directory. Here is the `SoapClient_relational.php` script:

```
<?php
 //File: SoapClient_relational.php
 require_once "obj2Arr.php";
 $wsdl = "http://localhost/WebServices/wsdl/po_relational.wsdl";
 $xmldoc = simplexml_load_file('purchaseOrder.xml');
 $xmlarr = obj2Arr($xmldoc);
 $client = new SoapClient($wsdl);
 try {
  print $result=$client->placeOrder($xmlarr);
 }
 catch (SoapFault $exp) {
  print $exp->getMessage();
 }
?>
```

Note that the above script assumes the `obj2Arr.php` script discussed in Chapter 2 is in the `WebServices/ch3` directory. So, make sure to copy it there from the `WebServices/ch2` directory.

The code for the `SoapServer_relational.php` script is as follows:

```
<?php
//File: SoapServer_relational.php
require_once "purchaseOrder_relational.php";
$wsdl= "http://localhost/WebServices/wsdl/po_relational.wsdl";
$srv= new SoapServer($wsdl);
$srv->setClass("purchaseOrder");
$srv->handle();
?>
```

As you can see, both the client and server use the `po_relational.wsdl` WSDL definition document. When creating `po_relational.wsdl`, you can use `po_imp.wsdl` discussed in Chapter 2 as the base, changing only the value of the `location` attribute in the `soap:address` element to the location of the `SoapServer_relational.php` script.

Once you've done all that, you can execute the `SoapClient_relational.php` script. If everything goes as planned, you will see a **PO inserted!** message. To make sure it has been done, you might issue a query against any or each of the tables created as discussed at the beginning of this section. If, for example, you issue queries against the `orders` and `items` tables from the MySQL Command Line Tool, you should see the following output:

```
MySQL Command Line Client

mysql>
mysql>
mysql> SELECT * FROM orders;
+-----------+
| pono      |
+-----------+
| 108128476 |
+-----------+
1 row in set (0.00 sec)

mysql> SELECT * FROM items;
+----+-----------+--------+----------+-------+
| id | pono      | partId | quantity | price |
+----+-----------+--------+----------+-------+
|  3 | 108128476 |    743 |   4.0000 | 15.50 |
|  4 | 108128476 |    235 |   7.0000 | 15.75 |
+----+-----------+--------+----------+-------+
2 rows in set (0.00 sec)

mysql> _
```

As you can see in the previous figure, the items table contains two rows, each of which represents a purchased item of the order whose `pono` is `108128476`.

Using Oracle Database XE

As the title implies, this section discusses how to build data-centric services on top of Oracle Database XE—a free edition of Oracle Database.

Like any other edition of Oracle Database, Oracle XE fully supports Oracle XML DB, a set of Oracle XML features enabling you to transform, construct, and natively store XML data, thus opening a whole spectrum of opportunities to process SOAP messages inside the database. However, note that to follow the examples discussed in this section, as well as all Oracle-related examples throughout this book, you are not in fact limited to using Oracle XE—any edition of Oracle Database will do.

If there's one thing to say why Oracle is a better choice than MySQL when it comes to data-centric services, it's that Oracle provides native XML support, while MySQL lacks it. With Oracle, you can handle the lion's share of data processing performed by your data-centric service inside the database while still meeting the principles of service-orientation.

Using XML Schemas with Oracle XML DB

While the most common usage of an XML schema is to validate that a certain XML document conforms to the definitions defined by that XML schema, Oracle also allows you to use XML schemas to automatically generate the storage for a certain set of XML documents.

As stated earlier, when using an Oracle database, you can store the data processed by the service in XML format, taking advantage of the native XML support. To achieve this, you first need to create an XMLType storage structure within the database. The simplest way to create an XMLType storage structure in Oracle XML DB is by registering an appropriate XML schema against the database. As a part of the registration process, Oracle automatically creates storage for a particular set of XML documents, based on the information provided by the schema.

So, you might want to create and register an XML schema against the database in order to:

- Build the storage for XML documents conforming the schema
- Set up business rules on XML content of conforming documents
- Validate XML documents conforming the schema

Turning back to the example discussed in the *Storing XML Data in Relational Tables* section, you can re-design it to use Oracle instead of MySQL, creating the storage for incoming PO XML documents by registering an XML schema. However, before you can do that, you need to grant the `ALTER SESSION` privilege to the database user with which you are going to connect to your Oracle database. Assuming that you have `xmlusr/xmlusr` user created as discussed in Chapter 2 in the *Setting Up the Database* section, you can issue the following `GRANT` statement from SQL*Plus:

```
CONN /as sysdba
GRANT ALTER SESSION TO xmlusr;
```

Once you're done, you can connect as `xmlusr/xmlusr` user to the database and then issue the PL/SQL block shown below.

> However, note that if you are using the command-line version of SQL*Plus and not the Windows GUI one, you won't be able to just copy and paste this block of code. So, you may find it a bit laborious to manually enter it. One way around this problem is to take advantage of SQL*Plus's ability to execute scripts created by an external editor. For example, you might issue the following command: `EDIT po_schema` from SQL*Plus to invoke your system's default text editor with the `po_schema.sql` script automatically created. Then, you paste the PL/SQL block shown below in the script and close it, saving the changes made. The next step is to run the newly created `po_schema.sql` script by issuing the following SQL*Plus command: `START po_schema`.

```
BEGIN
 DBMS_XMLSCHEMA.registerschema(
  'po.xsd',
  '<?xml version="1.0"?>
  <schema targetNamespace="http://localhost/WebServices/schema/po/"
        xmlns="http://www.w3.org/2001/XMLSchema"
        xmlns:types1="http://localhost/WebServices/schema/po/"
        xmlns:xdb="http://xmlns.oracle.com/xdb">
   <element name="purchaseOrder" type ="types1:purchaseOrder_typ"
           xdb:defaultTable="ORDERS"
           xdb:columnProps=
               "CONSTRAINT po_pkey PRIMARY KEY (XMLDATA.PONO)"/>
   <complexType name="purchaseOrder_typ"
                                  xdb:SQLType="PURCHASEORDER_TYP">
    <sequence>
      <element name="pono" type="string" xdb:SQLName="PONO"
                                  xdb:SQLType="VARCHAR2"/>
      <element name="shipTo" type="types1:AddressType" />
      <element name="billTo" type="types1:AddressType"/>
      <element name="items" type="types1:LineItemsType"/>
    </sequence>
   </complexType>
   <complexType name="AddressType">
    <sequence>
     <element name="name" type="string"/>
     <element name="street" type="string"/>
```

```
        <element name="city" type="string"/>
        <element name="state" type="string"/>
        <element name="zip" type="int"/>
        <element name="country" type="NMTOKEN" />
       </sequence>
      </complexType>
      <complexType name="LineItemsType">
       <sequence>
       <element minOccurs="0" maxOccurs="unbounded" name="item"
                                type="types1:LineItemType" />
       </sequence>
      </complexType>
      <complexType name="LineItemType">
       <sequence>
         <element name="partId" type="int"/>
         <element name="quantity" type="decimal"/>
         <element name="price" type="decimal"/>
       </sequence>
      </complexType>
    </schema >',
    TRUE,
    TRUE,
    FALSE,
    TRUE
  );
END;
/
```

As you can see in the above PL/SQL block, the `registerSchema` procedure from the `DBMS_XMLSCHEMA` PL/SQL package takes two arguments. The first one represents the name under which you want to register the schema against the database and the second one represents the XML schema itself.

Looking through the `po.xsd` XML schema discussed here, you may notice that it is very similar to the `po.xsd` XML schema discussed in Chapter 2 in the *Importing XML Schemas into WSDL Documents* section. You simply added the `xmlns:xdb="http://xmlns.oracle.com/xdb"` namespace as an attribute to the `schema` element, which allowed you to use Oracle XML schema annotations within the schema.

Oracle XML schema annotations are used to influence the underlying objects automatically generated by Oracle during the schema registration process. For example, the `xdb:defaultTable` annotation is used to explicitly define the name of the XMLType table generated to store XML documents conforming to the schema.

Another interesting annotation used here is `xdb:columnProps`. In this example, you use this annotation to define a primary key on the `PONO` element mapped to the `orders` table generated here.

Also note the use of the `xdb:SQLName` annotation. You use it to explicitly specify the name of the generated SQL object type. Otherwise, Oracle will use system-generated names. In this particular example, you use the `xdb:SQLName` annotation when defining the `PONO` element. This makes it possible for you to use a certain name when defining the primary key on the `orders` table, as discussed above.

Now, you might want to look into the underlying objects implicitly created by Oracle during the registration process. To start with, you might examine the `orders` table. To do this, you might issue the following query:

```
DESC orders
```

This should produce the following output:

```
Name                                       Null?    Type
 ---------------------------------------- -------- ------------------
TABLE of
    SYS.XMLTYPE(
      XMLSchema "po.xsd"
      Element "purchaseOrder")
    STORAGE Object-relational TYPE "PURCHASEORDER_TYP"
```

The above shows that the `orders` table is of XMLType, which, in this case, is persisted as the `purchaseorder_typ` custom object type. Now, you might want to check out the `purchaseorder_typ` type. This can be done as follows:

```
DESC purchaseorder_typ
```

This should produce the following output:

```
 purchaseorder_typ is NOT FINAL
 Name                                    Null?    Type
 --------------------------------------- -------- -----------------
--
 SYS_XDBPD$                                       XDB.XDB$RAW_LIST_T
 PONO                                             VARCHAR2(4000 CHAR)
 shipTo                                           AddressType268_T
 billTo                                           AddressType268_T
 items                                            LineItemsType266_T
```

As you can see, the `purchaseorder_typ` type includes several attributes. The `PONO` has been explicitly defined in the schema, while the names of other attributes are system-generated.

To learn more about using the XML schema feature with Oracle, you can refer to Oracle Documentation: *Oracle XML DB Developer's Guide*, chapters *XML Schema Storage and Query: Basic* and *XML Schema Storage and Query: Advanced.*

It is interesting to note that you can always delete the `po.xsd` XML registered against the database using the `DBMS_XMLSCHEMA.deleteSchema` procedure as shown below:

```
BEGIN
  DBMS_XMLSCHEMA.deleteSchema(
  SCHEMAURL => 'po.xsd',
  DELETE_OPTION => dbms_xmlschema.DELETE_CASCADE_FORCE);
END;
/
```

In that case, all the underlying objects created during the schema registration process will be automatically deleted.

Turning back to the `orders` XMLType table automatically generated during the `po.xsd` XML schema registration, you may be wondering how to insert rows in that table. Since the `po.xsd` schema declares a target namespace, a PO XML document being inserted must use the `schemaLocation` attribute in the root element to identify the XML schema. So, the correct definition of the `purchaseOrder` root element should be as follows:

```
<po:purchaseOrder
     xmlns:po="http://localhost/WebServices/schema/po/"
     xmlns:xsi="http://www.w3.org/2001/XMLSchema-instance"
     xsi:schemaLocation="http://localhost/WebServices/schema/po/
po.xsd">
   <pono>108128476</pono>
   ...
</po:purchaseOrder>
```

Now that you have created the database objects for natively storing PO XML documents and have an idea of how to store these documents into the database, it's time to move on and create the PHP handler class that will send incoming POs to the database. Here is the `purchaseOrder_schema.php` script containing the PHP handler class for this example:

```
<?php
 //File purchaseOrder_schema.php
 require_once 'obj2Dom.php';
 class purchaseOrder {
```

```
    function placeOrder($po) {
     $args['xmlns:po']='http://localhost/WebServices/schema/po/';
     $args['xmlns:xsi']='http://www.w3.org/2001/XMLSchema-instance';
     $args['xsi:schemaLocation']=
                    'http://localhost/WebServices/schema/po/ po.xsd';
     $obj = new obj2Dom('po:purchaseOrder', $args);
     $obj->trans2Dom($po);
     $po=$obj->printDomTree();
     if(!$conn = oci_connect('xmlusr', 'xmlusr', '//localhost/XE')){
        throw new SoapFault("Server","Failed to connect to database");
     };
     $sql = "INSERT INTO orders
                VALUES(XMLType(:po).createSchemaBasedXML('po.xsd'))";
     $query = oci_parse($conn, $sql);
     oci_bind_by_name($query, ':po', $po);
     if (!oci_execute($query)) {
         $err=oci_error($query);
         throw new SoapFault("Server","Failed to insert PO
                                              ".$err['message']);
     };
     $msg='<rsltMsg>PO inserted!</rsltMsg>';
     return $msg;
    }
  }
?>
```

As you can see in the above listing, the `placeOrder` method uses an instance of the `obj2Dom` class stored in the `obj2Dom.php` file. If you recall from Chapter 2, this class is used to convert an `stdClass` instance to XML and is discussed in the *Converting SOAP Messages' Payloads to XML* section. To use the `obj2Dom` class in this example, you should copy the `obj2Dom.php` script from the `/WebServices/ch2` directory to `/WebServices/ch3` and then modify the class constructor as follows:

```
<?php
//File: /WebServices/ch3/obj2Dom.php
class obj2Dom {
...
 public function __construct($rootElmName='root', $args)
 {
  $this->dom = new DomDocument('1.0');
  $root = $this->dom->createElement($rootElmName);
  $this->rootNode = $this->dom->appendChild($root);
  if ($args) {
   foreach($args as $key => $value){
```

```
        $this->rootNode->setAttribute($key, $value);
      }
    }
  }
  ...
}
```

In this code, you modify the obj2Dom class constructor so that it takes one more parameter, through which you will pass in the array containing the attributes to be set to the root element of the DOM document being constructed. You iterate over this associative array using the foreach construct, transforming the array's key/value pairs to the attributes of the root element.

The next step is to create the SOAP client and SOAP server. For this example, you can create the SoapClient_schema.php and SoapServer_schema.php scripts, using the SoapClient_relational.php and SoapServer_relational.php discussed in the *Storing XML Data in Relational Tables* section as the base. Besides the names, the SOAP client and server scripts created here should differ from the preceding ones only in that the new SOAP client and server scripts should use the new po_schema.wsdl document, rather than po_relational.wsdl used by the preceding pair. The po_schema.wsdl WSDL document in turn should be different from po_relational.wsdl only in that the location attribute of the soap:address element in po_schema.wsdl references the SoapServer_schema.php SOAP server script.

Once you set up all the above scripts and WSDL document, you can test the service by executing the SoapClient_schema.php script. This should output a **PO inserted!** message in your browser.

To make sure the row has been inserted into the orders table, you might issue the following query from SQL*Plus:

```
SET LONG 10000
SELECT * FROM orders;
```

As a result, you should see a screen similar to that shown in the following figure:

```
Run SQL Command Line
SQL> SET LONG 10000
SQL>
SQL> SELECT * FROM orders;

SYS_NC_ROWINFO$
--------------------------------------------------------------------------------

<?xml version="1.0"?>
<po:purchaseOrder xmlns:po="http://localhost/WebServices/schema/po/" xmlns:xsi="

http://www.w3.org/2001/XMLSchema-instance" xsi:schemaLocation="http://localhost/

WebServices/schema/po/ po.xsd">
  <pono>108128476</pono>
  <shipTo>
    <name>Janet Thomson</name>
    <street>11 Maple Street</street>
    <city>Small Valley</city>
    <state>VA</state>
    <zip>23037</zip>

SYS_NC_ROWINFO$
--------------------------------------------------------------------------------

    <country>US</country>
  </shipTo>
  <billTo>
    <name>Tony Jamison</name>
```

Now, if you try to execute the `SoapClient_schema.php` script again, you will get the following error message:

```
Failed to insert PO ORA-00001: unique constraint (XMLUSR.PO_PKEY)
violated
```

If you recall from the `SoapClient_schema.php` code, this script, when executed, uses the same PO XML document derived from the `purchaseOrder.xml` file. The fact is that an attempt to insert the same document into the `orders` table violates the primary key constraint defined on the `PONO` attribute.

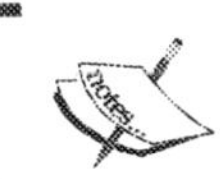

In a real-world scenario, though, the above normally doesn't happen, since the SOAP client script is supposed to send another document each time it is executed.

XML Schema Validation Considerations

With a large number of consumers using your service, you might need to check to see if an XML document, which a consumer sends to the service, contains appropriate data. One way to handle this task is to use constraining facets in the schema. For example, you might rewrite the `po.xsd` XML schema discussed in the preceding schema, applying constraining facets to some complex types used there.

However, before you can do this you first have to delete the XML schema as shown below:

```
BEGIN
  DBMS_XMLSCHEMA.deleteSchema(
  SCHEMAURL => 'po.xsd',
  DELETE_OPTION => dbms_xmlschema.DELETE_CASCADE_FORCE);
END;
/
```

Now, you can register the updated version of the `po.xsd` XML schema by issuing the following statement. Again, you can simplify entering the statement with the help of the `EDIT` and `START` SQL*Plus commands, as discussed at the beginning of the preceding section.

```
BEGIN
 DBMS_XMLSCHEMA.registerschema(
  'po.xsd',
  '<?xml version="1.0"?>
  <schema targetNamespace="http://localhost/WebServices/schema/po/"
        xmlns="http://www.w3.org/2001/XMLSchema"
        xmlns:types1="http://localhost/WebServices/schema/po/"
        xmlns:xdb="http://xmlns.oracle.com/xdb">
   <element name="purchaseOrder" type ="types1:purchaseOrder_typ"
           xdb:defaultTable="ORDERS"
           xdb:columnProps=
               "CONSTRAINT po_pkey PRIMARY KEY (XMLDATA.PONO)"/>
   <complexType name="purchaseOrder_typ"
                       xdb:SQLType="PURCHASEORDER_TYP">
    <sequence>
      <element name="pono" type="string" xdb:SQLName="PONO"
                       xdb:SQLType="VARCHAR2"/>
      <element name="shipTo" type="types1:AddressType" />
      <element name="billTo" type="types1:AddressType"/>
      <element name="items" type="types1:LineItemsType"/>
    </sequence>
   </complexType>
   <complexType name="AddressType">
    <sequence>
     <element name="name" type="string"/>
     <element name="street" type="string"/>
     <element name="city" type="string"/>
     <element name="state" >
       <simpleType>
        <restriction base="string">
```

```
            <pattern value="[A-Z]{2}"/>
           </restriction>
          </simpleType>
        </element>
        <element name="zip" type="int"/>
        <element name="country" type = "NMTOKEN"/>
       </sequence>
      </complexType>
      <complexType name="LineItemsType">
       <sequence>
       <element minOccurs="0" maxOccurs="unbounded" name="item"
                        type="types1:LineItemType" />
       </sequence>
      </complexType>
      <complexType name="LineItemType">
       <sequence>
         <element name="partId" type="int"/>
         <element name="quantity">
          <simpleType>
           <restriction base="decimal">
            <fractionDigits value="3"/>
            <totalDigits value="8"/>
           </restriction>
          </simpleType>
         </element>
         <element name="price">
          <simpleType>
           <restriction base="decimal">
            <fractionDigits value="2"/>
            <totalDigits value="12"/>
           </restriction>
          </simpleType>
         </element>
       </sequence>
      </complexType>
     </schema >',
     TRUE,
     TRUE,
     FALSE,
     TRUE
   );
  END;
  /
```

As you can see, the above `po.xsd` XML schema contains restriction blocks for some elements, which are highlighted.

After the po.xsd XML schema is registered, you can insert PO XML documents into the orders table. The simplest way to do this is to execute the SoapClient_schema.php script used in the preceding example. You should have no problem with this.

Now, suppose you want to insert a PO document whose price element contains an inappropriate value. For that purpose, you might modify a PO XML document stored in the purchaseOrder.xml as follows:

```
<purchaseOrder >
    <pono>108128477</pono>
   ...
   <items>
      <item>
       <partId>743</partId>
       <quantity>4</quantity>
       <price>15.58787897897</price>
      </item>
   ...
   </items>
</purchaseOrder>
```

It is interesting to note that Oracle will insert the above document, but the value of the price element will be automatically rounded to two decimal places, as specified in the XML schema for this element. As a result, the price element in the document stored in the orders table will contain the rounded value as shown below:

```
   ...
   <items>
      <item>
       <partId>743</partId>
       <quantity>4</quantity>
       <price>15.59</price>
      </item>
   ...
```

In fact, when a PO XML document is inserted into the orders table, Oracle actually performs a partial validation of that document against the po.xsd XML schema registered as discussed previously. What this means in practice is that Oracle will not trigger an error if, for example, the value of an element in the document being validated violates the pattern associated with that element in the schema. Suppose you are inserting the following document:

```
<purchaseOrder >
    <pono>108128478</pono>
```

```
  ...
   <shipTo>
    <name>Janet Thomson</name>
    <street>11 Maple Street</street>
    <city>Small Valley</city>
    <state>VA6</state>
    <zip>23037</zip>
    <country>US</country>
  </shipTo>
  ...
</purchaseOrder>
```

Although the value of the `state` element in the above document doesn't conform to the string pattern defined in the `po.xsd` XML schema for this element, the document will be inserted.

To handle this problem, you can force Oracle to perform a full XML schema validation upon inserting a new row into the `orders` table. To achieve this goal, you can define a `BEFORE INSERT` trigger on the `orders` table, explicitly calling the `schemaValidate` method of `XMLType` from within the trigger. This can be done by issuing the following statement from SQL*Plus:

```
CREATE OR REPLACE TRIGGER po_valid
BEFORE INSERT ON orders
FOR EACH ROW
DECLARE
  xmldoc XMLType;
BEGIN
  xmldoc := :new.OBJECT_VALUE;
  XMLType.schemaValidate(xmldoc);
END;
/
```

Now, if you execute the `SoapClient_schema.php` script again, you should see the following error message:

```
Failed to insert PO ORA-31154: invalid XML document ORA-19202: Error
occurred in XML processing LSX-00333: literal "VA6" is not valid with
respect to the pattern ORA-06512: at "SYS.XMLTYPE", line 345 ORA-
06512: at "XMLUSR.PO_VALID", line 5 ORA-04088: error during execution
of trigger 'XMLUSR.PO_VALID'
```

If you don't want to provide the user with such detailed information about the problem that occurred, you might set the `Exception` clause in the trigger as follows:

```
DROP TRIGGER po_valid;

CREATE OR REPLACE TRIGGER po_valid
BEFORE INSERT ON orders
FOR EACH ROW
DECLARE
  xmldoc XMLType;
BEGIN
  xmldoc := :new.OBJECT_VALUE;
  XMLType.schemaValidate(xmldoc);
  EXCEPTION
   WHEN OTHERS THEN
       RAISE_APPLICATION_ERROR(-20001, 'Failed to insert a row
                                        into the orders table');
END;
/
```

In this case, the `SoapClient_schema.php` script, when executed, should produce the following error message:

```
Failed to insert PO ORA-20001: Failed to insert a row into the orders
table ORA-06512: at "XMLUSR.PO_VALID", line 8 ORA-04088: error during
execution of trigger 'XMLUSR.PO_VALID'
```

Remember that performing full validation slows things down, affecting the performance of `INSERT` operations. It is recommended that you use full validation only if absolutely necessary.

It is interesting to note that you can always drop the `po_valid` trigger created as shown above, without affecting the data stored in the `orders` table. To do this, you can issue the following statement:

```
DROP TRIGGER po_valid;
```

Once the trigger has been dropped, you turn back to the situation in which Oracle performs only a partial validation upon inserting a new row into the `orders` table.

Defining Parameter-Driven Operations on Data-Centric Services

In the *Defining Parameter-Driven Operations* section in Chapter 2, you saw an example of encapsulating the underlying logic of a parameter-driven service operation in a PHP handler class. If you recall from that example, the `getOrder` method of the `orderInfo` PHP handler class took two arguments. Depending on the value of the second parameter, `getOrder` returned either an entire PO XML document or the status information on the document.

In a real-world scenario you may need to pass more than one parameter to the generic method representing a parameter-driven operation. The example discussed in the following two sections shows how you can encapsulate several parameters in XML, and then pass that XML structure as a parameter of a parameter-driven operation.

Defining XSD Types for Parameters

To start, you need to define an XML schema describing the XML structure that will be used to encapsulate parameters passed to the `getOrder` method of the `orderInfo` PHP handler class.

Here is the `po_xmlparams.xsd` XML schema document defining the `params` complex type element. It is assumed that you save this document in the `WebServices/schema` directory:

```
<?xml version='1.0'?>
<schema targetNamespace="http://localhost/WebServices/schema/
poxmlparams/"
        xmlns="http://www.w3.org/2001/XMLSchema"
        xmlns:types1="http://localhost/WebServices/schema/
poxmlparams/">
  <element name="params">
   <complexType>
     <sequence>
       <element minOccurs="0" maxOccurs="unbounded" name="param"
type="types1:paramType" />
     </sequence>
   </complexType>
  </element>
  <complexType name="paramType">
    <sequence>
      <element name="key" type="string"/>
      <element name="value" type="string"/>
    </sequence>
```

```
    </complexType>
  </schema >
```

An XML document conforming to this schema might look like the following:

```
  <params>
   <param>
    <key>po</key>
    <value>status</value>
   </param>
   ...
  </params>
```

Note that the number of `param` elements in this construction is unbounded, so you can use as many of these elements as needed.

The next step is to define the WSDL document describing the service. To be able to define a message part of the `params` type in a WSDL document, you need to import the `po_xmlparams.xsd` XML schema shown previously. So, the `po_xmlparams.wsdl` document stored in the `WebServices/wsdl` directory might look as follows:

```
  <?xml version="1.0" encoding="utf-8"?>
  <definitions name ="poInfoService"
              xmlns:http="http://schemas.xmlsoap.org/wsdl/http/"
              xmlns:soap="http://schemas.xmlsoap.org/wsdl/soap/"
              xmlns:xsd="http://www.w3.org/2001/XMLSchema"
              xmlns:prm=
                      "http://localhost/WebServices/schema/poxmlparams/"
              xmlns="http://schemas.xmlsoap.org/wsdl/"
              targetNamespace=
                              "http://localhost/WebServices/wsdl/poInfo">
      <import
        namespace="http://localhost/WebServices/schema/poxmlparams/"
                  location=
                "http://localhost/WebServices/schema/po_xmlparams.xsd" />
      <message name="getOrderInfoInput">
          <part name="pono" element="xsd:string"/>
          <part name="par" element="prm:params"/>
      </message>
      <message name="getOrderInfoOutput">
          <part name="body" element="xsd:string"/>
      </message>
      <portType name="poInfoServicePortType">
          <operation name="getOrder">
             <input message="tns:getOrderInfoInput"/>
             <output message="tns:getOrderInfoOutput"/>
```

```
        </operation>
    </portType>
    <binding name="poInfoServiceBinding"
                         type="tns:poInfoServicePortType">
        <soap:binding style="rpc"
                transport="http://schemas.xmlsoap.org/soap/http"/>
        <operation name="getOrder">
           <soap:operation
             soapAction="http://localhost/WebServices/ch3/getOrder"/>
           <input>
               <soap:body use="literal"/>
           </input>
           <output>
               <soap:body use="literal"/>
           </output>
        </operation>
    </binding>
    <service name="poInfoService">
        <port name="poInfoServicePort"
                         binding="tns:poInfoServiceBinding">
           <soap:address location=
        "http://localhost/WebServices/ch3/SoapServer_xmlparams.php"/>
        </port>
    </service>
</definitions>
```

As you can see, the input message defined in the above document consists of two parts. The first part, named `pono`, describes the first argument of the `getOrder` method exposed by the service. The second one, named `params`, represents the XML structure defined in the `po_xmlparams.xsd` document, which will be used as the second parameter of the `getOrder` method.

Moving Conditional Logic into the Database

Turning back to the `orderInfo` class discussed in the *Defining Parameter-Driven Operations* section in Chapter 2, you may recall that the `getOrder` method of that class contains the conditional `switch` block responsible for using an appropriate `SELECT` statement, depending on the parameter passed to `getOrder`. Now you can rewrite the `getOrder` method, moving the conditional logic to the database. However, before you can do this, you have to create a stored function in the database, which will be invoked from within `getOrder`.

Here is how you can create such a PL/SQL stored function from SQL*Plus. Once again, you can simplify entering the following statement by using the `EDIT` and `START` SQL*Plus commands, as discussed at the beginning of the *Using XML Schemas with Oracle XML DB* section earlier.

```
CREATE OR REPLACE FUNCTION getPOInfo (pono IN VARCHAR2, par IN
VARCHAR2)
RETURN VARCHAR2
IS
  stat  VARCHAR2(15);
  doc VARCHAR2(2000);
BEGIN
  CASE par
    WHEN 'status' THEN
     BEGIN
       SELECT status INTO stat FROM poStatusInfo WHERE pono=pono;
       RETURN stat;
     END;
    WHEN 'doc' THEN
     BEGIN
       SELECT doc INTO doc FROM purchaseOrders WHERE
                extractValue(XMLType(doc),
                '/purchaseOrder/pono')=pono AND rownum=1;
       RETURN doc;
     END;
    ELSE
       RETURN 'undefined';
  END CASE;
END;
/
```

In the above code, the `CASE` PL/SQL statement is used to take a different action for each alternative. You used the `switch` PHP construct in the `getOrder` method to achieve the same goal.

Note that you are explicitly limiting the `SELECT` statement in the `WHEN 'doc'` clause to one row being returned. In this particular example, though, it's redundant as long as, if you recall from the *Using XML Schemas with Oracle XML DB* section, a unique constraint is set on `pono`.

Now that you have the `getPOInfo` PL/SQL stored function created, you can copy the `orderInfo.php` script from the `WebServices/ch2` directory to `WebServices/ch3`, and then modify it as follows:

```
<?php
 //File orderInfo.php
 class orderInfo {
   function getOrder($pono, $par) {
     if(!$conn = oci_connect('xmlusr', 'xmlusr', '//localhost/XE')){
         throw new SoapFault("Server","Failed to connect to database");
     };
     foreach ($par->param as $value)
     {
       $arr[$value->key]=$value->value;
     }
     $sql="BEGIN :rslt:=".$arr['proc']."(:pono, :arg); END;";
     $query = oci_parse($conn, $sql);
     oci_bind_by_name($query, ':pono', $pono);
     oci_bind_by_name($query, ':arg', $arr['arg']);
     oci_bind_by_name($query, ':rslt', $rslt, 2000);
     if (!oci_execute($query)) {
         $err=oci_error($query);
         throw new SoapFault("Server","Failed to execute query
                                                  ".$err['message']);
     };
     return $rslt;
   }
 }
?>
```

If you recall, an argument of a complex XSD type passed to an exposed function is extracted from the SOAP envelope on the sever side and then transformed to an instance of the `stdClass` built-in PHP class. In this example, you use the `foreach` construct to iterate over the `stdClass` structure representing parameters passed in with the second argument of `getOrder`, transforming that structure to an easy-to-use array.

Also it's worth noting the use of the fourth optional parameter in the `oci_bind_by_name` function binding the `$rslt` output variable to a placeholder in the query. By specifying `2000`, you set the maximum length for the result value returned by the `getPOInfo` PL/SQL stored function invoked within the query. Otherwise, you would get the following error message:

```
Failed to execute query ORA-06502: PL/SQL: numeric or value error:
character string buffer too small ORA-06512: at line 1
```

If you want the getPOInfo PL/SQL function to return a result value that exceeds 4000 characters, consider using the CLOB Oracle data type instead of VARCHAR2, which is limited to 4000.

The next step is to create the SOAP server that will expose the getOrder method of the orderInfo class. For this purpose, you need to create the SoapServer_xmlparams.php script in the WebServices/ch3 directory as follows:

```
<?php
 //File: SoapServer_xmlparams.php
 require_once "orderInfo.php";
 $wsdl= "http://localhost/WebServices/wsdl/po_xmlparams.wsdl";
 $srv= new SoapServer($wsdl);
 $srv->setClass("orderInfo");
 $srv->handle();
?>
```

Before you can test the poInfoService service discussed here, you need to create a client script. Here is the SoapClient_xmlparams.php script that you should create in the WebServices/ch3 directory:

```
<?php
 //File: SoapClient_xmlparams.php
 require_once "obj2Arr.php";
 $wsdl = "http://localhost/WebServices/wsdl/po_xmlparams.wsdl";
 $client = new SoapClient($wsdl);
 $pono='108128476';
 $xmlpar = simplexml_load_file('params.xml');
 $xmlarr = obj2Arr($xmlpar);
 try {
  print $result=$client->getOrder($pono, $xmlarr);
 }
 catch (SoapFault $exp) {
  print $exp->getMessage();
 }
?>
```

As you can see, the above client script takes the second parameter for the getOrder method from the params.xml file, which is supposed to be in the WebServices/ch3 directory and, in this particular case, might look like this:

```
<params>
 <param>
  <key>proc</key>
```

```
    <value>getPOInfo</value>
   </param>
   <param>
    <key>arg</key>
    <value>doc</value>
   </param>
  </params>
```

The above document will be passed to the `getOrder` method as the second parameter. The document contains two `param` elements representing parameters that will be utilized within `getOrder`.

Now you are ready to test the `poInfoService` service. To do this, you should execute `SoapClient_xmlparams.php`. Since the value of the `arg` parameter in the `params.xml` file is `doc`, your browser should display the PO XML document stored in the `purchaseOrders` table, whose `pono` is `108128476`.

Alternatively, if the value of the `arg` parameter in the `params.xml` document were `status`, your browser would simply display: **shipped**, which represents the status of the PO document, as specified in the `poStatusInfo` table.

This example assumes that you have created the `poStatusInfo` table as shown in the *Defining Parameter-Driven Operations* section in Chapter 2.

Finally, if the value of the `arg` parameter is neither `doc` nor `status`, your browser will simply display: **undefined**.

Summary

The purpose of this chapter was to show you how to design data-centric services with PHP and either of the two most popular databases today: MySQL and Oracle. The chapter began with a concise discussion of how to choose an appropriate database to be used in your data-centric service, touching upon options provided by MySQL and Oracle database servers. Then it quickly moved to the practical themes of using MySQL and Oracle as back-end databases in data-centric services. The chapter not only discussed how to map relational databases to services, but also using native XML databases in the database-backed services, providing concise and up-to-date coverage of the Oracle XML features.

In this chapter, you also learned that a database can not only be used as a repository to store payload content, but also as an efficient means for performing data processing, thus allowing you to move some underlying logic from the PHP handler class into the database.

4

Building Web Service Applications

With a service-oriented approach you can expose the logic of your application as a collection of loosely coupled services. To achieve this, you might not even need to restructure the existing code to extend your application through a service-oriented architecture. Often, all you need to do is to build a set of agile services upon the existing application structures such as classes utilized within the application. Once you have a collection of services, the next step is to combine them into a composite solution, preserving the key principles of service-orientation.

In this chapter, you will learn how to:

- Combine a set of services into a composition without defining an orchestration process
- Define a controller service providing parameter-driven operations upon more granular services
- Expose methods of an existing class as Web service operations
- Use the same PHP class as the handler class of several services
- Secure services built with PHP SOAP extension

Defining Parameter-Driven Operations on Fine-Grained Services

The ability of loosely coupled services to be reused and combined into composite solutions is one of the most important things in the service-oriented paradigm. While the WS-BPEL orchestration language provides a standard mechanism for services' interactions, there is often a need to combine some services into a composite solution that doesn't rely upon an orchestration engine.

For example, you might want to design a controller service providing a generic interface and relying upon several granular services responsible for performing the real work. The granular services might be invoked directly from within the PHP handler class of the coarse service. The information about the granular services might be stored in a separate XML document loaded dynamically during run time.

The following sections explain in detail how you might build a service providing generic and parameter-driven operations upon several fine-grained services, rather than directly upon classes or individual functions encapsulating entity-specific logic as discussed in the preceding chapters. In the example discussed here, the service providing a parameter-driven operation delegates the work to some other granular services that perform the real work.

The following figure depicts an example of a service composition using a parameter-driven controller service.

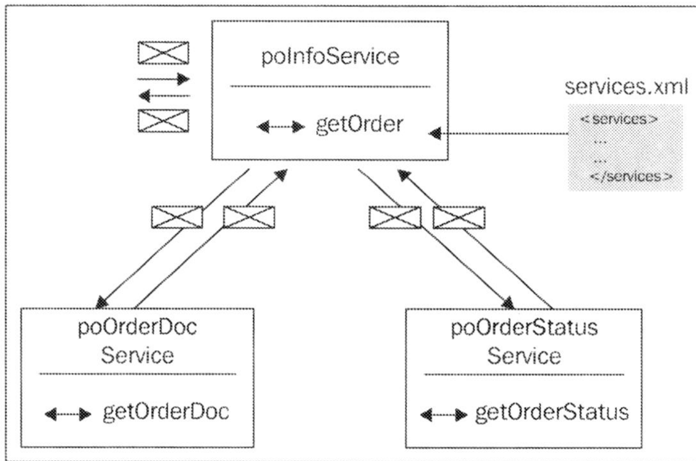

As you can see in the figure, the `poInfoService` coarse-grained service providing generic operation, namely `getOrder`, employs the two granular services: `poOrderDocService` and `poOrderStatusService` specified in the `services.xml` document.

One word of warning though. While such a granular design makes life easier for the service consumers and conforms to the service-oriented principles, this approach assumes the additional overhead of transferring and handling SOAP messages involved between the coarse service (`poInfoService` in this example) and more granular services (`poOrderDocService` and `poOrderStatusService`) performing the real work. You should take this kind of issue into account when choosing a level of granularity to be used in your solution. If an operation, which you consider to expose as a granular service, has no reuse potential, it would be a good idea not to implement it as an individual service.

Putting Info on Fine-Grained Services in a Separate XML File

As mentioned earlier, for better reusability, information about fine-grained services to be utilized from within a more coarse-grained service may be stored in a separate file, thus allowing for dynamic binding between the services involved.

For example, you might create the following XML document, which contains information about the `poOrderDocService` and `poOrderStatusService` services mentioned above. It is assumed that you save this document as `services.xml` in the `WebServices\ch4` directory:

```
<services>
 <service>
  <name>poOrderDocService</name>
  <wsdl>http://localhost/WebServices/wsdl/po_orderdoc.wsdl</wsdl>
  <function>getOrderDoc</function>
  <param>doc</param>
 </service>
 <service>
  <name>poOrderStatusService</name>
  <wsdl>http://localhost/WebServices/wsdl/po_orderstatus.wsdl</wsdl>
  <function>getOrderStatus</function>
  <param>status</param>
 </service>
</services>
```

The information about the fine-grained services encapsulated in the above XML document can be then used in the logic of a parameter-driven operation belonging to a more coarse-grained service.

You might load this information from within PHP as follows:

```
$srv = simplexml_load_file('services.xml');
$srv=obj2Arr($srv);
foreach ($srv['service'] as $value)
{
  $srvarr[$value['param']]=array("wsdl" => $value['wsdl'],
                                 "func" => $value['function']);
}
```

As a result, you will have the following two-dimensional array:

```
array(2) {
  ["doc"]=>
  array(2) {
    ["wsdl"]=>
    string(50) "http://localhost/WebServices/wsdl/po_orderdoc.wsdl"
    ["func"]=>
    string(11) "getOrderDoc"
  }
  ["status"]=>
  array(2) {
    ["wsdl"]=>
    string(53)
         "http://localhost/WebServices/wsdl/po_orderstatus.wsdl"
    ["func"]=>
    string(14) "getOrderStatus"
  }
}
```

As mentioned, when represented in an array like this, the information about granular services can be easily used at run time within the code encapsulating the underlying logic of the coarse service utilizing these granular services. In the *Creating the Coarse-Grained Service* section later, you will see how all this really works in practice.

Building Fine-Grained Services

Turning back to the service combination depicted in the previous figure, let's start by defining the WSDL describing the `poOrderDocService` granular service providing the operation `getOrderDoc`. Consider the following WSDL document, which you should save as `po_orderdoc.wsdl` in the `WebServices\wsdl` directory:

```
<?xml version="1.0" encoding="utf-8"?>
<definitions name ="poOrderDocService"
```

```
            xmlns:http="http://schemas.xmlsoap.org/wsdl/http/"
            xmlns:soap="http://schemas.xmlsoap.org/wsdl/soap/"
            xmlns:xsd="http://www.w3.org/2001/XMLSchema"
            xmlns="http://schemas.xmlsoap.org/wsdl/"
            targetNamespace=
                    "http://localhost/WebServices/wsdl/poOrderDoc">
    <message name="getOrderDocInput">
        <part name="pono" element="xsd:string"/>
    </message>
    <message name="getOrderDocOutput">
        <part name="body" element="xsd:string"/>
    </message>
    <portType name="poOrderDocServicePortType">
        <operation name="getOrderDoc">
           <input message="tns:getOrderDocInput"/>
           <output message="tns:getOrderDocOutput"/>
        </operation>
    </portType>
    <binding name="poOrderDocServiceBinding"
               type="tns:poOrderDocServicePortType">
        <soap:binding style="rpc"
               transport="http://schemas.xmlsoap.org/soap/http"/>
        <operation name="getOrderDoc">
           <soap:operation
          soapAction="http://localhost/WebServices/ch4/getOrderDoc"/>
           <input>
               <soap:body use="literal"/>
           </input>
           <output>
               <soap:body use="literal"/>
           </output>
        </operation>
    </binding>
    <service name="poOrderDocService">
        <port name="poOrderDocServicePort"
               binding="tns:poOrderDocServiceBinding">
           <soap:address
location="http://localhost/WebServices/ch4/SOAPServer_orderdoc.php"/>
        </port>
    </service>
</definitions>
```

As you can see, this WSDL document describes the `poOrderDocService` service that supports the `getOrderDoc` operation assuming one input and one output parameter, both of which are of simple XSD type `string`.

The next step is to implement the PHP handler class to be used with the `poOrderDocService` service described by this WSDL document. The code for this class is as follows, which you need to save in the `orderDoc.php` script file in the `WebServices\ch4` directory:

```
<?php
 //File orderDoc.php
 class orderDoc {
   function getOrderDoc($pono) {
    if(!$conn = oci_connect('xmlusr', 'xmlusr', '//localhost/XE')){
        throw new SoapFault("Server","Failed to connect to
         database");
    };
    $sql="SELECT doc FROM purchaseOrders WHERE
       extractValue(XMLType(doc), '/purchaseOrder/pono')=:pono
        AND rownum=1";
    $query = oci_parse($conn, $sql);
    oci_bind_by_name($query, ':pono', $pono);
    if (!oci_execute($query)) {
        $err=oci_error($query);
        throw new SoapFault("Server","Failed to execute query
          ".$err['message']);
    };
    oci_fetch($query);
    $rslt = oci_result($query, 'DOC');
    return $rslt;
   }
 }
?>
```

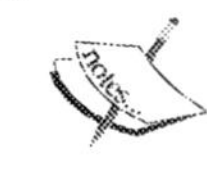

This example assumes that you have the `purchaseOrders` table created as discussed in Chapter 2 in the *Setting Up the Database* section.

Finally, you need to create the SOAP server script for the `poOrderDocService` service. Here is the `SoapServer_orderdoc.php` script that you also should save in the `WebServices\ch4` directory:

```
<?php
 //File: SoapServer_orderdoc.php
```

```
 require_once "orderDoc.php";
 $wsdl= "http://localhost/WebServices/wsdl/po_orderdoc.wsdl";
 $srv= new SoapServer($wsdl);
 $srv->setClass("orderDoc");
 $srv->handle();
?>
```

Now that you have finished building the `poOrderDocService` service, you can move on to the other fine-grained service: `poOrderStatusService`.

First, you might want to create the WSDL document describing the `poOrderStatusService` service. Looking at `po_orderdoc.wsdl` shown at the beginning of this section, you might now create the `po_orderstatus.wsdl` WSDL document on your own, specifying `getOrderStatus` as the operation name and `SoapServer_orderstatus.php` as the SOAP server to be used.

Then, you create the `SoapServer_orderstatus.php` SOAP server script, specifying the newly created `po_orderstatus.wsdl` as the WSDL and setting the `orderStatus` class stored in the `orderStatus.php` script as the PHP handler class for the service. So, make sure to create the `orderStatus.php` script, as follows:

```
<?php
 //File orderStatus.php
 class orderStatus {
   function getOrderStatus($pono) {
    if(!$conn = oci_connect('xmlusr', 'xmlusr', '//localhost/XE')){
        throw new SoapFault("Server","Failed to connect to
                             database");
    };
    $sql="SELECT status FROM poStatusInfo WHERE pono=:pono";
    $query = oci_parse($conn, $sql);
    oci_bind_by_name($query, ':pono', $pono);
    if (!oci_execute($query)) {
        $err=oci_error($query);
        throw new SoapFault("Server","Failed to execute query
                            ".$err['message']);
    };
    oci_fetch($query);
    $rslt = oci_result($query, 'STATUS');
    return $rslt;
   }
 }
?>
```

As you can see, the query used in this script is issued against the `poStatusInfo` database table created and filled with data as discussed in the *Defining Parameter-Driven Operations* section in Chapter 2.

Creating the Coarse-Grained Service

Now that you have the `poOrderDocService` and `poOrderStatusService` granular services created, the next step in building a composite solution as depicted in the previous figure is to design the `poInfoService` coarse controller service.

You might want to start by creating the WSDL definition document describing the `poInfoService` service that provides the generic and parameter-driven operation `getOrder`. For this purpose, you might create the `po_orderinfo.wsdl` WSDL document as follows:

```
<?xml version="1.0" encoding="utf-8"?>
<definitions name ="poInfoService"
            xmlns:http="http://schemas.xmlsoap.org/wsdl/http/"
            xmlns:soap="http://schemas.xmlsoap.org/wsdl/soap/"
            xmlns:xsd="http://www.w3.org/2001/XMLSchema"
            xmlns="http://schemas.xmlsoap.org/wsdl/"
            targetNamespace=
                         "http://localhost/WebServices/wsdl/poInfo">
    <message name="getOrderInfoInput">
        <part name="pono" element="xsd:string"/>
        <part name="par" element="xsd:string"/>
    </message>
    <message name="getOrderInfoOutput">
        <part name="body" element="xsd:string"/>
    </message>
    <portType name="poInfoServicePortType">
        <operation name="getOrder">
           <input message="tns:getOrderInfoInput"/>
           <output message="tns:getOrderInfoOutput"/>
        </operation>
    </portType>
    <binding name="poInfoServiceBinding"
            type="tns:poInfoServicePortType">
        <soap:binding style="rpc"
            transport="http://schemas.xmlsoap.org/soap/http"/>
        <operation name="getOrder">
           <soap:operation
             soapAction="http://localhost/WebServices/ch4/getOrder"/>
           <input>
```

```
                <soap:body use="literal"/>
            </input>
            <output>
                <soap:body use="literal"/>
            </output>
        </operation>
    </binding>
    <service name="poInfoService">
        <port name="poInfoServicePort"
                binding="tns:poInfoServiceBinding">
            <soap:address location=
        "http://localhost/WebServices/ch4/SOAPServer_orderinfo.php"/>
        </port>
    </service>
</definitions>
```

The next step is to create the PHP handler class for the `poInfoService` Web service described by the above WSDL document. Consider the `orderInfo.php` script shown as follows:

```
<?php
 //File orderInfo.php
 require_once "obj2Arr.php";
 class orderInfo {
   function getOrder($pono, $par) {
    $srv = simplexml_load_file('services.xml');
    $srv=obj2Arr($srv);
    foreach ($srv['service'] as $value)
    {
      $srvarr[$value['param']]=array("wsdl" => $value['wsdl'],
                              "func" => $value['function']);
    }
    $client = new SoapClient($srvarr[$par]['wsdl']);
    try {
     $rslt=$client->$srvarr[$par]['func']($pono);
    }
    catch (SoapFault $exp) {
     throw new SoapFault("Server", $exp->getMessage());
    }
    return $rslt;
   }
 }
?>
```

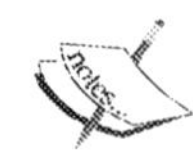

The `orderInfo.php` script shown uses the `obj2Arr` function originally introduced in Chapter 2 in the *Structuring Complex Data for Sending* section. So, you need to copy the `obj2Arr.php` script from the `WebServices/ch2` to `WebServices/ch4` directory.

As you can see, the `getOrder` method invokes an appropriate service specified in the `services.xml` document, depending on the parameter passed in as the second argument. To achieve this, it first loads the information from `services.xml` and then converts it to an easy-to-use associative array, as discussed in the *Putting Info on Fine-Grained Services in a Separate XML File* section earlier in this chapter.

If the `getOrder` method receives `doc` as the second argument, then it invokes the `poOrderDocService` service. If receives `status` as the second argument, then it invokes the `poOrderStatusService` service. If the value of the second argument is neither `doc` nor `status`, a SOAP fault is thrown.

This example shows you how to combine a set of services into a composition by means of logic encapsulated within the PHP handler class of the controller service, without actually orchestrating. When proceeding with this example in the next chapter, you will learn how to achieve the same general result using WS-BPEL, an orchestration language.

Now that you have created the PHP handler class for the `poInfoService` Web service, the next step is to create a SOAP server that will expose the methods of the handler class to consumers. For this purpose, you might create the `SoapServer_orderinfo.php` script as follows:

```
<?php
 //File: SoapServer_orderinfo.php
 require_once "orderInfo.php";
 $wsdl= "http://localhost/WebServices/wsdl/po_orderinfo.wsdl";
 $srv= new SoapServer($wsdl);
 $srv->setClass("orderInfo");
 $srv->handle();
?>
```

Testing the Application

Finally, you need to write a client to test the `poInfoService` service exposing the `getOrder` parameter-driven operation. For this purpose, you might build the `SoapClient_orderinfo.php` SOAP client script in the `WebServices\ch4` directory.

The `SoapClient_orderinfo.php` script might look as follows:

```
<?php
 //File: SoapClient_orderinfo.php
 $wsdl = "http://localhost/WebServices/wsdl/po_orderinfo.wsdl";
 $client = new SoapClient($wsdl);
 $pono='108128476';
 $par = 'doc'; //can be either 'doc' or 'status'
 try {
  print $result=$client->getOrder($pono, $par);
 }
 catch (SoapFault $exp) {
  print $exp->getMessage();
 }
?>
```

When executed, the `SoapClient_orderinfo.php` SOAP client script shown above should output the entire PO XML document whose `pono` is `108128476`. Now if you change the value of the `$par` variable in the above code to `status`, the script will return the message saying **shipped**.

This example assumes that the `purchaseOrders` table created as discussed in Chapter 2 in the *Setting Up the Database* section contains a row representing a PO XML document whose `pono` is `108128476`. Such a row will appear in the table when you have tested the PO Web service as discussed in the *Testing the Service* section in Chapter 2. It also assumes that the `poStatusInfo` table has a row containing the status information about the above PO XML document. This row should have been inserted in `poStatusInfo` as shown in the *Defining Parameter-Driven Operations* section in Chapter 2.

Exposing Application Logic as a Web Service

To make existing application logic available via a Web service—while achieving loose coupling, one of the most important principles of service-orientation—you first will need to decompose the business logic of your application into a series of lightweight and independent services to be then utilized within a composite service-oriented solution. It is interesting to note that an SOA solution may be built upon the existing application structures, often without the need to change those structures.

In the following section, you will see an example of how to define a set of services upon a single PHP class, associating each service operation with a certain method of the class.

Sharing the Same PHP Handler Class Between Services

The preceding example used two different PHP handler classes for the two fine-grained services discussed there. In practice, though, there is often a need to expose methods belonging to the same PHP class using different services, thus sharing the same handler class between these services. This sort of situation often arises when you need to build a collection of light services upon an existing PHP class.

Continuing with the preceding example, you might put the `getOrderStatus` and `getOrderDoc` methods belonging to the `orderDoc` and `orderStatus` classes respectively within the same PHP class, say `orderClass`. At the same time, these two methods will still be exposed by the `poOrderDocService` and `poOrderStatusService` services respectively. Diagrammatically, this might look like the following figure:

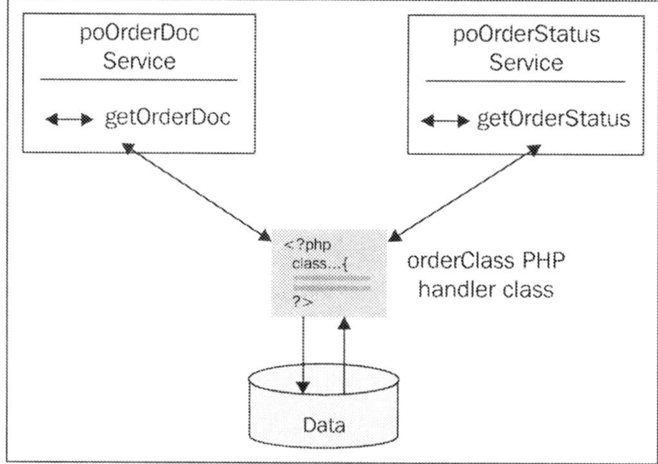

To achieve the above functionality, you don't need to modify the `orderInfo` PHP handler class of the `poInfoService` coarse-grained service employing the `poOrderDocService` and `poOrderStatusService` services, nor its SOAP server script. The only thing you need to change is the `services.xml` configuration file providing information about the above fine-grained services, assuming you're using the variations of these services that have been slightly updated to work with this example.

When modifying the poOrderDocService and poOrderStatusService services to be used in this example, you probably will not want to change the names of services and functions to be exposed. If so, in services.xml you will have to change only the names of the WSDL documents to the ones describing the updated fine-grained services. As a result, the updated services.xml document might look as follows:

```
<services>
 <service>
  <name>poOrderDocService</name>
  <wsdl>http://localhost/WebServices/wsdl/
                                        po_orderdoc_share.wsdl</wsdl>
  <function>getOrderDoc</function>
  <param>doc</param>
 </service>
<service>
  <name>poOrderStatusService</name>
  <wsdl>http:
      //localhost/WebServices/wsdl/po_orderstatus_share.wsdl</wsdl>
  <function>getOrderStatus</function>
  <param>status</param>
 </service>
</services>
```

In the downloadable ZIP archive, this file is stored as __services.xml in the WebServices\ch4 directory. When moving on to this example, though, make sure to rename this document to services.xml.

As you can see, the above assumes that you create the po_orderstatus_share.wsdl and po_orderdoc_share.wsdl WSDL definition documents based on the po_orderstatus.wsdl and po_orderdoc.wsdl documents, specifying SoapServer_orderdoc_share.php and SoapServer_orderstatus_share.php as the SOAP servers respectively.

Then, you create the SoapServer_orderdoc_share.php and SoapServer_orderstatus_share.php SOAP server scripts, setting the orderClass class stored in the orderClass.php script as the PHP handler class for both the services.

It is interesting to note that although both poOrderDocService and poOrderStatusService services are set upon the same PHP handler class, each service operation is associated with a specific class method.

The following figure gives a graphical depiction of this design:

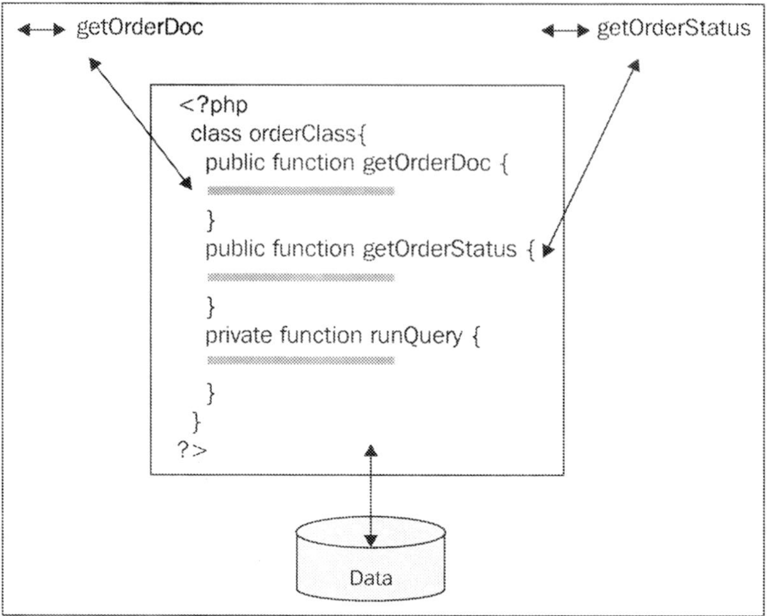

As you can see in the figure, the `orderClass` class, besides the `getOrderStatus` and `getOrderDoc` public methods, includes the `runQuery` private method to which you moved all the code performing database-related tasks. The `orderClass.php` script containing the `orderClass` class might look as follows:

```
<?php
 //File orderClass.php
 class orderClass {
   private function runQuery($sql, $pono, $par)
   {
    if(!$conn = oci_connect('xmlusr', 'xmlusr', '//localhost/XE')){
        throw new SoapFault("Server","Failed to connect to
                             database");
    };
    $query = oci_parse($conn, $sql);
    oci_bind_by_name($query, ':pono', $pono);
    if (!oci_execute($query)) {
        $err=oci_error($query);
        throw new SoapFault("Server","Failed to execute query
                            ".$err['message']);
    };
    oci_fetch($query);
    $rslt = oci_result($query, $par);
    return $rslt;
```

```
    }
    public function getOrderDoc($pono) {
     $sql="SELECT doc FROM purchaseOrders WHERE
            extractValue(XMLType(doc), '/purchaseOrder/pono')=:pono
            AND rownum=1";
     return $this->runQuery($sql, $pono, 'DOC');
    }
    public function getOrderStatus($pono) {
     $sql="SELECT status FROM poStatusInfo WHERE pono=:pono";
     return $this->runQuery($sql, $pono, 'STATUS');
    }
  }
?>
```

To put the above class into action, you should execute the `SoapClient_orderinfo.php` SOAP client script discussed in the *Testing the Application* section earlier. As a result, your browser should output the entire PO XML document whose `pono` is `108128476`.

It is important to realize that although both `poOrderDocService` and `poOrderStatusService` services are set upon the same PHP handler class, you cannot use, say, a `poOrderDocService` instance to call the `getOrderStatus` method of the handler class. If you try to do this from within, say, the `getOrder` method of the `orderInfo` class discussed in the *Creating the Coarse-Grained Service* section, you will receive the following error message:

```
Function ("getOrderStatus") is not a valid method for this service
```

To understand why it works this way, you should look into the `po_orderdoc.wsdl` WSDL document describing the `poOrderDocService` service. This WSDL document was shown at the beginning of the *Building Fine-Grained Services* section earlier. Looking through this document, you may notice that it defines only one operation, namely `getOrderDoc`. What this means in practice is that any attempt to call another operation via the `poOrderDocService` service will result in an error like the one shown above.

Choosing the Appropriate Level of Service Granularity

When designing services to be utilized within an SOA solution, it's always a good idea to look at the situation with a big-picture view of your future projects. It is important to figure out if there's long-term potential with exposing a certain piece of business logic as an individual service. If you determine that there is little benefit in building a service upon a certain piece of existing logic, it will be wise to pass on this. For example, if you have two classes built one upon another, in most cases, you don't need to define a service or services on each of these classes. Instead, it would be a good idea to use the top class as the PHP handler class for the service or services being built. The following example illustrates how you might define two services upon the same class, which in turn uses another class containing database-specific code.

Examining the `orderClass` class discussed in the preceding section, you may notice that the code responsible for interacting with the database is encapsulated in a separate private method. Despite this fact, the `orderClass` still depends on a certain database, namely Oracle. To eliminate dependency on a certain database, you might rewrite the `orderClass` so that it provides a generic interface, delegating the real work to methods belonging to another class. Graphically it might look like the following figure:

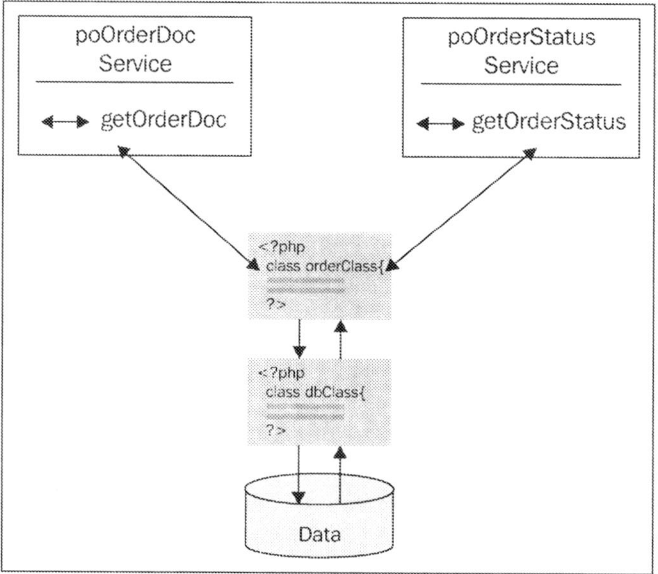

> In real object-oriented solutions, it is particularly common for one class use another one, which is responsible for performing a specific task or tasks. Actually, a class may be built upon a hierarchy of classes. In this particular example, the `dbClass` underlying class performs the database-specific work, while the `orderClass` upfront class is used as the PHP handler class for two services, namely `poOrderDocService` and `poOrderDocService`.

Now that you have an idea of how the `orderClass/dbClass` combination works, let's look at the code. The code for the `orderClass` class is as follows:

```
<?php
 //File __orderClass.php
 require_once "dbClass.php";
 class orderClass {
   public function getOrderDoc($pono) {
    $dbObj = new dbClass();
    return $dbObj->getOrderDoc($pono);
   }
   public function getOrderStatus($pono) {
    $dbObj = new dbClass();
    return $dbObj->getOrderStatus($pono);
   }
 }
?>
```

In the downloadable ZIP archive, this file is stored as `__orderClass.php` in the `WebServices\ch4` directory. When moving on to this example, though, make sure to rename this document to `orderClass.php`.

As you can see, the above variation of the `orderClass` simply provides a generic interface, containing no database-specific code. So, the `dbClass` class performing the real database work can be implemented to communicate with the database you need, not necessarily Oracle. For example, you might have the following `dbClass` class to interact with MySQL:

```
<?php
//File dbClass.php
 class dbClass {
   public function getOrderDoc($pono) {
    $sql="SELECT doc FROM purchaseOrders WHERE
          extractValue(doc, '/purchaseOrder/pono')=? LIMIT 1";
    return $this->runQuery($sql, $pono);
   }
   public function getOrderStatus($pono) {
    $sql="SELECT status FROM poStatusInfo WHERE pono=?";
    return $this->runQuery($sql, $pono);
   }
   private function runQuery($sql, $pono)
   {
    if(!$conn = new mysqli('localhost', 'usr', 'pswd', 'my_db')){
        throw new SoapFault("Server","Failed to connect to
          database");
```

```
        };
        $stmt = $conn->prepare($sql);
        $stmt->bind_param('s', $pono);
        if (!$result = $stmt->execute()) {
            throw new SoapFault("Server","Failed to execute query");
        };
        $stmt->bind_result($rslt);
        $stmt->fetch();
        return $rslt;
      }
  }
```

This example assumes that you have created the `purchaseOrders` table in the `my_db` MySQL database and then populated that table with the data as discussed in the *Building a Service Interacting with MySQL* section in Chapter 3. Also you may notice that the `getOrderStatus` method used here assumes that you have a `poStatusInfo` table in the `my_db` MySQL database, and this table is supposed to contain a row whose `pono` attribute is `108128476`. Since the `poStatusInfo` table has not been created before, you should create it and populate with the data now. To do this, you can issue the following SQL statements from MySQL Command Line Client:

```
use my_db;
CREATE TABLE poStatusInfo(
    pono VARCHAR(9),
    status VARCHAR(15)
);
INSERT INTO poStatusInfo VALUES(
    '108128476',
    'shipped'
);
```

To test the updated application, you can execute the `SoapClient_orderinfo.php` SOAP client script discussed in the *Testing the Application* section. Assuming that the `$par` variable in the script is still set to `doc`, you should see in your browser the PO XML document whose `pono` is `108128476`.

To summarize this example: Theoretically, you might, of course, expose the database-specific code encapsulated in the `dbClass` class as a distinct service, thus adding another level of service granularity. However, it would not be efficient in this situation, since such a service, if created, would never be used independently of the `poOrderDocService` and `poOrderStatusService` services based on the `orderClass` generic class, thus having no reuse potential as a distinct service.

Securing Services

One problem with the services discussed so far is that they are not secure. For example, no authentication is required when consuming the PO Web service discussed in the *Building Service Providers and Service Requestors* section in Chapter 2. What this means is that anyone may consume the service and submit a PO document, without having to provide any credentials. In a real-world situation, you probably might want only legitimate users to have the ability to consume the service.

As you may recall from the *Building Service Providers and Service Requestors* section in Chapter 2, the PO Web service, when invoked, is supposed to perform the following four steps:

1. Receive a PO document in XML format
2. Validate the PO against the appropriate XML schema
3. Store the PO in the database
4. Send a response message to the requestor

Going one step further, you might add a security check to the above scenario. That would be the second step, performed just after receiving the SOAP package containing a PO document and before validating the received document. So, the above scenario will now look as follows:

1. Receive a PO document in XML format
2. Perform a security check
3. Validate the PO against the appropriate XML schema
4. Store the PO in the database
5. Send a response message to the requestor

The following sections discuss how you might implement the second step in the above scenario.

Implementing Message-Level Security

One simple way to secure the PO Web service would be to provide legitimate users with a token. This approach assumes that each SOAP message containing a PO document sent by a consumer will contain a username/password pair, which is checked against the database when it arrives at the service provider.

While this approach allows the service provider to obtain the information about the consumer to make an authorization decision, a significant disadvantage is that the credentials passed within the message are actually independent of the message payload, and thus, once obtained by a malicious user, may be used to consume the service on behalf of a legitimate user. Of course, you can still use SSL to ensure transport-level security. Often, though, a SOAP message sent from a service consumer to a service provider is processed by an intermediate service or services, running the risk of a malicious user stealing the password travelling with the message.

This section discusses how you might work around the above issue by using a hash generated from the value of a particular element or elements of the PO document being transmitted with the message, rather than sending a fixed token. On the client, you might include that hash as part of the SOAP message payload also containing the PO document as the other part. The server in turn is responsible for retrieving the hashed token from the message and checking whether this hash corresponds to the PO that arrived in the same message. Depending on the algorithm used to generate a hash, each new PO document may come with a potentially different hashed token, which makes it harder for a malicious user to illegally access the service.

> It is important to realize that the above security mechanism does not ensure a private way to transfer the data, since the payload of a SOAP message being transmitted is not encrypted. As for data integrity, you may be fully confident that the message has not been modified in transit only if the hash transmitted within the message was generated upon the entire payload rather than some parts of it. What does this security mechanism do then? Well, it prevents unauthorized users from consuming the service. That is it.

Diagrammatically, the security mechanism discussed here might look like the following figure:

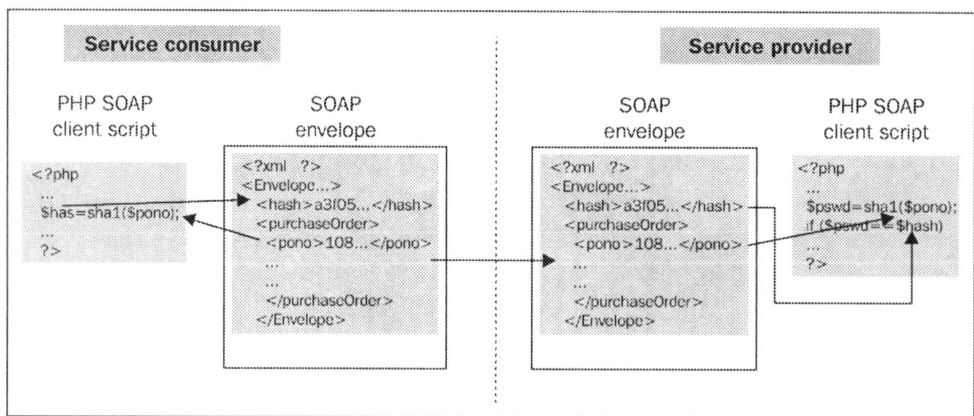

Here is the PHP code you might use to generate the `sha1` hash upon the value of the `pono` element of a PO XML document:

```
$xmlpo = simplexml_load_string($po);
$pono = $xmlpo->purchaseOrder->pono;
$hash=sha1($pono);
```

While the previous figure illustrates an example assuming that the hash is generated upon the value of the `pono` element only, in reality, however, the hash might be built upon any other PO document's element or, even better, upon a combination of elements. The more elements are involved and the more complicated the hashing algorithm is, the harder it will be for a malicious user to guess that algorithm. When choosing elements for hashing, it is always a good idea to consider the element whose value uniquely identifies the document, since it will be most likely used as the primary key when storing the document in the database. So utilizing the `pono` in this particular example is essential, since an attempt to submit a new PO document with the same `pono` will fail due to the primary key constraints placed upon the database table holding incoming PO documents.

However, for simplicity the `purchaseOrder` table being used in this example and created as discussed in Chapter 2 in the *Setting Up the Database* section doesn't have a primary key constraint. In practice, though, you would definitely use a more complicated database table for storing PO XML documents, like the `orders` table created during the process of the `po.xsd` XML schema registration as discussed in Chapter 3, in the *Using XML Schemas with Oracle XML DB* section. If you recall, the `orders` table has the primary key defined on the `pono` attribute.

As you can see, with the above approach, you don't even need to create and hold the security accounts in the database, since the security measures are incorporated in a SOAP message itself, thus enabling message-level security.

As an alternative to including credentials in the SOAP message body, you might include them in the SOAP message headers. To achieve this with the PHP SOAP extension, you might use the following predefined classes: `SoapHeader` and `SoapVar`. Using SOAP message headers to send secure messages, as well as implementing WS-Security authentication, is discussed in detail later, in the *Using SOAP Message Headers* and *Using WS-Security for Message-Level Security* sections.

In the remainder of this section, you will learn how to implement a secure version of the PO Web service, based on the approach outlined above.

The first step is to create the WSDL document for the updated PO Web service. For that, you might create the following document and save it as `po_secure.wsdl` in the `WebServices\wsdl` directory:

```
<?xml version="1.0" encoding="utf-8"?>
<definitions name ="poServiceSecure"
            xmlns:http="http://schemas.xmlsoap.org/wsdl/http/"
            xmlns:soap="http://schemas.xmlsoap.org/wsdl/soap/"
            xmlns:xsd="http://www.w3.org/2001/XMLSchema"
            xmlns="http://schemas.xmlsoap.org/wsdl/"
            targetNamespace="http://localhost/WebServices/wsdl/po_
secure.wsdl">
    <message name="getPlaceOrderInput">
        <part name="hash" element="xsd:string"/>
        <part name="po" element="xsd:string"/>
    </message>
    <message name="getPlaceOrderOutput">
        <part name="body" element="xsd:string"/>
    </message>
    <portType name="poServiceSecurePortType">
        <operation name="placeOrder">
           <input message="tns:getPlaceOrderInput"/>
           <output message="tns:getPlaceOrderOutput"/>
        </operation>
    </portType>
    <binding name="poServiceSecureBinding"
                  type="tns:poServiceSecurePortType">
        <soap:binding style="rpc"
                  transport="http://schemas.xmlsoap.org/soap/http"/>
        <operation name="placeOrder">
           <soap:operation
           soapAction="http://localhost/WebServices/ch4/placeOrder"/>
           <input>
               <soap:body use="literal"/>
           </input>
           <output>
               <soap:body use="literal"/>
           </output>
        </operation>
    </binding>
    <service name="poServiceSecure">
        <port name="poServiceSecurePort"
                  binding="tns:poServiceSecureBinding">
           <soap:address
```

```
      location="http://localhost/WebServices/ch4/SoapServer_secure.php"/>
            </port>
        </service>
    </definitions>
```

As you can see, this WSDL assumes two message parts in the input message of the `placeOrder` operation defined here. So, make sure that the binding style defined in the document is `rpc`.

Next, you might want to create the PHP handler class representing the underlying logic of the service discussed here. For that, you might create the following `purchaseOrder.php` script in the `WebServices\ch4` directory:

```
<?php
 //File purchaseOrder_secure.php
 class purchaseOrder {
   public function placeOrder($hash, $po) {
    if(!$conn = oci_connect('xmlusr', 'xmlusr', '//localhost/XE')){
       throw new SoapFault("Server","Failed to connect to database");
    };
    $xmlpo = simplexml_load_string($po);
    $pono = $xmlpo->pono;
    $pswd=sha1($pono);
    $this->checkOrder($hash, $pswd);
    $sql = "INSERT INTO purchaseOrders VALUES(:po)";
    $query = oci_parse($conn, $sql);
    oci_bind_by_name($query, ':po', $po);
    if (!oci_execute($query)) {
        throw new SoapFault("Server","Failed to insert PO");
    };
    $msg='<rsltMsg>PO inserted!</rsltMsg>';
    return $msg;
   }
   private function checkOrder($hash, $pswd) {
    if ($pswd!=$hash) {
        throw new SoapFault("Server","You're not authorized to
                                     consume this service");
    }
   }
 }
?>
```

In this `purchaseOrder` class, in the first highlighted code block you load the PO XML document as a `SimpleXMLElement` object and then extract the value of the `pono` element. Next, you generate the `sha1` hash upon the extracted `pono` and call the `checkOrder` private method of `purchaseOrder`. The code for this method is also highlighted in the listing and is used to check to see whether the hash generated here is equal to the hash that arrived with the message. If there is a mismatch, a `SoapFault` exception is thrown.

The implementation of the SOAP server script to be used in this example is straightforward. It is assumed that you save the following SOAP server script as `SoapServer_secure.php` in the `WebServices/ch4` directory:

```
<?php
 //File: SoapServer_secure.php
 require_once "purchaseOrder_secure.php";
 $wsdl= "http://localhost/WebServices/wsdl/po_secure.wsdl";
 $srv= new SoapServer($wsdl);
 $srv->setClass("purchaseOrder");
 $srv->handle();
?>
```

Now that you have the service created, all that's left is to build a client script to test the newly created service. For that, you might create the `SoapClient_secure.php` client script shown below:

```
<?php
 //File: SoapClient_secure.php
 $wsdl = "http://localhost/WebServices/wsdl/po_secure.wsdl";
 $xmldoc = simplexml_load_file('purchaseOrder.xml');
 $pono = $xmldoc->pono;
 $hash=sha1($pono);
 $podoc=$xmldoc->asXML();
 $client = new SoapClient($wsdl);
 try {
  print $result=$client->placeOrder($hash, $podoc);
 }
 catch (SoapFault $exp) {
  print $exp->getMessage();
 }
?>
```

Before you can execute this SOAP client script, you need to have a `purchaseOrder.xml` document containing a PO XML document. For that, you might use the one shown in Chapter 2, in the *Building the Service Requestor* section. So, make sure to copy the `purchaseOrder.xml` document from the `WebServices\ch2` to `WebServices\ch4` directory.

In this client script, you extract the value of the `pono` element from the PO loaded as a `SimpleXMLObject` from `purchaseOrder.xml`, and then generate an `sha1` hash upon the extracted value. The generated hash and the PO document converted into a string are then passed to the `placeOrder` SOAP function as arguments.

Unlike the above client, the following one uses a more complicated algorithm for generating the hash. In particular, it generates an `sha1` hash upon the `pono` and `shipName` concatenated together.

```
<?php
 //File: __SoapClient_secure.php
 $wsdl = "http://localhost/WebServices/wsdl/po_secure.wsdl";
 $xmldoc = simplexml_load_file('purchaseOrder.xml');
 $pono = $xmldoc->pono;
 $shipName = $xmldoc->shipTo->name;
 $mix=$pono.$shipName;
 $hash=sha1($mix);
 $podoc=$xmldoc->asXML();
 $client = new SoapClient($wsdl);
 try {
  print $result=$client->placeOrder($hash, $podoc);
 }
 catch (SoapFault $exp) {
  print $exp->getMessage();
 }
?>
```

Now if you try to run the `__SoapClient_secure.php` script shown above, you should get the following error message:

```
You're not authorized to consume this service
```

This is because you haven't changed the authentication algorithm on the server side yet. To handle this task, you might modify the `purchaseOrder_secure.php` script as shown overleaf (the script has been cut down to save space):

For the full version, see the `__purchaseOrder_secure.php` script in the `WebServices\ch4` directory of the downloadable ZIP archive accompanying this book. However, before you put the script into action, make sure to rename it to `purchaseOrder_secure.php`.

```
<?php
 //File __purchaseOrder_secure.php
 class purchaseOrder {
   public function placeOrder($hash, $po) {
     ...
     $xmlpo = simplexml_load_string($po);
     $pono = $xmlpo->pono;
     $shipName = $xmlpo->shipTo->name;
     $mix=$pono.$shipName;
     $pswd=sha1($mix);
     $this->checkOrder($hash, $pswd);
     ...
   }
  ...
 }
?>
```

Now the mechanism of generating the hash on the client agrees with the one used on the server. So, if you now run the `__SoapClient_secure.php` script, you should not have a problem.

Using SOAP Message Headers

In the preceding section you saw an example of how you might implement message-level security by including a hash generated upon the data from the document being transmitted into the message. The mechanism discussed there assumed that you pass the hash generated as part of the message payload, which means you had to define another part of the input message in the WSDL document in order to carry the hash. However, sending the hash as part of the payload is probably not a good idea, because the hash, acting as a security measure in this case, can be considered metadata rather than user data transmitted within the SOAP message payload.

If you recall from the *Communicating via SOAP* section in Chapter 1, SOAP assumes that you will use the header element of a message to carry metadata associated with that message. So, turning back to the example discussed here, it would be wise to put the hash in the header of the message.

The following figure gives a graphical depiction of the process that takes place on the server side when a secure message arrives.

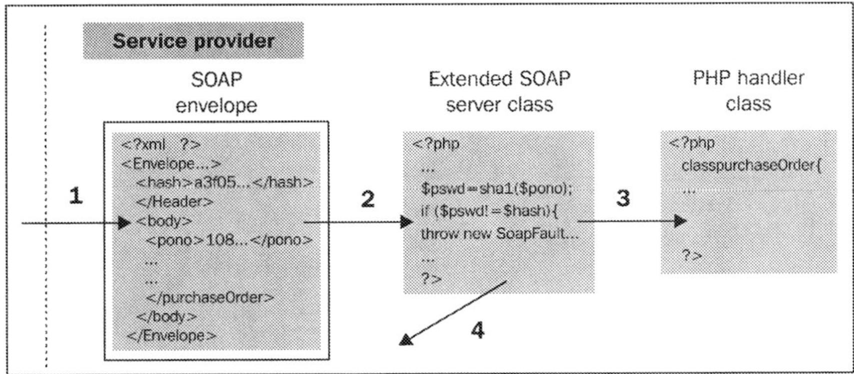

Here is the explanation of the steps in the figure:

- Step 1: The service provider receives the message containing a PO document as the payload and the hash as a header.
- Step 2: The overridden `handle` method of an extended SOAP server class checks whether the hash that arrived with the message as a header is equal to the hash generated upon the `pono` element of the PO document composing the message payload.
- Step 3: If the check performed in Step 2 returns true, the SOAP server passes the PO document to an instance of the PHP handler class for further processing.
- Step 4: Otherwise, the server stops processing the message, throwing a SOAP exception.

An important point about the security mechanism discussed here is that the SOAP server processes the hash passed in as a header of the message before the message payload is sent to the handler class for processing. So, if the hash passed in is not equal to the hash generated upon the value of the `pono` element of the PO document that arrived as the payload, then the server generates a SOAP fault exception and stops processing the message.

The rest of this section discusses how to implement a service acting as outlined in the above scenario.

As usual, let's start with creating the WSDL document for the updated `poServiceSecure`. For that, create the `po_headers.wsdl` document in the `WebServices\ch4` directory, which might look as follows:

```
<?xml version="1.0" encoding="utf-8"?>
<definitions name ="poServiceSecure"
             xmlns:http="http://schemas.xmlsoap.org/wsdl/http/"
             xmlns:soap="http://schemas.xmlsoap.org/wsdl/soap/"
             xmlns:xsd="http://www.w3.org/2001/XMLSchema"
             xmlns="http://schemas.xmlsoap.org/wsdl/"
             targetNamespace=
                  "http://localhost/WebServices/wsdl/po_headers.wsdl">
    <message name="getPlaceOrderInput">
        <part name="po" element="xsd:string"/>
    </message>
    <message name="getPlaceOrderOutput">
        <part name="body" element="xsd:string"/>
    </message>
    <portType name="poServiceSecurePortType">
        <operation name="placeOrder">
           <input message="tns:getPlaceOrderInput"/>
           <output message="tns:getPlaceOrderOutput"/>
        </operation>
    </portType>
    <binding name="poServiceSecureBinding"
                   type="tns:poServiceSecurePortType">
        <soap:binding style="document"
                   transport="http://schemas.xmlsoap.org/soap/http"/>
        <operation name="placeOrder">
           <soap:operation
           soapAction="http://localhost/WebServices/ch4/placeOrder"/>
           <input>
               <soap:body use="literal"/>
           </input>
           <output>
               <soap:body use="literal"/>
           </output>
        </operation>
    </binding>
    <service name="poServiceSecure">
        <port name="poServiceSecurePort"
                    binding="tns:poServiceSecureBinding">
           <soap:address
 location="http://localhost/WebServices/ch4/SoapServer_headers.php"/>
```

```
            </port>
        </service>
    </definitions>
```

There are a couple of points worth noting about the WSDL document shown opposite. First, the input message of the `placeOrder` operation defined here consists of one part only—you don't need to define the `hash` part any more, since you're not going to transmit a hash as part of the message payload. Second, you may use the binding style `document`, since the input message payload is going to contain only a PO document.

```
<?php
 //File purchaseOrder_headers.php
 class purchaseOrder {
   public function placeOrder($po) {
    if(!$conn = oci_connect('xmlusr', 'xmlusr', '//localhost/XE')){
       throw new SoapFault("Server","Failed to connect to database");
    };
    $sql = "INSERT INTO purchaseOrders VALUES(:po)";
    $query = oci_parse($conn, $sql);
    oci_bind_by_name($query, ':po', $po);
    if (!oci_execute($query)) {
        throw new SoapFault("Server","Failed to insert PO");
    };
    $msg='<rsltMsg>PO inserted!</rsltMsg>';
    return $msg;
   }
 }
?>
```

The `secSoapServer` class is shown in the following snippet that extends the `SoapServer` predefined SOAP extension class, overriding the parent's `handle` method. It is assumed that you save this class as `secSoapServer.php` in the `WebServices\ch4` directory.

```
<?php
 //File: secSoapServer.php
 class secSoapServer extends SoapServer {
  function handle($req) {
   $env = simplexml_load_string($req);
   $hash= $env->xpath('//ns1:hash');
   $hash = (string) $hash[0];
   $po= $env->xpath('//po');
   $po = simplexml_load_string((string)$po[0]);
   $pono = $po->xpath('//pono');
```

```
    $pono = (string)$pono[0];
    $pswd=sha1($pono);
    if ($pswd!=$hash) {
        throw new SoapFault("Server","You're not authorized to
                              consume this service");
    };
    parent::handle();
  }
}
?>
```

In the overridden `handle` method, you first convert the value of the argument passed in to the method and representing the request message received by the server into a `SimpleXMLElement` object, which makes it possible for you to access the request message as XML. In particular, you use the `xpath` `SimpleXMLElement` method to access the hash encapsulated within the message header block. Using the same method, you obtain the message payload, specifying `//po` as the path argument for the `xpath` method. If you recall from the `po_headers.wsdl` document discussed earlier in this section, `po` is the name of the input message part that represents the message payload. Next, you load the obtained payload as another `SimpleXMLElement` object that you then use to access the `pono` element in the PO document representing the payload. It's explained later in this section why you have to create another `SimpleXMLElement` object to access the payload, rather than accessing it via the `SimpleXMLElement` object created earlier and representing the entire message. Finally, to make use of the parent `handle` method functionality, you explicitly call this method.

Now that you have the `secSoapServer` class created, you can put it into action with the following SOAP server script, which you should save as `SoapServer_headers.php` in the `WebServices/ch4` directory:

```
<?php
//File: SoapServer_headers.php
 require_once "purchaseOrder_headers.php";
 require_once "secSoapServer.php";
 $wsdl= "http://localhost/WebServices/wsdl/po_headers.wsdl";
 $srv= new secSoapServer($wsdl);
 $srv->setClass("purchaseOrder");
 $srv->handle($HTTP_RAW_POST_DATA);
?>
```

To test the newly created service, you might create and then execute the following client script:

```
<?php
 //File: SoapClient_headers.php
 $wsdl = "http://localhost/WebServices/wsdl/po_headers.wsdl";
 $xmldoc = simplexml_load_file('purchaseOrder.xml');
 $pono = $xmldoc->pono;
 $hash=sha1($pono);
 $header = new SOAPHeader('http://localhost/WebServices/ch4/headers',
                         'hash', $hash);
 $client = new SoapClient($wsdl);
 $client->__setSOAPHeaders($header);
 $podoc=$xmldoc->asXML();
 try {
  print $result=$client->placeOrder($podoc);
 }
 catch (SoapFault $exp) {
  print $exp->getMessage();
 }
?>
```

As you no doubt have guessed, the highlighted code in the above script is used to set up the header block in the request message being sent to the server. In this particular example, the header block transports the hash used as a security measure.

Now let's turn back to the `secSoapServer` class, discussed a bit earlier in this section. Examining the `handle` method overridden in this class, you may wonder why you would want to use another `SimpleXMLElement` object to access the payload, despite the fact that you already have a `SimpleXMLElement` object representing the entire message. To understand why you have to do it this way, it would be a good idea to look at the request message passed to the `handle` method for processing.

There are several ways in which you can do this. For example, you might make use of the `__getLastRequest` method of a `SoapClient` on the client side as discussed in Chapter 2, in the *Using PHP SOAP Extension Tracing Capabilities* section. As a result, you should get the following message:

```
<SOAP-ENV:Envelope ...>
  <SOAP-ENV:Header>
   <ns1:hash>da30b3a3056d477be870db86a140a4a36cf7b243</ns1:hash>
  </SOAP-ENV:Header>
  <SOAP-ENV:Body>
   <po>
    &lt;?xml version="1.0"?&gt;
```

```
        &lt;purchaseOrder&gt;
         &lt;pono&gt;108128476&lt;/pono&gt;
         &lt;billTo&gt;
          ...
        &lt;/purchaseOrder&gt;
      </po>
    </SOAP-ENV:Body>
  </SOAP-ENV:Envelope>
```

So, to extract the hash from the above message you use the following code in the `handle` method:

```
$env = simplexml_load_string($pack);
$hash= $env->xpath('//ns1:hash');
$hash = (string) $hash[0];
```

However, since the PO document composing the message payload contains HTML entities, obtaining the value of the `pono` element of the PO is a bit tricky. First, you obtain the string representing the PO and containing HTML entities. Next, you load this string as a `SimpleXMLElement` object and then get the `pono` element with the `xpath` method as follows:

```
$po= $env->xpath('//po');
$po = simplexml_load_string((string)$po[0]);
$pono = $po->xpath('//pono');
$pono = (string)$pono[0];
```

This is not the case, though, if the message payload is defined as XML rather than a string. For example, you might use the following WSDL document to describe the `poServiceSecure` service discussed here:

```
<definitions name ="poServiceSecure"
             xmlns:http="http://schemas.xmlsoap.org/wsdl/http/"
             xmlns:soap="http://schemas.xmlsoap.org/wsdl/soap/"
             xmlns:xsd="http://www.w3.org/2001/XMLSchema"
             targetNamespace=
                   "http://localhost/WebServices/wsdl/po_headers.wsdl"
             xmlns:xsd1="http://localhost/WebServices/schema/po/"
             xmlns="http://schemas.xmlsoap.org/wsdl/">
    <import namespace="http://localhost/WebServices/schema/po/"
                location="http://localhost/WebServices/schema/po.xsd"
  />
    <message name="getPlaceOrderInput">
        <part name="po" element="xsd1:purchaseOrder"/>
    </message>
...
</definitions>
```

In this case, the request message issued by a consumer of poServiceSecure would look as follows:

```
<SOAP-ENV:Envelope ...>
  <SOAP-ENV:Header>
   <ns1:hash>da30b3a3056d477be870db86a140a4a36cf7b243</ns1:hash>
  </SOAP-ENV:Header>
  <SOAP-ENV:Body>
   <SOAP-ENV:placeOrder>
    <po>
     <pono>108128476</pono>
     <shipTo>
      ...
    </po>
   </SOAP-ENV:placeOrder>
  </SOAP-ENV:Body>
</SOAP-ENV:Envelope>
```

This simplifies things at the server end. Now, the code extracting the hash and the value of the pono element in the overridden handle method of secSoapServer might look as follows:

```
$env = simplexml_load_string($pack);
$hash= $env->xpath('//ns1:hash');
$hash = (string) $hash[0];
$pono= $env->xpath('//pono');
$pono = (string)$pono[0];
```

In the above example, you use only one SimpleXMLElement object, loading the entire request message into it and then extracting first the hash and then the value of the pono element of the PO document composing the message payload.

Using WS-Security for Message-Level Security

While the security approach discussed in the preceding section may be efficient in many PHP SOAP extension-based solutions and is easy to maintain, it does not represent a standard security mechanism.

If you want to employ a standard SOAP security mechanism, consider WS-Security, a core security specification describing a mechanism for implementing message-level security, providing the means of encapsulating security measures in SOAP messages.

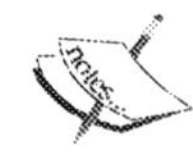

For more information on WS-Security, you can visit the OASIS Web Services Security (WS-Security) page containing links to specification documents. This page can be found at: `http://www.oasis-open.org/committees/tc_home.php?wg_abbrev=wss`.

Actually, the PHP SOAP extension provides no support for WS-Security. To take advantage of the technology, you have to explicitly create the required WS-Security headers and put them into the SOAP message. The header of the message in this case should look as follows:

```
<SOAP-ENV:Header>
 <ns1:Security
       xmlns:ns1="http://schemas.xmlsoap.org/ws/2003/06/secext">
  <ns1:UsernameToken>
   <ns1:Username>yourusername</ns1:Username>
   <ns1:Password>yourpassword</ns1:Password>
  </ns1:UsernameToken>
 </ns1:Security>
</SOAP-ENV:Header>
```

It is interesting to note that WS-Security is not the only WS-* specification that utilizes message headers—virtually all WS-* specifications do that. For example, WS-Addressing transports message exchange information with SOAP headers.

Now that you know what a WS-Security header looks like, let's create a client script that would be able to post messages containing such a header.

To start with, you need to create two classes that will be used in the process of creating a WS-Security header. The first class should look as follows:

```
<?php
 //File: UsernameToken.php
 class UsernameToken {
  private $Username;
  private $Password;
   public function __construct($Username, $Password) {
    $this->Username = $Username;
    $this->Password = $Password;
  }
 }
?>
```

When creating an instance of this class you will have to specify the username and password to be encapsulated in the WS-Security header being created.

The second class should look as follows:

```
<?php
 //File: varUsernameToken.php
 class varUsernameToken {
  private $UsernameToken;
  public function __construct($UsernameToken) {
    $this->UsernameToken = $UsernameToken;
  }
 }
?>
```

This class will be used to create a `SoapVar` variable from an instance of the `UsernameToken` class discussed previously.

Assuming that you have saved the above classes in the `UsernameToken.php` and `varUsernameToken.php` scripts respectively, you can now create the following client script:

```
<?php
 //File: SoapClient_wssecurity.php
 require_once 'UsernameToken.php';
 require_once 'varUsernameToken.php';
 //setting up the variables
 $ns1 = 'http://schemas.xmlsoap.org/ws/2003/06/secext';
 $wsdl = "http://localhost/WebServices/wsdl/po_headers.wsdl";
 //generating the hash
 $xmldoc = simplexml_load_file('purchaseOrder.xml');
 $pono = $xmldoc->pono;
 $hash=sha1($pono);
 //building WS-Security tags
 $usr = new SoapVar('usr', XSD_STRING,null,null,null,$ns1);
 $pswd = new SoapVar('pswd', XSD_STRING,null,null,null,$ns1);
 $tok = new UsernameToken($usr, $pswd);
 $token = new SoapVar($tok, SOAP_ENC_OBJECT,null,null,'UsernameToken'
,$ns1);
 $varToken = new varUsernameToken($token);
 $token = new SoapVar($varToken, SOAP_ENC_OBJECT,null,null,'UsernameT
oken',$ns1);
 $header = new SOAPHeader($ns1, 'Security', $token);
 //creating the client
 $client = new SoapClient($wsdl, array('trace' => 1));
```

```
    $client->__setSOAPHeaders($header);
    $podoc=$xmldoc->asXML();
    try {
     print $result=$client->placeOrder($podoc);
    }
    catch (SoapFault $exp) {
     print $exp->getMessage();
    }
    print "REQUEST:\n".$client->__getLastRequest()."\n";
?>
```

As you might guess, the highlighted block of code is responsible for setting up a WS-Security header to be sent with the request message. You define a `SoapVar` object upon an instance of the `UsernameToken` class defined earlier, and then use this `SoapVar` object when defining an instance of the `varUsernameToken` class. The latter in turn is used when defining another `SoapVar` object, which is then passed to the `SoapHeader` constructor.

For simplicity, this client script uses the same WSDL document as in the preceding example. This means that when you execute the above client, the `SoapServer_headers.php` server script discussed in the preceding section will be invoked. So, the authentication will fail, because the `secSoapServer` class utilized within `SoapServer_headers.php` is not supposed to work with a WS-Security header. In a real-world scenario, though, it is assumed that the receiver understands WS-Security.

However, the purpose of the client script discussed here is to show how you can set up a WS-Security header rather than how you can handle it on the server side. To achieve this goal, you create a `SoapClient` in debugging mode, and then use the `__getLastRequest` method to print out the request message. In this case, the request message will be printed regardless of whether the server fails to process the message or not.

> To complete this example, though, you might create the SOAP server that will understand WS-Security headers. For that, you might want to create a class that extends the `SoapServer` class, similar to `secSoapServer` used in the preceding example, in order to handle WS-Security headers on the server side.

All that's left is to run the script to check to see what the request message being generated looks like. When examining the request message, you should notice that it contains the header block shown at the beginning of this section.

Summary

In this chapter, you looked at how to build a composite solution based on Web services, without using an orchestration engine. You saw an example of how information about the fine-grained services to be utilized from within a more coarse-grained service may be stored in a separate file, thus allowing for dynamic binding between the services involved. You also learned how SOAP headers can be used to transport metadata. In particular, you looked at different approaches to implementing message-level security, including the one based on WS-Security.

In the next chapter, you will start getting your hands dirty with WS-BPEL, looking at how to utilize single services built with the PHP SOAP extension within a WS-BPEL process service.

5

Composing SOA Solutions with WS-BPEL

When building a WS-BPEL process, you in fact define the way in which different services forming a composition interact with one another. With WS-BPEL you actually create new services from the existing ones, since a WS-BPEL process can be considered a service itself. If the business requirements change, you can easily modify your WS-BPEL service by changing its process definition document.

In this chapter, you will look at how to build, deploy, and test the WS-BPEL process services. In particular, you'll see the following:

- The general structure of a WS-BPEL process definition
- Utilizing the basic constructs of WS-BPEL language when designing process definitions
- Using ActiveBPEL open-source engine as a means of executing WS-BPEL process definitions
- Building and deploying a simple WS-BPEL process service that returns a hello message to the consumer
- Combining a set of fine-grained services into a coarse-grained one with WS-BPEL

Getting Started with WS-BPEL

As mentioned in the *WS-BPEL* section in Chapter 1, WS-BPEL orchestration language enables you to define business processes based on Web services, describing the message exchange behavior between the parties involved.

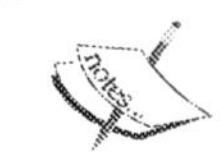

It is recommended that you read the *WS-BPEL* section in Chapter 1 before proceeding to this chapter.

The following three sections provide a brief look at WS-BPEL again, concentrating on how it works and the general structure of a WS-BPEL definition.

How it Works

In Chapter 1, you also learned that WS-BPEL utilizes several XML specifications, where WSDL is the most significant one. Practically speaking, being a service itself, a WS-BPEL process should have a corresponding WSDL document describing it to its consumers. Thus, both a WS-BPEL process service and the partner services utilized within that process are exposed via WSDL.

The following figure illustrates the above interaction model diagrammatically:

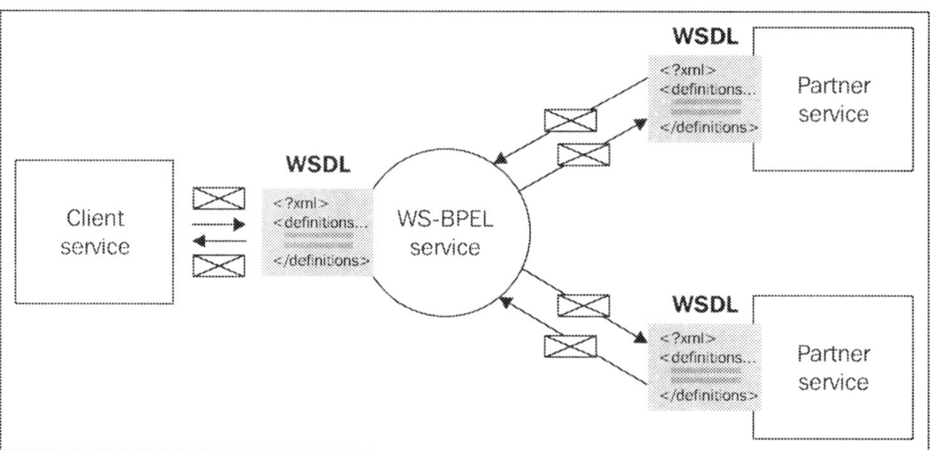

Although the diagram in this figure doesn't tell you about the mechanisms behind WS-BPEL, it can be used as an aid to understand how a WS-BPEL process service fits into the big picture of a composite solution based on using WS-BPEL orchestration. In particular, it shows you that a WS-BPEL process service, like any other service, exposes its functionality through a WSDL interface and thus can be invoked by a client created in WSDL mode.

> Actually, there are several ways in which a WS-BPEL process service can be invoked. For example, a WS-BPEL process may be invoked from within another WS-BPEL process, thus being a part of another orchestration. For simplicity, the examples in this chapter show how to invoke a WS-BPEL process by a client script built with the PHP SOAP extension.

When creating a WS-BPEL service you create a WS-BPEL definition that will then be executed against a WS-BPEL engine, while a partner service built with the PHP SOAP extension will be executed against a PHP engine. The following figure gives a graphical depiction of this situation:

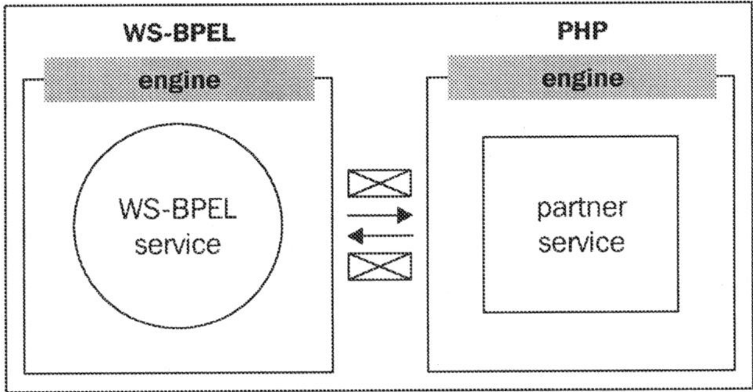

A WS-BPEL engine reads an executable WS-BPEL process definition, as well as other documents such as WSDL and XSD and waits for an incoming request message from a consumer of the WS-BPEL process. When such a message arrives, it creates an instance of the process, executing, and interacting with partner services as described in the process definition.

The Structure of a WS-BPEL Definition

If you recall from the *WS-BPEL Processes* section in Chapter 1, a WS-BPEL business process definition specifies how to co-ordinate the interactions between an instance of that process and its partner services. This section discusses the structure of a WS-BPEL definition document, providing a brief description of the most important WS-BPEL language constructs.

Graphically, the general structure of a WS-BPEL process definition might look like the following figure:

```
<process...>
  <partnerLinks>
    ...
  </partnerLinks>
  <variables>
    ...
  </variables>
  <faultHandlers>
    ...
  </faultHanders>
  <sequence>
    <receive.../>
    <invoke.../>
    <reply...>
      ...
  </sequence>
</process>
```

As you can see in the figure, a WS-BPEL definition represents an XML document containing WS-BPEL language constructs performing the process logic. A WS-BPEL definition, as well as some other documents related to the process definition are then deployed to a WS-BPEL engine against which that process definition will be executed.

Here are the most important WS-BPEL constructs used when defining WS-BPEL definitions:

WS-BPEL construct	**Description**
`process`	This is the root element of a WS-BPEL process definition and uses attributes to declare a number of the process-related namespaces.
`partnerLinks`	Contains a set of `partnerLink` elements. Each `partnerLink` element establishes the relationship between the process service and one of its partners.
`variables`	Contains a set of variable elements. Each variable element defines a variable used by the process.
`faultHandlers`	Contains fault handlers that describe the actions to be taken in response to the faults that may arise during the process execution.

WS-BPEL construct	Description
`sequence`	Contains one or more activities performed one after another, as they appear within the construct. In a complex scenario, several sequences maybe grouped within the flow construct, which enables concurrency and synchronization.
`flow`	Enables concurrency between the activities enclosed within this construct. For example, you may start several invoke activities concurrently, enabling synchronization dependencies between them.
`receive`	Receives a message from a partner client service. Usually, this activity is used with the `createInstance` attribute set to `yes` in order to instantiate the business process.
`invoke`	Calls the partner service specified by the `partnerLink` attribute of the activity.
`reply`	Sends a response message to the request received by a receive activity, assuming a request-response operation is involved.
`assign`	Contains the from and to pairs wrapped in a copy element, which are used to update the values of variables defined within the variables section.
`If`	Allows you to add conditional logic to your process definition. By using nested `elseif` elements and an optional `else` element, you can define one or more conditional branches within the `if` activity. Note that `if/elseif/else` are new WS-BPEL 2.0 elements. In BPEL4WS 1.1, you use `switch/case/otherwise` instead.
`throw`	Explicitly throws a named fault inside the business process. You can optionally use the `faultVariable` attribute to specify a variable with the fault data. A thrown fault should be then handled by a corresponding fault handler defined within a `faultHandlers` construct.

The example in the following section shows how to use the above mentioned WS-BPEL constructs in a WS-BPEL process definition.

An Example of a WS-BPEL Definition

Suppose you want to define a WS-BPEL process that will return the required information about the specified order. For simplicity's sake, the WS-BPEL process discussed in this section will interact with a single partner service implemented in PHP. In particular, the process will utilize the `poOrderDocService` partner service discussed in the *Building Fine-Grained Services* section in Chapter 4. If you recall, the `poOrderDocService` service returns the entire `po` document whose `pono` is equal to the one specified in the request message sent by a consumer.

So, this example assumes no conditional logic in the WS-BPEL process, since it has a very simple structure—the only information returned about the specified order is going to be the entire document representing that order.

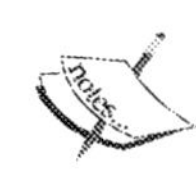

When continuing with this example in the *Implementing Service-Oriented Orchestrations* section later in this chapter, you will learn how to utilize another partner service, namely `poOrderStatusService`, which is discussed in the *Building Fine-Grained Services* section in Chapter 4. Then, you will look at how to enhance the process definition by adding conditional logic responsible for determining what partner service should be invoked.

Schematically, the above design might look as follows:

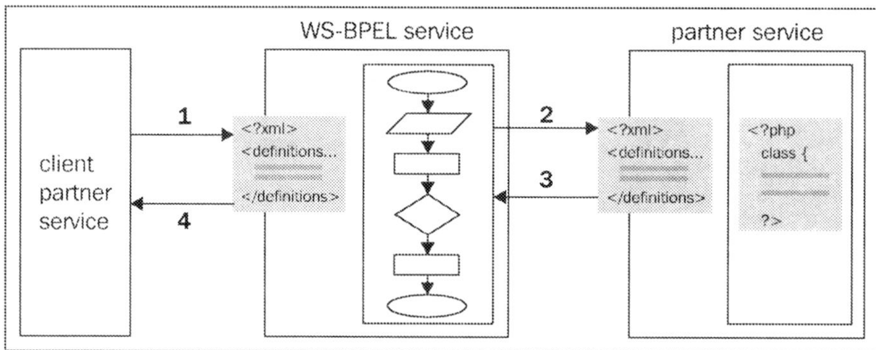

Here is the explanation of the steps in the figure, from the WS-BPEL process instance's standpoint:

- Step 1: The WS-BPEL process receives a request message from the client partner service. This is done with the help of the `receive` WS-BPEL language construct. In fact, this is the first step in the lifecycle of a WS-BPEL process instance, since a new instance of the business process is created upon receiving a request message from the client.
- Step 2, 3: The business process invokes the partner service implemented with PHP. This example assumes a synchronous request-response operation between the process and the client. That is why both Steps 2 and 3 can be implemented using a single `invoke` activity in the WS-BPEL process.
- Step 4: The business process replies to the client's request made in Step 1. To do this, the `reply` activity can be used.

As you no doubt have realized, the WS-BPEL process depicted in the figure should include at least the following three activities:

- `receive`
- `invoke`
- `reply`

Before moving on to the WS-BPEL process definition though, let's look at the WSDL document that might be used to expose that process service to its consumers. This helps you understand the structure of the WS-BPEL process definition discussed latter in this section.

```
<?xml version="1.0" encoding="UTF-8"?>
<definitions name="poInfo"
    targetNamespace="http://localhost:8081/active-bpel/services/
poInfoService.wsdl"
    xmlns:tns="http://localhost:8081/active-bpel/services/
poInfoService.wsdl"
    xmlns:plnk="http://schemas.xmlsoap.org/ws/2003/05/partner-link/"
    xmlns:xsd="http://www.w3.org/2001/XMLSchema"
    xmlns:ns2="http://localhost/WebServices/wsdl/poOrderDoc"
    xmlns="http://schemas.xmlsoap.org/wsdl/">
  <import namespace="http://localhost/WebServices/wsdl/poOrderDoc"
          location="http://localhost/WebServices/wsdl/
             po_orderdoc.wsdl"/>
  <types>
    <schema attributeFormDefault="qualified"
            elementFormDefault="qualified"
            targetNamespace=
     "http://localhost:8081/active-bpel/services/poInfoService.wsdl"
            xmlns="http://www.w3.org/2001/XMLSchema">
      <element name="poInfoRequest">
        <complexType>
          <sequence>
            <element name="input" type="xsd:string"/>
          </sequence>
        </complexType>
      </element>
     </schema>
  </types>
  <message name="poInfoResponseMessage">
    <part name="payload" type="xsd:string"/>
  </message>
  <message name="poInfoRequestMessage">
```

```
      <part name="payload" element="tns:poInfoRequest"/>
    </message>
    <portType name="poInfoPT">
      <operation name="getInfo">
        <input message="tns:poInfoRequestMessage"/>
        <output message="tns:poInfoResponseMessage"/>
      </operation>
    </portType>
    <plnk:partnerLinkType name="poInfoLT">
     <plnk:role name="poInfoProviderRole">
        <plnk:portType name="tns:poInfoPT"/>
     </plnk:role>
    </plnk:partnerLinkType>
    <plnk:partnerLinkType name="poDocLT">
     <plnk:role name="poDocProviderRole">
        <plnk:portType name="ns2:poOrderDocServicePortType"/>
     </plnk:role>
    </plnk:partnerLinkType>
  </definitions>
```

The most interesting thing to note about the above WSDL definition is that it contains no `binding` and `service` sections. As you will learn later in this chapter, the WS-BPEL engine will generate these definitions implicitly, thus providing the client service with the required binding information.

Another important thing to note here is that the above WSDL imports another WSDL document, namely `po_orderdoc.wsdl`, which describes the `poOrderDocService` partner service.

The `po_orderdoc.wsdl` WSDL document is discussed in the *Building Fine-Grained Services* section in Chapter 4.

If you recall from Chapter 4, the `po_orderdoc.wsdl` document defines the `poOrderDocServicePortType` port type used in the above document when defining the `poDocLT` partner link type. This partner link type along with the other one—`poInfoLT`, which was described previously and is used to represent the interaction between the business process and the client service—are then used when defining partner links in the WS-BPEL process definition discussed below.

Now that you have looked through the WSDL document describing the WS-BPEL process depicted in the previous figure, it's time to look at the WS-BPEL process definition itself. For the purpose of this discussion, the WS-BPEL process definition document is divided into pieces, each of which is explained in detail.

Like any other WS-BPEL definition, this process definition starts with the `process` root element, establishing the namespaces related to the process:

```
<?xml version="1.0" encoding="UTF-8"?>
<process xmlns="http://docs.oasis-open.org/wsbpel/2.0/process/
executable"
     xmlns:ns1=
      "http://localhost:8081/active-bpel/services/poInfoService.wsdl"
     xmlns:ns2="http://localhost/WebServices/wsdl/poOrderDoc"
     xmlns:xsd="http://www.w3.org/2001/XMLSchema"
     name="poInfo.bpel"
     suppressJoinFailure="yes"
     targetNamespace="http://poInfo.bpel">
```

Next, you import WSDL definitions that are used in the WS-BPEL definition. In particular, you import the WSDL document describing the process to its consumers and the WSDL describing the `poOrderDocService` partner service:

```
<import importType="http://schemas.xmlsoap.org/wsdl/"
        location="wsdl/poInfo.wsdl"
        namespace=
 "http://localhost:8081/active-bpel/services/poInfoService.wsdl"/>
<import importType="http://schemas.xmlsoap.org/wsdl/"
        location=
              "http://localhost/WebServices/wsdl/po_orderdoc.wsdl"
        namespace="http://localhost/WebServices/wsdl/poOrderDoc"/>
```

Looking through the above snippet, you may be wondering why the `location` attribute related to the WSDL describing the WS-BPEL process doesn't contain a full path to the document. The fact is that this example assumes that the process will be deployed to an ActiveBPEL engine. As you will learn in the *Your First ActiveBPEL Project* section later in this chapter, the WSDL describing the WS-BPEL process is included in the `wsdl` folder within the deployment archive, so that you can refer to that WSDL as shown in the above example.

The next step is to define the partner links representing relationships between the WS-BPEL process and its partners:

```
<partnerLinks>
   <partnerLink myRole="poInfoProviderRole" name="poInfoProvider"
                          partnerLinkType="ns1:poInfoLT"/>
   <partnerLink name="poDocRequester"
   partnerLinkType="ns1:poDocLT" partnerRole="poDocProviderRole"/>
</partnerLinks>
```

In the partnerLinks section, you define two partner links. The first one specifies the relationship between the process and its client. The second one specifies the relationship between the process and the partner service.

If you recall from the *Basic Principles of Service Orientation* section in Chapter 1, statelessness is one of the key principles of service orientation, meaning that services don't maintain their state specific to an activity. As mentioned, building stateless fine-grained services encourages loose coupling, reusability, and composability. However, when you combine services into an SOA application you are likely interested in building a solution that supports stateful interactions between partners. To achieve this goal in WS-BPEL, you use variables. In the following variables section, you define variables that will then be used to store state information between the process interactions:

```
<variables>
   <variable messageType=
         "ns1:poInfoRequestMessage" name="poInfoRequestMessage"/>
   <variable messageType=
         "ns1:poInfoResponseMessage" name="poInfoResponseMessage"/>
   <variable messageType=
         "ns2:getOrderDocInput" name="poDocRequestMessage"/>
   <variable messageType=
         "ns2:getOrderDocOutput" name="poDocResponseMessage"/>
</variables>
```

Now you are ready to define the sequence activity, which instructs the WS-BPEL engine to start sequential processing of the activities nested within it.

```
<sequence>
```

The first activity you employ within the sequence is receive, which specifies the partnerLink containing the myRole used to receive a request message from a client service. The payload of the request message will be passed to the poInfoRequestMessage variable specified by the variable attribute of the receive activity:

```
   <receive createInstance="yes"
            operation="getInfo"
            partnerLink="poInfoProvider"
            portType="ns1:poInfoPT"
            variable="poInfoRequestMessage"/>
```

As you can see, the createInstance attribute of the receive activity is set to yes, meaning that performing this activity will instantiate the business process.

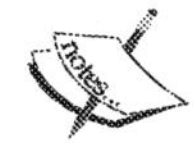

Actually, using the `createInstance` attribute with a `receive` or `pick` activity is the only way in which you can create an instance of a WS-BPEL process.

Next, you copy the value of the `input` element, which is nested within the XML fragment held in the `poInfoRequestMessage` variable to the `pono` part of the `poDocRequestMessage` variable as shown below:

```
<assign>
   <copy>
      <from part="payload" variable="poInfoRequestMessage">
         <query>ns1:input</query>
      </from>
      <to part="pono" variable="poDocRequestMessage"/>
   </copy>
</assign>
```

Now you are ready to invoke the `poOrderDocService` partner service, using the `invoke` activity, as shown below:

```
<invoke inputVariable="poDocRequestMessage"
        outputVariable="poDocResponseMessage"
        operation="getOrderDoc"
        partnerLink="poDocRequester"
        portType="ns2:poOrderDocServicePortType ">
</invoke>
```

You specify the `poDocRequestMessage` variable set in the preceding step as the input variable and specify the `poDocResponseMessage` variable as the output variable in the above `invoke` activity. Also note that the `operation` attribute of the activity is set to `getOrderDoc`, which, as you may recall from Chapter 4, is the name of the operation specified in the `po_orderdoc.wsdl` WSDL document describing the `poOrderDocService` service.

It is important to understand that a partner service invoked during the course of the process execution maybe a WS-BPEL process service itself. In such a case, the parent WS-BPEL process is used to describe cross-business process interactions performed via WSDL interfaces.

Once this invoke activity has been performed, the poDocResponseMessage output variable should contain the result message returned by the poOrderDocService partner service. Before you can define the reply activity that will complete the operation started by the receive activity defined at the beginning of the sequence, you should copy the value of the doc part of the poDocResponseMessage variable to the payload part of poInfoResponseMessage. One way to do this is as follows :

```
<assign>
   <copy>
      <from>$poDocResponseMessage.doc</from>
      <to>$poInfoResponseMessage.payload</to>
   </copy>
</assign>
```

Now you can define the reply activity that will be associated with the receive activity defined at the beginning of the sequence:

```
        <reply operation="getInfo"
               partnerLink="poInfoProvider"
               portType="ns1:poInfoPT"
               variable="poInfoResponseMessage"/>
    </sequence>
</process>
```

The reply activity is the last one in this WS-BPEL definition. After this activity is completed, you explicitly end the sequence and then the process.

As mentioned, the above process, after it has been deployed to a WS-BPEL engine, is executed when a client sends a request message to it. The request message should contain the pono whose value is then passed to the poOrderDocService partner service invoked from within the process. The poOrderDocService service, in turn, returns the entire po document with the specified pono. The process then returns this document to the client that instantiated the process. That is it.

Using ActiveBPEL Engine

Now that you have a grasp of WS-BPEL and have seen an example of a WS-BPEL definition, it's time to look at how you can put it into action. To achieve this goal, you first need to obtain and install a WS-BPEL engine against which you will execute your WS-BPEL processes.

The ActiveBPEL engine is an open-source implementation of a WS-BPEL engine implemented in Java. To get a brief introduction to the ActiveBPEL engine, you can refer to the *ActiveBPEL Open Source Engine* page at `http://www.active-endpoints.com/open-source-active-bpel-Intro.htm`.

An ActiveBPEL process will run in a standard servlet container. So, before you can install the ActiveBPEL engine, you should have a servlet container installed and configured properly on your computer. Diagrammatically, this architecture might look like the following figure:

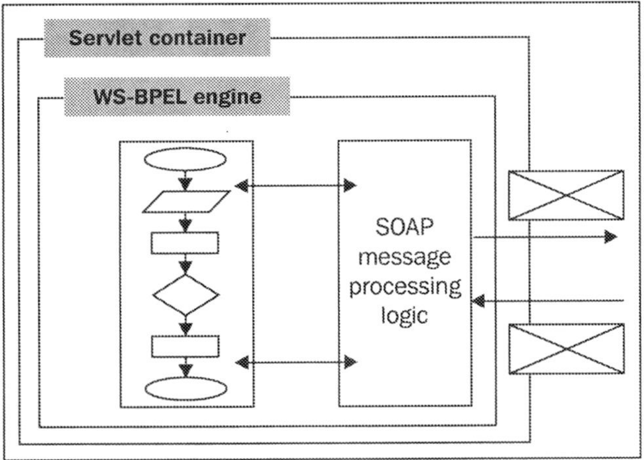

Note that although the ActiveBPEL engine should run under any standard servlet container, it has been tested with Apache Tomcat 5.x. So, this chapter assumes that you install the ActiveBPEL engine upon Apache Tomcat 5.x. For more details on installing the ActiveBPEL engine, you can visit the *Installing and Configuring the ActiveBPEL Engine* page that can be found at `http://www.active-endpoints.com/installation-guide.htm` or refer the *Installing ActiveBPEL Engine* section in Appendix A at the end of this book.

When using the ActiveBPEL engine, it is assumed that you manually build a WS-BPEL definition to be executed against the engine. Thus, you need to have some knowledge of WS-BPEL language constructs and how to build them within a process definition. The *Your First ActiveBPEL Project* section later in this chapter discusses in detail how to build and then deploy a WS-BPEL process service to the ActiveBPEL engine.

In reality, you likely will want to use a visual WS-BPEL tool for building and deploying WS-BPEL solutions. However, even by using a visual tool for WS-BPEL development such as ActiveBPEL Designer discussed in the next chapter, you won't be that efficient without knowledge of how to manually build a WS-BPEL definition.

Taking Advantage of the ActiveBPEL Open-Source Engine Project

As mentioned, the ActiveBPEL engine is an open-source project. Actually, you can use the ActiveBPEL engine under either an Open-Source License or a Commercial License that can be acquired by contacting Active Endpoints, Inc.

The Open-Source License assumes that you develop open-source applications. In this case, the ActiveBPEL engine is licensed free of charge.

For commercial applications, the ActiveBPEL enterprise software, which includes ActiveBPEL engine, is licensed for a fee, under the terms of a commercial license agreement.

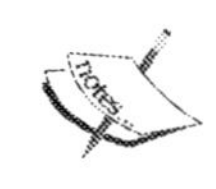

To learn more about Active Endpoints' licensing polices, you can visit the *ActiveBPEL Open Source Licensing Policies* page at `http://www.active-endpoints.com/open-source-license.htm`.

Your First ActiveBPEL Project

One easy way to get started with ActiveBPEL engine is to play with the samples that can be obtained from Active Endpoints' Website.

The samples can be obtained from the ActiveBPEL Samples page at `http://www.active-endpoints.com/active-bpel-samples.htm`.

One disadvantage of the above approach is that the samples may rely on partner services built with Java, rather than with PHP. Moreover, if you have just started with WS-BPEL, many of the samples may look too complicated to you. So, in the following sections you will learn how to build an ActiveBPEL project from scratch. For simplicity's sake, the WS-BPEL process in the ActiveBPEL project discussed in the next sections will not utilize partner services. It is going to be a hello WS-BPEL process that receives a name from the client service and returns a corresponding hello message back to the client. Then, in the *Implementing Service-Oriented Orchestrations* section, you will see how to implement and then deploy a WS-BPEL process service that interacts with partner services.

Structure of the Business Process Archive (BPR) to be Deployed to the ActiveBPEL Engine

Before delving into the details of building the documents composing an ActiveBPEL project, let's look at how these documents should be combined to create a structure that will be deployed to the ActiveBPEL engine.

To deploy a WS-BPEL process so that it can then be executed against an ActiveBPEL engine, you need to create a deployment archive containing all the required documents. This archive document must be a JAR archive with extension `bpr`, and must have the following structure:

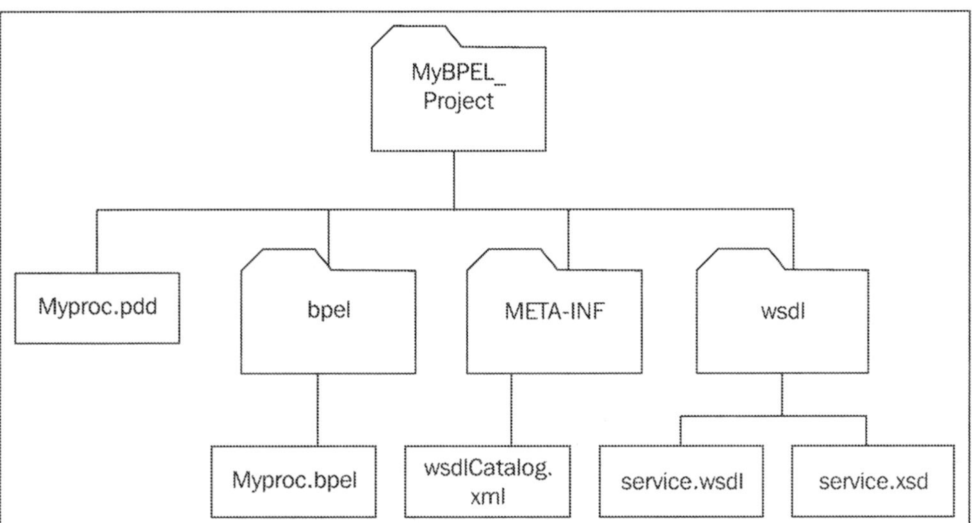

As you can see in the figure, the archive contains the root folder and three subfolders in it. You are free to choose any name for the root folder, while the names of subfolders are predefined:

BPR archive folder	Description
bpel	Contains the WS-BPEL definition document that, using WS-BPEL language constructs, describes the behavior and interactions of a process instance.
META-INF	Contains the wsdlCatalog.xml document, which is a catalog of the WSDL and XML schema definitions related to the WS-BPEL process and stored in the wsdl folder of the archive.
wsdl	Contains the WSDL and XML schema definitions related to the WS-BPEL process.

Also worth noting is the Process Deployment Descriptor (PDD) file that is located in the root directory of the deployment archive. This document contains information about the process to be deployed, which is required for the ActiveBPEL engine to perform the deployment.

Turning back to the hello project discussed here, you need to create a folder in your file system, to which you may give a custom name, say, `hello`. Next, you need to create the `META-INF`, `bpel`, and `wsdl` folders within the `hello` folder.

The following four sections take you through creating the documents composing the `bpr` archive of a hello WS-BPEL process service. Then, in the *Deploying the WS-BPEL Process Service* section, you will see how to combine these documents into a `bpr` archive and then deploy it to the ActiveBPEL engine.

Designing WSDL for the WS-BPEL Process Service

As stated earlier, a WS-BPEL process can be considered as a service, since it provides a WSDL interface to its consumers. So, it would be a good idea to start developing a WS-BPEL process with creating the WSDL definition describing this process service to its clients.

[If you recall, designing WSDL definitions for composite services built with WS-BPEL was already discussed in the *WSDL Definitions for Composite Services* section in Chapter 1.]

Here is the `hello.wsdl` document that you should save in the `wsdl` folder of your project, created as discussed in the preceding section:

```
<?xml version="1.0" encoding="UTF-8" ?>
<definitions targetNamespace="http://localhost:8081/active-bpel/
services/hello"
       xmlns:tns="http://localhost:8081/active-bpel/services/hello"
       xmlns="http://schemas.xmlsoap.org/wsdl/"
```

```
        xmlns:soap="http://schemas.xmlsoap.org/wsdl/soap/"
        xmlns:xsd="http://www.w3.org/2001/XMLSchema"
        xmlns:plnk="http://schemas.xmlsoap.org/ws/2003/05/partner-
                                                              link/">
  <!-- abstract characteristics of the WS-BPEL process service -->
  <message name="inputMessage">
     <part name="firstName" type="xsd:string"/>
  </message>
  <message name="outputMessage">
     <part name="hello" type="xsd:string"/>
  </message>
  <portType name="helloServicePT">
     <operation name="hello">
        <input name="inputMessage" message="tns:inputMessage"/>
        <output name="outputMessage" message="tns:outputMessage"/>
     </operation>
  </portType>
  <!-- partnerLinkType section representing interaction
                  between the WS-BPEL service and its client -->
  <plnk:partnerLinkType name="helloPartnerLinkType">
     <plnk:role name="helloServiceRole">
         <plnk:portType name="tns:helloServicePT"/>
     </plnk:role>
  </plnk:partnerLinkType>
  </definitions>
```

As you can see, this WSDL document doesn't contain deployment information (binding and address information). The fact is that the client services will use a modified version of the above WSDL document. Based on the above WSDL, the ActiveBPEL engine will dynamically generate the document containing the required binding and address information.

The highlighted block in the above WSDL represents the `partnerLinkType` construct within which you define the relationship between the WS-BPEL process and its consumer (client service).

Actually, you must specify a `partnerLinkType` construct for each partner service involved. In this particular case, though, the WS-BPEL process has only one partner, its consumer, thus, you specify only one `partnerLinkType` construct in the WSDL document describing the WS-BPEL process service.

Creating the WSDL Catalog

Now that you have the WSDL document describing the WS-BPEL process service created, you can move on and create the `wsdlCatalog.xml` document in the `META-INF` directory of the project. This document contains information about all the WSDL and XML schema definitions to be used. In this particular case, thought, it contains only one entry, which refers to the `hello.wsdl` document shown in the preceding section.

```
<?xml version="1.0" encoding="UTF-8"?>
<wsdlCatalog>
 <wsdlEntry location="wsdl/hello.wsdl"
            classpath="wsdl/hello.wsdl" />
</wsdlCatalog>
```

The ActiveBPEL engine will use information from this document to find the `hello.wsdl` WSDL document within the BPR deployment archive discussed in the *Deploying the WS-BPEL Process Service* section later.

Designing the WS-BPEL Process Definition

The next step in building the hello project discussed here is to implement the WS-BPEL process definition. Here is the `hello.bpel` definition that you have to save in the `bpel` folder of the project:

```
<?xml version="1.0" encoding="UTF-8"?>
<process name="hello"
         xmlns=
            "http://schemas.xmlsoap.org/ws/2003/03/business-process/"
         xmlns:bpws=
            "http://schemas.xmlsoap.org/ws/2003/03/business-process/"
         xmlns:lns="http://localhost:8081/active-bpel/services/hello"
         xmlns:xsd="http://www.w3.org/2001/XMLSchema"
         suppressJoinFailure="yes"
         targetNamespace="http://hello">
   <partnerLinks>
      <partnerLink myRole="helloServiceRole" name="customer"
                          partnerLinkType="lns:helloPartnerLinkType"/>
   </partnerLinks>
   <variables>
      <variable messageType="lns:inputMessage" name="inputMessage"/>
      <variable messageType="lns:outputMessage"
                                    name="outputMessage"/>
   </variables>
   <sequence>
```

```
        <receive createInstance="yes"
                 operation="hello"
                 partnerLink="customer"
                 portType="lns:helloServicePT"
                 variable="inputMessage"/>
        <assign>
           <copy>
             <from expression="concat( 'Hello, ',
            bpws:getVariableData('inputMessage', 'firstName'),'!' )"/>
             <to part="hello" variable="outputMessage"/>
           </copy>
        </assign>
        <reply operation="hello"
               partnerLink="customer"
               portType="lns:helloServicePT"
               variable="outputMessage"/>
     </sequence>
  </process>
```

The `partnerLinks` section contains `partnerLink` sections establishing relationships with the partner services that interact with the business process during the course of its execution. In the above document, the `partnerLinks` section contains only one entry—the one that represents the relationship between the process service and the client service. In this case, you use the `myRole` attribute in the `partnerLink` element because the WS-BPEL process service is the service provider to the client service.

It is important to note that the name specified in the `partnerLinkType` attribute of the `partnerLink` element is equal to the one specified in the corresponding `partnerLinkType` section in the `hello.wsdl` document discussed earlier.

The sequence of activities defined within the `sequence` construct is fairly straightforward. The first one is the `receive` activity that is used to handle a request message sent by a client service. By setting the `createInstance` attribute of the `receive` activity to `yes`, you instruct the ActiveBPEL engine to create a process instance when this activity receives a request message.

The next activity defined within the `sequence` construct is `assign`. Here you actually generate the output message, based on the information that arrived with the input message.

Finally, you define the `reply` activity, which is responsible for sending the output message to the client service.

Creating the Process Deployment Descriptor (PDD) Document

Now that you have the WSDL and WS-BPEL definitions created, you need to create the Process Deployment Descriptor (PDD) document that contains the information required for the ActiveBPEL engine to deploy the process service discussed here. Here is the `hello.pdd` document that you should save in the root folder of the project:

```
<?xml version="1.0" encoding="UTF-8"?>
<process name="bpelns:hello"
         location="bpel/hello.bpel"
         xmlns=
          "http://schemas.active-endpoints.com/pdd/2004/09/pdd.xsd"
         xmlns:bpelns="http://hello"
         xmlns:wsa="http://schemas.xmlsoap.org/ws/2003/03/addressing">
<partnerLinks>
  <partnerLink name="customer">
   <myRole allowedRoles="" binding="RPC"
          service="helloServicePT"/>
  </partnerLink>
</partnerLinks>
<wsdlReferences>
  <wsdl location="wsdl/hello.wsdl"
    namespace="http://localhost:8081/active-bpel/services/hello"/>
</wsdlReferences>
</process>
```

As you can see, the above `pdd` document includes the `partnerLinks` section containing the `partnerLink` section related to the one defined in the process definition discussed in the preceding section.

Deploying the WS-BPEL Process Service

Now that you have all the project components ready, it's time to move on and deploy the WS-BPEL process to the ActiveBPEL engine. This section provides a description of the deployment of the WS-BPEL process discussed above.

Before you can deploy the newly created WS-BPEL process service, you have to create the Business Process Archive (BPR). To do this, you might use the operating-system command prompt. First, you need to change the current directory to the root directory of the project and then issue the following command:

```
jar cf hello.bpr *.pdd META-INF bpel wsdl
```

As a result of this command, you should have a deployable `hello.bpr` Business Process Archive (BPR). All that's left is to copy that file to the `$CATALINA_HOME/bpr` directory created during the installation of the ActiveBPEL engine.

Once you copy the BPR archive to the `$CATALINA_HOME/bpr` directory, the ActiveBPEL engine will implicitly deploy the WS-BPEL process, provided there are no typos in the files included in the archive.

One way to make sure that the process has been successfully deployed is to look at the deployment log. To do this, you can use the BPEL Administrative Console graphical tool installed by default during the ActiveBPEL engine installation as shown in the following figure:

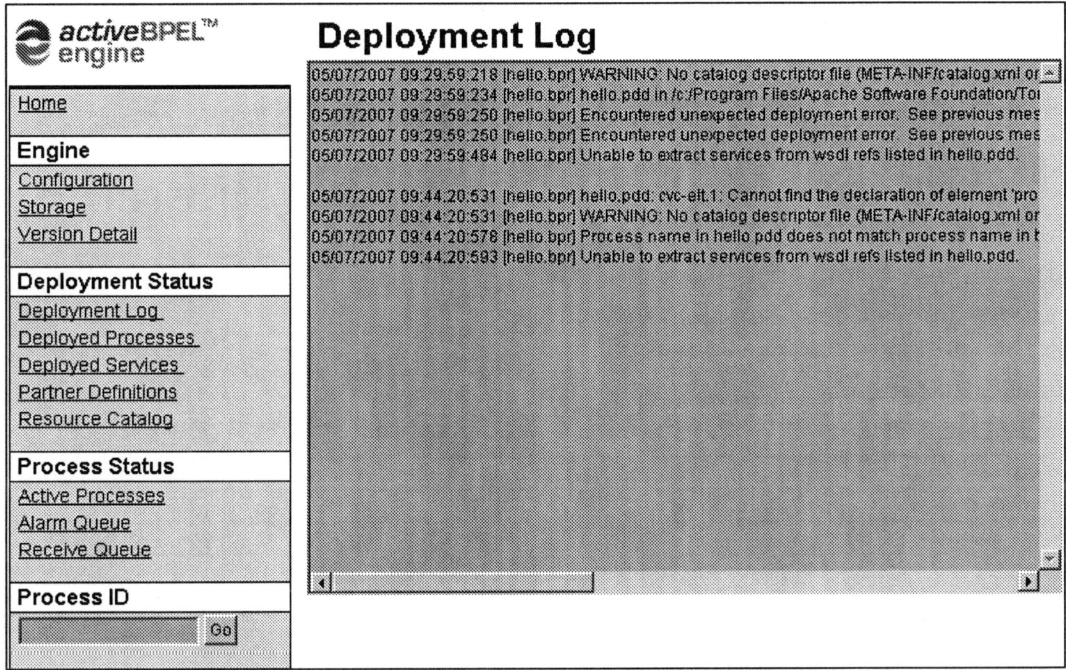

To load the BPEL Administrative Console (also known as BpelAdmin), enter the following URL in your browser:

```
http://localhost:8081/BpelAdmin
```

This URL assumes that you have installed your Tomcat server at `http://localhost:8081/`. The fact is that the Oracle XML DB HTTP server runs on port 8080 by default. So, if you have an Oracle database installed on your machine, you can choose another port when installing a Tomcat server; say, 8081.

Once you have loaded BpelAdmin, you can open the **Deployment Log** page by clicking the **Deployment Log** link available in the **Deployment Status** group. As a result, you might see the page shown below.

If the deployment fails, the information provided on the **Deployment Log** page may help you figure out what's wrong. In that case, you need to fix the problem and then rebuild the deployment archive.

If the process has been successfully deployed, you should see the following message in the Deployment Log box:

```
05/22/2007 08:59:27:328 [hello.bpr] [hello.wsdl] Added resource mapped
to location hint: wsdl/hello.wsdl
05/22/2007 08:59:28:812 [hello.bpr] [hello.pdd] Successfully deployed.
```

Now you can click the **Deployed Services** link from the **Deployment Status** group to look at the information related to the deployed service. The Deployed Services page should look like the following figure:

Deployed Services

Name	Process Name	Binding	Partner Link
helloServicePT	hello	RPC	customer

Another way to make sure that the process service has been successfully deployed is to enter the following URL:

```
http://localhost:8081/active-bpel/services/helloServicePT?wsdl
```

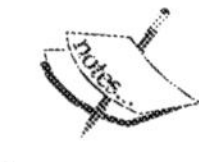

If you recall from the `hello.pdd` discussed in the *Creating the Process Deployment Descriptor (PDD) Document* section earlier, `helloServicePT` is specified as the service name of the process service.

As a result, the browser should output the following WSDL definition:

```
<?xml version="1.0" encoding="UTF-8" ?>
<definitions targetNamespace=
                  "http://localhost:8081/active-bpel/services/hello"
       xmlns="http://schemas.xmlsoap.org/wsdl/"
       xmlns:plnk=
            "http://schemas.xmlsoap.org/ws/2003/05/partner-link/"
       xmlns:soap="http://schemas.xmlsoap.org/wsdl/soap/"
       xmlns:tns="http://localhost:8081/active-bpel/services/hello"
       xmlns:xsd="http://www.w3.org/2001/XMLSchema">
   <message name="outputMessage">
    <part name="hello" type="xsd:string" />
   </message>
   <message name="inputMessage">
    <part name="firstName" type="xsd:string" />
   </message>
   <portType name="helloServicePT">
    <operation name="hello">
     <input message="tns:inputMessage" name="inputMessage" />
     <output message="tns:outputMessage" name="outputMessage" />
    </operation>
   </portType>
   <binding name="helloServicePTBinding" type="tns:helloServicePT">
    <soap:binding style="rpc"
          transport="http://schemas.xmlsoap.org/soap/http"
          xmlns:soap="http://schemas.xmlsoap.org/wsdl/soap/" />
    <operation name="hello">
     <soap:operation soapAction="" style="rpc"
       xmlns:soap="http://schemas.xmlsoap.org/wsdl/soap/" />
      <input>
       <soap:body
         encodingStyle="http://schemas.xmlsoap.org/soap/encoding/"
          use="encoded" xmlns:soap=
            "http://schemas.xmlsoap.org/wsdl/soap/" />
      </input>
      <output>
       <soap:body
         encodingStyle="http://schemas.xmlsoap.org/soap/encoding/"
          use="encoded" xmlns:soap=
         "http://schemas.xmlsoap.org/wsdl/soap/" />
      </output>
    </operation>
```

```
</binding>
<service name="helloServicePT">
 <port binding="tns:helloServicePTBinding"
                              name="helloServicePTPort">
   <soap:address location=
        "http://localhost:8081/active-bpel/services/helloServicePT"
         xmlns:soap="http://schemas.xmlsoap.org/wsdl/soap/" />
 </port>
</service>
</definitions>
```

As you can see, the above document is based on the `hello.wsdl` WSDL document discussed in the *Designing WSDL for the WS-BPEL Process Service* section earlier. The ActiveBPEL engine implicitly generated the `binding` and `service` definitions, thus making it possible for a client partner service to consume the process service discussed here.

Testing the WS-BPEL Process Service

Now that the hello process service has been deployed and you know how to obtain the WSDL document describing this service to its clients, it's time to test it. For that, you might create and then run the following PHP script:

```
<?php
 //File: SoapClient_hello.php
 $client = new SoapClient("http://localhost:8081/active-
                          bpel/services/helloServicePT?wsdl");
 try {
  print($client->hello('Larry'));
 }
 catch (SoapFault $e) {
  print $e->getMessage();
 }
?>
```

When executed, the above script should invoke the hello process service discussed in the preceding sections, and output the following hello message:

```
Hello, Larry!
```

Implementing Service-Oriented Orchestrations

The hello process service we have discussed is a simplified example of a WS-BPEL process service. It doesn't use partner services to get the job done, simply composing a hello message based on the data sent by the client. In contrast, a real-world WS-BPEL process may invoke a lot of partner services during its execution.

The following sections take you through creating the documents composing the `bpr` archive of a poInfo WS-BPEL process service that interacts with two partner services. The partner services used in this example are the following: `poOrderDocService` and `poOrderStatusService`—both are discussed in the *Building Fine-Grained Services* section in Chapter 4. So, the following sections do not discuss how to create these services, since it is assumed that you have them already created.

The poInfo process service discussed here is invoked when a client sends a request message containing two parameters: `pono` and `par`. The first one specifies the `pono` of the order document on which you need to get information, while the second one specifies what kind of information should be returned, meaning two possible choices: the entire document or the status of the document.

Since you are going to deploy the poInfo process service to the ActiveBPEL engine, you first need to create the required folders in your file system for the project. For example, you may create the folder named `poInfo` and then create the `META-INF`, `bpel`, and `wsdl` folders within it.

Creating the WSDL Definition Describing the WS-BPEL Process

As usual, the first step in creating the service is to create the WSDL definition describing that service to its clients. Here is the `poInfo.wsdl` document that you should save in the `wsdl` folder created within the `poInfo` folder, which is the root folder for this project:

```
<?xml version="1.0" encoding="UTF-8"?>
<definitions name="poInfo"
    targetNamespace=
     "http://localhost:8081/active-bpel/services/poInfoService.wsdl"
    xmlns:tns=
     "http://localhost:8081/active-bpel/services/poInfoService.wsdl"
    xmlns:plnk="http://schemas.xmlsoap.org/ws/2003/05/partner-link/"
    xmlns:xsd="http://www.w3.org/2001/XMLSchema"
    xmlns:ns2="http://localhost/WebServices/wsdl/poOrderDoc"
```

```
    xmlns:ns3="http://localhost/WebServices/wsdl/poOrderStatus"
    xmlns="http://schemas.xmlsoap.org/wsdl/">
  <import namespace="http://localhost/WebServices/wsdl/poOrderDoc"
    location="http://localhost/WebServices/wsdl/po_orderdoc.wsdl"/>
  <import namespace="http://localhost/WebServices/wsdl/poOrderStatus"
    location="http://localhost/WebServices/wsdl/po_orderstatus.wsdl"/>
  <types>
    <schema attributeFormDefault="qualified"
            elementFormDefault="qualified"
            targetNamespace=
      "http://localhost:8081/active-bpel/services/poInfoService.wsdl"
            xmlns="http://www.w3.org/2001/XMLSchema">
      <element name="poInfoRequest">
        <complexType>
          <sequence>
            <element name="pono" type="xsd:string"/>
            <element name="par" type="xsd:string"/>
          </sequence>
        </complexType>
      </element>
     </schema>
  </types>
  <message name="poInfoResponseMessage">
    <part name="payload" type="xsd:string"/>
  </message>
  <message name="poInfoRequestMessage">
    <part name="payload" element="tns:poInfoRequest"/>
  </message>
  <portType name="poInfoPT">
    <operation name="getInfo">
      <input message="tns:poInfoRequestMessage"/>
      <output message="tns:poInfoResponseMessage"/>
    </operation>
  </portType>
  <plnk:partnerLinkType name="poInfoLT">
   <plnk:role name="poInfoProviderRole">
      <plnk:portType name="tns:poInfoPT"/>
   </plnk:role>
  </plnk:partnerLinkType>
  <plnk:partnerLinkType name="poDocLT">
   <plnk:role name="poDocProviderRole">
      <plnk:portType name="ns2:poOrderDocServicePortType"/>
   </plnk:role>
  </plnk:partnerLinkType>
  <plnk:partnerLinkType name="poStatusLT">
   <plnk:role name="poStatusProviderRole">
```

```
        <plnk:portType name="ns3:poOrderStatusServicePortType"/>
      </plnk:role>
    </plnk:partnerLinkType>
  </definitions>
```

As you can see, the above WSDL definition imports two definitions describing the `poOrderDocService` and `poOrderStatusService` partner services.

This example assumes that you have the `po_orderdoc.wsdl` and `po_orderstatus.wsdl` documents created as discussed in the in the *Building Fine-Grained Services* section in Chapter 4.

Note the use of the `poInfoRequest` complex type when defining the input message. This structure makes it possible for the client to send two parameters, namely `pono` and `par`, within a single request message.

Another important thing to note here is the use of three partner links. The first one defines the interaction between the WS-BPEL process service and its client, while the other two define the relationships between the WS-BPEL service and the `poOrderDocService` and `poOrderStatusService` partner services respectively.

Creating the WSDL Catalog

The next step is to create the `wsdlCatalog.xml` WSDL catalog document in the `META-INF` directory of the project. In this example, the document contains only one entry that refers to the `poInfo.wsdl` document discussed in the preceding section.

```
<?xml version="1.0" encoding="UTF-8"?>
<wsdlCatalog>
  <wsdlEntry location="wsdl/poInfo.wsdl"
             classpath="wsdl/poInfo.wsdl" />
</wsdlCatalog>
```

Creating the WS-BPEL Business Definition Containing Conditional Logic

The WS-BPEL definition you create in this example is a bit complicated than the one you saw in the *An Example of a WS-BPEL Definition* section at the beginning of this chapter. This is because the `poInfo.bpel` definition shown below contains conditional logic.

```
<?xml version="1.0" encoding="UTF-8"?>
<process xmlns="http://docs.oasis-open.org/wsbpel/2.0/process/
executable"
      xmlns:ns1=
       "http://localhost:8081/active-bpel/services/poInfoService.wsdl"
      xmlns:ns2="http://localhost/WebServices/wsdl/poOrderDoc"
      xmlns:ns3="http://localhost/WebServices/wsdl/poOrderStatus"
      xmlns:xsd="http://www.w3.org/2001/XMLSchema"
      name="poInfo.bpel"
      suppressJoinFailure="yes"
      targetNamespace="http://poInfo.bpel">
   <import importType="http://schemas.xmlsoap.org/wsdl/"
           location="wsdl/poInfo.wsdl"
           namespace=
     "http://localhost:8081/active-bpel/services/poInfoService.wsdl"/>
   <import importType="http://schemas.xmlsoap.org/wsdl/"
         location="http://localhost/WebServices/wsdl/po_orderdoc.wsdl"
         namespace="http://localhost/WebServices/wsdl/poOrderDoc"/>
   <import importType="http://schemas.xmlsoap.org/wsdl/"
      location="http://localhost/WebServices/wsdl/po_orderstatus.wsdl"
           namespace=
                 "http://localhost/WebServices/wsdl/poOrderStatus"/>

   <partnerLinks>
      <partnerLink myRole="poInfoProviderRole" name="poInfoProvider"
partnerLinkType="ns1:poInfoLT"/>
      <partnerLink name="poDocRequester" partnerLinkType="ns1:poDocLT"
partnerRole="poDocProviderRole"/>
      <partnerLink name="poStatusRequester" partnerLinkType="ns1:
poStatusLT" partnerRole="poStatusProviderRole"/>
   </partnerLinks>
   <variables>
      <variable messageType="ns1:poInfoRequestMessage" name="poInfoReq
uestMessage"/>
      <variable messageType="ns1:poInfoResponseMessage" name="poInfoRe
sponseMessage"/>
      <variable messageType="ns2:getOrderDocInput" name="poDocRequest
Message"/>
      <variable messageType="ns2:getOrderDocOutput" name="poDocRespon
seMessage"/>
      <variable messageType="ns3:getOrderStatusInput" name="poStatusRe
questMessage"/>
      <variable messageType="ns3:getOrderStatusOutput" name="poStatusR
esponseMessage"/>
   </variables>
```

```
<sequence>
  <receive createInstance="yes"
           operation="getInfo"
           partnerLink="poInfoProvider"
           portType="ns1:poInfoPT"
           variable="poInfoRequestMessage"/>
   <if>
    <condition>($poInfoRequestMessage.payload/ns1:par =
                                             'doc')</condition>
    <sequence>
     <assign>
      <copy>
         <from part="payload" variable="poInfoRequestMessage">
            <query>ns1:pono</query>
         </from>
         <to part="pono" variable="poDocRequestMessage"/>
      </copy>
     </assign>
     <invoke inputVariable="poDocRequestMessage"
           outputVariable="poDocResponseMessage"
           operation="getOrderDoc"
           partnerLink="poDocRequester"
           portType="ns2:poOrderDocServicePortType">
     </invoke>
     <assign>
      <copy>
         <from>$poDocResponseMessage.doc</from>
         <to>$poInfoResponseMessage.payload</to>
      </copy>
     </assign>
    </sequence>
    <elseif>
     <condition>($poInfoRequestMessage.payload/ns1:par =
                                            'status')</condition>
     <sequence>
     <assign>
      <copy>
         <from part="payload" variable="poInfoRequestMessage">
            <query>ns1:pono</query>
         </from>
         <to part="pono" variable="poStatusRequestMessage"/>
      </copy>
     </assign>
     <invoke inputVariable="poStatusRequestMessage"
```

```
                outputVariable="poStatusResponseMessage"
                operation="getOrderStatus"
                partnerLink="poStatusRequester"
                portType="ns3:poOrderStatusServicePortType">
          </invoke>
          <assign>
           <copy>
              <from>$poStatusResponseMessage.status</from>
              <to>$poInfoResponseMessage.payload</to>
           </copy>
          </assign>
         </sequence>
         </elseif>
         <else>
          <assign>
           <copy>
              <from>'Wrong input parameter. Should be either
                                      doc or status!'</from>
              <to>$poInfoResponseMessage.payload</to>
           </copy>
          </assign>
         </else>
        </if>
        <reply operation="getInfo"
               partnerLink="poInfoProvider"
               portType="ns1:poInfoPT"
               variable="poInfoResponseMessage"/>
    </sequence>
 </process>
```

The most interesting part of the above WS-BPEL process definition is the `if/elseif/else` construct. Schematically it looks like the following:

```
    <sequence>

       activities

       <if>
        <condition>...</condition>
        <sequence>

         activities

        </sequence>
      <elseif>
```

```
        <condition>...</condition>

        <sequence>

         activities

        </sequence>
       </elseif>
       <else>
        activity
       </else>
      </if>

      activities

    </sequence>
```

Note the use of the inner sequence constructs in the above structure. The fact is that WS-BPEL doesn't allow you to use more than one activity within `if` or `elseif` or `else` blocks. That is why you have to enclose a set of activities within any of those blocks with `sequence`.

Creating the PDD Document

Before you build the deployment archive for this project, you need to create the Process Deployment Descriptor document. Here is the `poInfo.pdd` document that you should save in the root folder of the project:

```
<?xml version="1.0" encoding="UTF-8"?>
<process xmlns="http://schemas.active-endpoints.com/pdd/2006/08/pdd.
xsd"
 xmlns:bpelns="http://poInfo.bpel"
 xmlns:wsa="http://schemas.xmlsoap.org/ws/2003/03/addressing"
 location="bpel/poInfo.bpel"
 name="bpelns:poInfo.bpel">
   <partnerLinks>
      <partnerLink name="poDocRequester">
         <partnerRole endpointReference="static">
            <wsa:EndpointReference xmlns:s=
                       "http://localhost/WebServices/wsdl/poOrderDoc">
             <wsa:Address>http://localhost/WebServices/ch4/
                                                SoapServer_orderdoc.php
                                                </wsa:Address>
             <wsa:ServiceName PortName=
        "poOrderDocServicePort">s:poOrderDocService</wsa:ServiceName>
```

```
            </wsa:EndpointReference>
         </partnerRole>
      </partnerLink>
      <partnerLink name="poStatusRequester">
         <partnerRole endpointReference="static">
            <wsa:EndpointReference xmlns:s=
              "http://localhost/WebServices/wsdl/poOrderStatus">
              <wsa:Address>http://localhost/WebServices/ch4/
                    SoapServer_orderstatus.php</wsa:Address>
                <wsa:ServiceName PortName="poOrderStatusServicePort">
                           s:poOrderStatusService</wsa:ServiceName>
            </wsa:EndpointReference>
         </partnerRole>
      </partnerLink>
      <partnerLink name="poInfoProvider">
         <myRole allowedRoles="" binding="RPC"
                                 service="poInfoService"/>
      </partnerLink>
   </partnerLinks>
   <wsdlReferences>
      <wsdl location=
                 "http://localhost/WebServices/wsdl/po_orderdoc.wsdl"
    namespace="http://localhost/WebServices/wsdl/poOrderDoc"/>
      <wsdl location=
               "http://localhost/WebServices/wsdl/po_orderstatus.wsdl"
    namespace="http://localhost/WebServices/wsdl/poOrderStatus"/>
      <wsdl location="wsdl/poInfo.wsdl" namespace=
     "http://localhost:8081/active-bpel/services/poInfoService.wsdl"/>
   </wsdlReferences>
</process>
```

As you can see, the above `pdd` document contains three `partnerLink` sections, each of which is related to the corresponding `partnerLink` section defined in the process definition discussed in the preceding section.

Deploying the WS-BPEL Process Service

Now that you have all the project components ready, you can create the deployment archive.

Using your operating-system command prompt, you should change the current directory to the root directory of the project, and then issue the following command:

```
jar cf poInfo.bpr *.pdd META-INF bpel wsdl
```

As a result, you should have a deployable `poInfo.bpr` archive. Make sure to copy that file to the `$CATALINA_HOME/bpr` directory to deploy it to the ActiveBPEL engine.

To make sure that the process has been successfully deployed, you can use the BPEL Administrative Console, loading the **Deployment Log** page. Or you can enter the following URL in your browser:

```
http://localhost:8081/active-bpel/services/poInfoService?wsdl
```

As a result, you should see the WSDL based on the `poInfo.wsdl` with the `service` and `binding` sections automatically added by the ActiveBPEL engine.

Testing the WS-BPEL Process Service

After the poInfo process service has been successfully deployed, it's time to test it. For that, you might create and then run the following PHP script:

```
<?php
 //File: SoapClient_poInfo.php
 $client = new SoapClient
  ("http://localhost:8081/active-bpel/services/poInfoService?wsdl");
 $xmldoc = '<wrapper><pono>108128476</pono><par>doc</par></wrapper>';
 $xmldoc = simplexml_load_string($xmldoc);
 try {
  print($client->getInfo($xmldoc));
 }
 catch (SoapFault $e) {
  print $e->getMessage();
 }
?>
```

This should output the entire `po` document whose `pono` is `108128476`. When setting the `$xmldoc` variable in the above script as shown below:

```
$xmldoc = '<wrapper><pono>108128476</pono><par>status</par></
                                                     wrapper>';
```

you should receive a short message: **shipped**, which indicates the status of the document.

Summary

As you have learned in this chapter, WS-BPEL can be used to build both simple WS-BPEL process services that do not rely on partner services and WS-BPEL orchestrations that combine single loosely coupled services into composite stateful applications. In particular, you saw an example of how to combine a set of fine-grained services into a coarse-grained one with WS-BPEL. The chapter also provided a description of the deployment of a WS-BPEL process to the ActiveBPEL engine.

Now that you have seen how a set of individual services can be combined into an SOA with WS-BPEL, it's time to move on and learn how the process of building SOA solutions can be simplified with the help of a WS-BPEL visual tool. That's the subject of the next chapter, in which we will look at the ActiveBPEL Designer, a free visual tool for creating and testing WS-BPEL-based solutions.

6
ActiveBPEL Designer

While the preceding chapter gave some background on WS-BPEL and focused mostly on how to write WS-BPEL code and then build deployable archives, this chapter discusses how you might simplify the process of creating WS-BPEL process services using the ActiveBPEL Designer—a free graphical tool for WS-BPEL process design, debugging, and simulation.

With the ActiveBPEL Designer, you can graphically orchestrate Web services into multi-step business processes (composite services). Being a fully-functional WS-BPEL development tool, the ActiveBPEL Designer provides a graphical drag-and-drop user interface that simplifies the process of creating a WS-BPEL process service.

In this chapter, you will learn how to create, deploy, and test WS-BPEL process services with the ActiveBPEL Designer. In particular, we will look at:

- ActiveBPEL Designer's user interface
- Building WS-BPEL processes using a drag-and-drop approach
- Building and deploying a hello WS-BPEL process service
- Combining a set of fine-grained services into a WS-BPEL-based composition

Getting Started with ActiveBPEL Designer

As you no doubt have guessed, the ActiveBPEL Designer is an efficient means when it comes to building composite applications based on the principles of service orientation. The following section touches upon the ActiveBPEL Designer's user interface. Then, you will learn how to build a hello WS-BPEL process service discussed in the preceding chapter, with the ActiveBPEL Designer.

For information on how to get and install the ActiveBPEL Designer, refer the *Installing ActiveBPEL Designer* section in the Appendix.

Overview of ActiveBPEL Designer's User Interface

ActiveBPEL Designer's user interface consists of a series of views, editors, palettes, toolbars, and menus.

The following figure shows what an ActiveBPEL Designer IDE might look like when you open it for the first time:

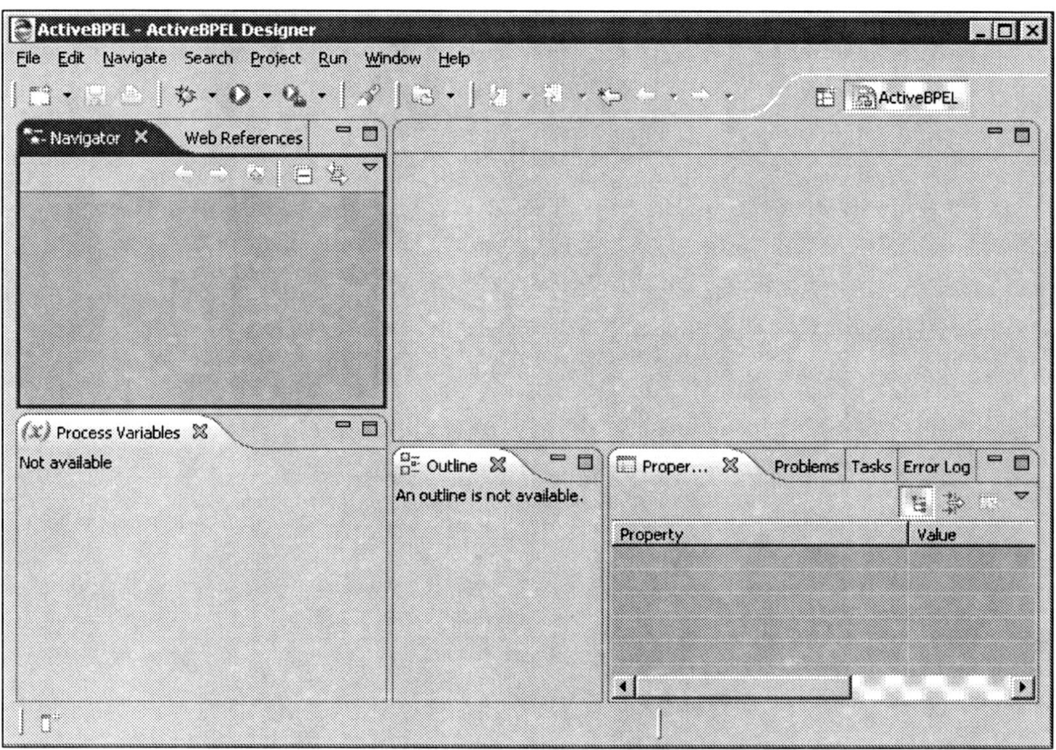

Looking at the ActiveBPEL Designer perspective, you may notice that it includes several views, each of which is designed to display information of a certain type. Here are the most important views belonging to the the ActiveBPEL Designer perspective:

ActiveBPEL Designer view	Description
Navigator	Enables you to manipulate projects and files. Through the Navigator, you can copy and paste files from the file system to projects.
Web References	Enables you to add Web references, each of which is either a Web Services Description Language (WSDL) document or XSD schema, making them available for all projects.
Process Variables	Displays the list of variables related to the WS-BPEL process you are working on.
Outline	Displays all the major components of the WS-BPEL process selected in the **Navigator**.
Properties	Displays names and values of properties of the resource selected in the ActiveBPEL Process Editor canvas.
Problems	Displays errors and warnings related to the validation of the WS-BPEL process you are working on.

To create a WS-BPEL process, you use the ActiveBPEL Process Editor. To build a WS-BPEL process with the ActiveBPEL Process Editor, you use a drag-and-drop approach, dragging required components from the Palette to the canvas.

The following figure shows what the ActiveBPEL Process Editor might look like:

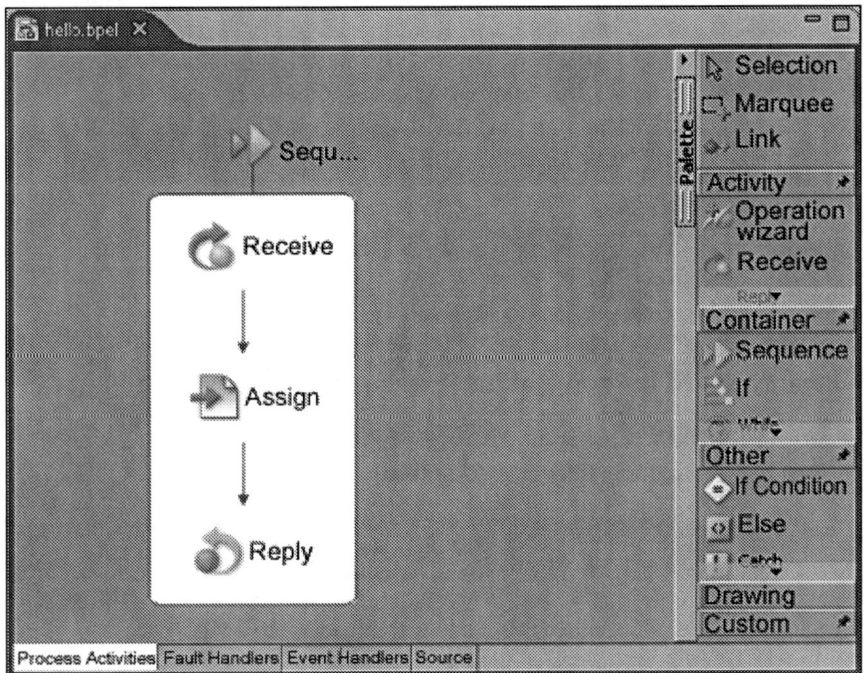

In the *Creating the WS-BPEL Process* section later, you will see the ActiveBPEL Process Editor in action when building a hello WS-BPEL process service.

Your First Project in ActiveBPEL Designer

The ActiveBPEL Designer is shipped with samples that might be used to start playing with. To quickly familiarize yourself with the ActiveBPEL Designer, you might take advantage of the ActiveBPEL Tutorial that is included in the Help contents shipped with Designer. The ActiveBPEL Tutorial consists of step-by-step instructions on how to build, deploy, run, and debug a sample process.

Creating the Project

When you need to create a new WS-BPEL process service with the ActiveBPEL Designer, the first step is to create a project. To do this, you might select **File | New | Project**, choose **Project** in the Wizard, and then click **Next**. In the next window of the Wizard as shown in the following figure, you should specify the name for the project. For the project discussed here, you might use **hello_designer** as the name.

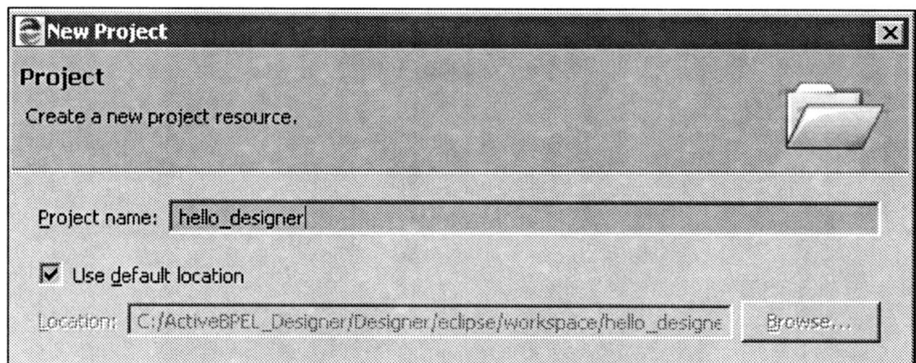

After you have specified the name of the project, click **Finish**.

The following figure illustrates what the Navigator view might look like after you've created the `hello_designer` project as discussed above.

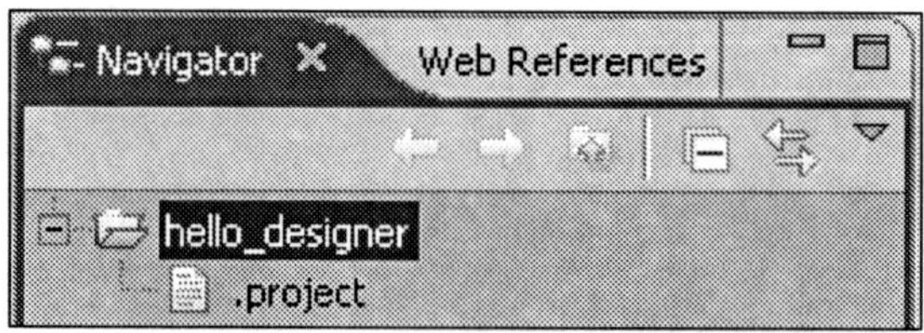

Adding the WSDL Definition

The next step is to add a WSDL document to this project. To keep things simple, you might use the `hello.wsdl` document discussed in the *Designing WSDL for the WS-BPEL Process Service* section in Chapter 5. It would be a good idea to copy this file to a single subfolder within your project. So, you first need to create that subfolder. This can be done via the **Navigator** shown in the previous figure:

- Right-click the **hello_designer** folder in the **Navigator**.
- In the pop-up menu, choose **New->Other...**
- In the first Wizard window, choose **Folder** and click **Next**.
- In the second Wizard window, type in **wsdl** as the name for the folder being created and click **Finish**.

Now that you have created the `wsdl` folder in your project, you can copy the `hello.wsdl` file to it. To achieve this goal, you might use the **Import...** wizard as follows:

- Right-click the newly created **wsdl** folder in the **Navigator**.
- In the pop-up menu, choose **Import...**
- In the first Wizard window, choose **File System** and click **Next**.
- In the second Wizard window, click the **Browse...** button to the right of the **From directory:** box and select the **wsdl** directory of the hello project discussed in Chapter 5. In the right pane, select **hello.wsdl** and click **Finish**.

As a result, the `hello.wsdl` document should appear in the `wsdl` folder created in the `hello_designer` folder.

Although you have the `hello.wsdl` WSDL document in the `wsdl` folder located within the root folder of your project, it doesn't mean that this WSDL will be automatically available within the project. To solve this problem, you need to add the `hello.wsdl` WSDL document as a Web Reference, thus creating a registry of namespaces, messages, and other elements defined in this WSDL document.

To add a Web Reference, you need to move on to the Web References view, which is placed next to the **Navigator**, and perform the following steps:

- Right-click within Web References view.
- In the pop-up menu, choose **Add Web Reference**.

- In the **Add Web Reference** dialog, click the **Browse Projects...** button and select **/hello_designer/wsdl/hello.wsdl**. As a result, the **Add Web Reference** dialog should look like the following figure. Then, to complete the operation, you should click **OK**.

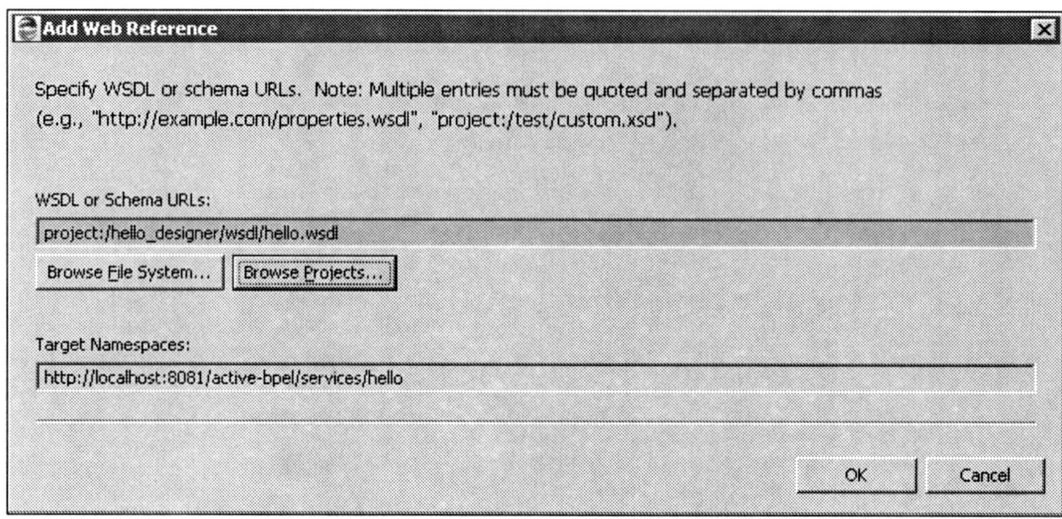

As a result, the **hello.wsdl** node should appear in the Web References view. Now if you expand this node by clicking the plus sign next to the file name, the Web References view should look like the following figure:

As you can see in the figure, the Web References view allows you to look through the structure of the WSDL document added as a Web Reference. In the next section, we look at how you might use the elements of a Web Reference when building a WS-BPEL process with a drag-and-drop approach.

Creating the WS-BPEL Process

Now that you have added the `hello.wsdl` document to the project and added it as a Web Reference, you can move on and build the WS-BPEL process definition. To do this, you should follow the steps below:

- Turn back to the Navigator view by clicking the **Navigator** tab.
- In the **Navigator**, right-click the **hello_designer** folder and select **New->BPEL Process**.
- In the Wizard dialog, enter **hello.bpel** in the **File name** box and click **Finish**. As a result, **hello.bpel** should appear in the **Navigator** within the **hello_designer** folder, and you also should see the **hello.bpel** tab in the ActiveBPEL Process Editor.
- Turn back to the Web References view by clicking the **Web References** tab.
- In the Web References view, expand **hello.wsdl** and then **helloServicePT**, which should contain the operation **hello**.
- Drag the **hello** operation from the Web References view to the **hello.bpel** canvas displayed within the ActiveBPEL Process Editor. As a result, the **Define Partner Link Type** dialog should appear.
- In the **Define Partner Link Type** dialog, click **Finish**. As a result, the **Operation:hello** dialog should appear.
- In the **Operation:hello** dialog, make sure that the **Receive-Reply** option is selected, and click **Finish**. As a result, the **Receive** and **Reply** activities will be automatically added to the canvas.
- Turn back to the Navigator view by clicking the **Navigator** tab.
- In the ActiveBPEL Process Editor, expand the **Palette** by putting the mouse cursor on its tab.
- In the **Palette**, choose **Sequence** from the **Container** section and put it on the canvas.
- Drag the **Receive** activity located on the canvas to the **Sequence** container created in the preceding step, so that the **Receive** activity is within the container.
- Drag the **Reply** activity located on the canvas to the **Sequence** container, so that the **Reply** activity is within the container and under the **Receive** activity.

- In the **Palette**, choose **Assign** from the **Activity** section and put it on the canvas under the **Receive** activity and above the **Reply** activity, within the **Sequence** container. The result should look like the following figure:

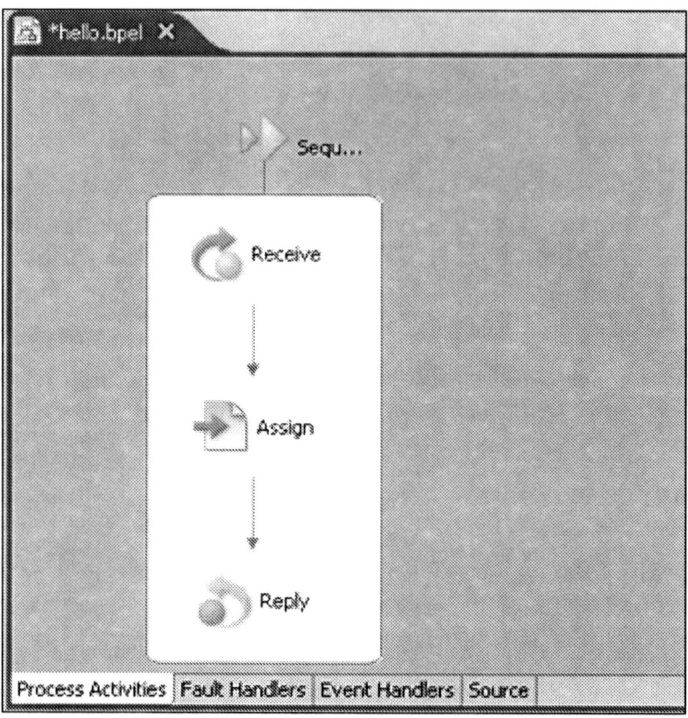

You have just built the **hello.bpel** WS-BPEL process whose visual representation is shown in the previous figure. The next step is to set up the properties of the activities composing the process to the appropriate values:

- On the canvas, select the **Receive** activity located within the **Sequence** container and open the Properties view by clicking the **Properties** tag located at the bottom of the ActiveBPEL Designer perspective.
- In the Properties view, change the value of the **Create Instance** property to **Yes**.
- On the canvas, select the **Assign** activity located within the **Sequence** container and get back to the Properties view.
- In the Properties view, click the **...** button to the right of the **value** field of the **Copy Operations** property. As a result, the **Copy Operations** dialog should appear.

- In the **Copy Operations** dialog, click the **New...** button. As a result, the **Copy Operation** dialog should appear.
- In the **Copy Operation** dialog, select **Expression** in the **Type** combo-box within the **From** group and then click the **...** button located to the right of the **Expression** box. As a result, the **Expression Builder** dialog should appear.
- In the **Expression Builder** dialog, enter the following expression in the **Expression** box: **concat('Hello, ', bpws:getVariableData('inputMessage', 'firstName'),'!')**, and click **OK**. As a result, you should get back to the **Copy Operation** dialog.
- In the **Copy Operation** dialog, move on to the elements within the **To** group and set the properties to the following values: **Type** to **Variable**; **Variable** to **outputMessage**, **Part** to **hello**. Once you've done all that, click **OK**. As a result, you should get back to the **Copy Operations** dialog.
- In the **Copy Operations** dialog, click **OK**.

Examining the expression you used in the above example, you may notice that the `getVariableData` function is used with the `bpws` prefix. If you recall from Chapter 5, in the `hello.bpel` process this prefix is associated with the following namespace:

```
http://schemas.xmlsoap.org/ws/2003/03/business-process/
```

So, you have to add the above namespace to the `hello.bpel` process discussed here. To do this, move on to the Outline view located at bottom part of the ActiveBPEL Designer perspective. The folllowing figure shows what the Outline view may look like:

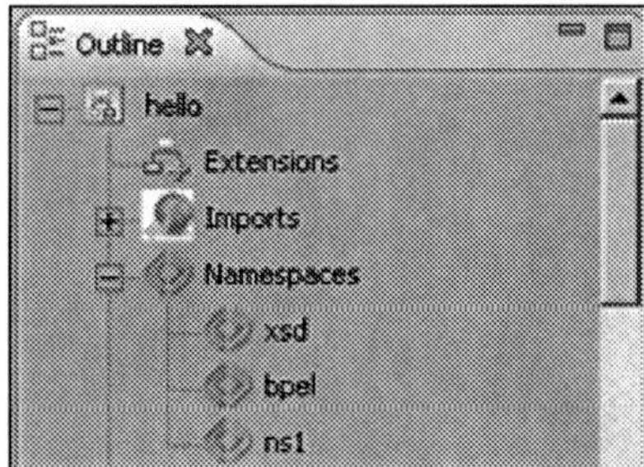

Now you should perform the following steps to set up the namespace mentioned above:

- In the Outline view, right-click the **Namespaces** node, which is under the **hello** node.
- In the pop-up menu, select **Add->Declaration->Namespace**.

- Move on to the Properties view and set the **Namespace** properties as follows: **Prefix** to **bpws**, and **URI** to **http://schemas.xmlsoap.org/ws/2003/03/business-process/**.

That is it. You can now save the `hello.bpel` process by selecting the **hello.bpel** in the ActiveBPEL Process Editor and then selecting **File->Save**. You also may want to look at the WS-BPEL code generated by the ActiveBPEL Designer for the `hello.bpel` document. To do this, click the **Source** tab in the ActiveBPEL Process Editor. The code for the `hello.bpel` document should look as follows:

```
<?xml version="1.0" encoding="UTF-8"?>
<!--
BPEL Process Definition
Edited using ActiveBPEL(tm) Designer Version 3.0.0 (http://www.active-endpoints.com)
-->
<bpel:process xmlns:bpel=
         "http://docs.oasis-open.org/wsbpel/2.0/process/executable"
xmlns:bpws="http://schemas.xmlsoap.org/ws/2003/03/business-process/"
xmlns:ns1="http://localhost:8081/active-bpel/services/hello" xmlns:
xsd="http://www.w3.org/2001/XMLSchema" name="hello" suppressJoinFailur
e="yes" targetNamespace="http://hello">
   <bpel:import importType="http://schemas.xmlsoap.org/wsdl/"
     location="wsdl/hello.wsdl"
     namespace="http://localhost:8081/active-bpel/services/hello"/>
   <bpel:partnerLinks>
      <bpel:partnerLink myRole="helloServiceRole" name="helloPartnerLi
nkType" partnerLinkType="ns1:helloPartnerLinkType"/>
   </bpel:partnerLinks>
   <bpel:variables>
      <bpel:variable messageType="ns1:inputMessage"
name="inputMessage"/>
      <bpel:variable messageType="ns1:outputMessage"
name="outputMessage"/>
   </bpel:variables>
   <bpel:sequence>
      <bpel:receive createInstance="yes" operation="hello" partnerLin
k="helloPartnerLinkType" portType="ns1:helloServicePT" variable="inpu
tMessage"/>
      <bpel:assign>
         <bpel:copy>
            <bpel:from>concat( 'Hello, ', bpws:getVariableData('inputM
essage', 'firstName'),'!')</bpel:from>
            <bpel:to part="hello" variable="outputMessage"/>
         </bpel:copy>
      </bpel:assign>
```

```
        <bpel:reply operation="hello" partnerLink="helloPartnerLinkType"
    portType="ns1:helloServicePT" variable="outputMessage"/>
      </bpel:sequence>
    </bpel:process>
```

Finally, make sure that the Problems view displays no error. If so, you can move on to the deployment phase discussed in the next two sections.

Creating the Deployment Descriptor

As you may recall from the *Creating the Process Deployment Descriptor (PDD) Document* section in Chapter 5, the Process Deployment Descriptor document holds the deployment information required for the ActiveBPEL engine to execute in the ActiveBPEL server environment. While the above section from Chapter 5 discusses how to manually build a descriptor document, this section shows you how to create a `pdd` with the ActiveBPEL Designer.

To create the `pdd` document for the hello WS-BPEL process discussed here, follow the steps below:

- In the Navigator view, right-click within the view to invoke the pop-up menu.
- In the pop-up menu, select **New->Deployment Descriptor** to open the **New Deployment Descriptor** dialog.
- In the **New Deployment Descriptor** dialog, open the **hello_designer** folder and select the **hello.bpel** document, so that it appears in the **Select BPEL Process file** textbox and click **Next**.
- In the next screen of the **New Deployment Descriptor** dialog, make sure that the **Deployment Platform** field is set to **ActiveBPEL Engine** and click **Next**.
- In the next screen of the **New Deployment Descriptor** dialog, select the **helloPartnerLinkType** in the **Partner Links:** listbox. Then, move on to the **MyRole** tab located at the bottom of the same window.
- On the **MyRole** tab, set the properties as follows: **Binding** to **RPC Literal**, **Service** to **helloService**, and click **Finish**.

After you've performed the above steps, the newly created descriptor document should appear in the ActiveBPEL Process Editor, and should look as follows:

```
<?xml version="1.0" encoding="UTF-8"?>
<process xmlns="http://schemas.active-
  endpoints.com/pdd/2006/08/pdd.xsd" xmlns:bpelns="http://hello"
  xmlns:wsa="http://schemas.xmlsoap.org/ws/2003/03/addressing"
  location="bpel/hello_designer/hello.bpel" name="bpelns:hello">
   <partnerLinks>
```

```
        <partnerLink name="helloPartnerLinkType">
           <myRole allowedRoles="" binding="RPC-LIT"
                                   service="helloService"/>
        </partnerLink>
     </partnerLinks>
     <references>
        <wsdl location="project:/hello_designer/wsdl/hello.wsdl"
         namespace="http://localhost:8081/active-bpel/services/hello"/>
     </references>
  </process>
```

> Since the hello WS-BPEL process discussed here doesn't utilize partner services, the above descriptor contains the only partner link—the one that represents the relationship between the process service and its client service.

In the above `pdd` document, pay attention to the value of the `location` attribute of the `wsdl` element. In particular, notice the use of `project:` followed by the path to the `hello.wsdl` file. The ActiveBPEL Designer thus specifies the location of the WSDL document making it possible for the ActiveBPEL engine to find this document within the deployment archive, regardless of the actual location to which that deployment archive will be deployed.

Creating the Deployment Archive

Now that you have all the project components created, you are ready to create the Business Process Archive file required to deploy the newly created hello WS-BPEL process service to an ActiveBPEL server.

Since it's always a good idea to create a deployment archive file in a separate folder, let's do it before creating the archive file:

- In the Navigator view, right-click the **hello_designer** folder.
- In the pop-up menu, select **New->Other...**
- In the first screen of the **New** wizard, select the **Folder** node in the box, and click **Next**.
- In the next screen of the wizard, make sure that the **Enter or select the parent folder** editbox contains **hello_designer**. If so, enter **bpr** in the **Folder name** editbox, and click **Finish**.

After performing these steps, the `bpr` folder should appear within the **hello_designer** folder in the Navigator. Now you can create the deployment archive for the hello WS-BPEL process service and deploy it to the ActiveBPEL engine by following the steps below:

- In the Navigator view, right-click the **hello_designer** folder.
- In the pop-up menu, select **Export...**
- In the **Export** dialog, make sure that **Business Process Archive File** under **ActiveBPEL** node is selected and click **Next**.
- In the **Export Business Process Archive** dialog, make sure that the checkbox on the left of the **hello.pdd** node within the **hello_designer** folder is checked on.
- In the **Export Business Process Archive** dialog, move on to the **BPR file** textbox and enter the following into it: **C:\ActiveBPEL_Designer\Designer\eclipse\workspace\hello_designer\bpr\hello_designer.bpr**.

Depending on the directory in which you installed the ActiveBPEL Designer, you may have another path to the `Designer\eclipse\workspace\hello_designer\bpr` folder.

- In the **Export Business Process Archive** dialog, move on to the **Deployment** group. In the **Type** combobox, select **File**. Next, move on to the **Deployment location** textbox and enter the following into it: **C:\Program Files\Apache Software Foundation\Tomcat 5.5\bpr**, and click **Finish**.

In fact, the ActiveBPEL Designer comes with the Tomcat/ActiveBPEL Server to which you can deploy your WS-BPEL process services. This particular example though, assumes that you are using the same Tomcat server and ActiveBPEL engine running on it, as you used in Chapter 5 meaning the Tomcat/ActiveBPEL Server is installed separately from the ActiveBPEL Designer.

To make sure that the hello WS-BPEL process service has been deployed to the ActiveBPEL engine successfully, enter and then check out the following page generated by Axis:

```
http://localhost:8081/active-bpel/services
```

In this page, you should see the following nodes among others:

helloService (wsdl)

hello

If so, the hello WS-BPEL process service discussed here has been deployed successfully.

Deploying the WS-BPEL Service to the ActiveBPEL Server Shipped with ActiveBPEL Designer

As mentioned, you don't have to install another ActiveBPEL engine on your machine in order to test WS-BPEL processes you build with ActiveBPEL Designer. The fact is that the ActiveBPEL Designer comes with the ActiveBPEL engine running under Apache Tomcat.

This section discusses how to deploy the hello WS-BPEL service discussed above to the ActiveBPEL Server shipped with the ActiveBPEL Designer.

To start with, you need to run the ActiveBPEL Server. However, before you can do this, make sure that another Web server is not running on the port that your ActiveBPEL Server is going to use.

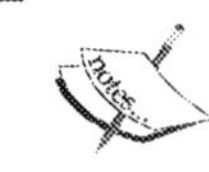

If you have an Oracle database installed on your machine, the 8080 port is likely used by the Oracle XML DB HTTP server. If so, choose another port for your Tomcat server; say, 8081.

Suppose you want to run the ActiveBPEL Server shipped with the ActiveBPEL Designer on port 8081. To do this, you first need to perform the following preliminary steps:

- Change `8080` in the `ActiveBPEL Designer\Server\ActiveBPEL_Tomcat\conf\server.xml` document to `8081`.
- Stop the Tomcat server that you have installed to follow examples provided in Chapter 5, since this server is running on the same port: 8081.

With all that done, you can start the ActiveBPEL Server that comes with ActiveBPEL Designer. To achieve this, you have two choices: you can do either of:

- Click the **Start** button on the Windows taskbar, select **Programs->Active Endpoints->ActiveBPEL Designer->Start ActiveBPEL Tomcat Server**.
- In the `ActiveBPEL Designer\Server\ActiveBPEL_Tomcat\bin` folder double-click the `startup.bat` file.

The Tomcat server shipped with the ActiveBPEL Designer runs in a command window, which you may minimize.

To make sure that the ActiveBPEL Server is running, you can launch the ActiveBPEL Administration Console by entering the following URL in your browser:

`http://localhost:8081/BpelAdmin`

If you recall from Chapter 5, the ActiveBPEL Administration Console is a graphical tool shipped with the ActiveBPEL engine. This tool makes it easier to work with the WS-BPEL processes deployed to the ActiveBPEL engine.

Now that you have the ActiveBPEL Server shipped with ActiveBPEL Designer running on your computer, you can move on and deploy the hello WS-BPEL process service to it. To achieve this goal, you should export the deployment archive for the hello process, as follows:

- In the Navigator view, right-click the **hello_designer** folder.
- In the pop-up menu, select **Export...**
- In the **Export** dialog, make sure that **Business Process Archive File** under the **ActiveBPEL** node is selected and click **Next**.
- In the **Export Business Process Archive** dialog, make sure that the checkbox on the left of the **hello.pdd** node within the **hello_designer** folder is checked on.
- In the **Export Business Process Archive** dialog, move on to the **BPR file** textbox and enter the following into it: **C:\ActiveBPEL_Designer\Designer\eclipse\workspace\hello_designer\bpr\hello_designer.bpr**.

Once again, you may have another path to the `Designer\eclipse\workspace \hello_designer\bpr` folder, depending on the ActiveBPEL Designer installation directory.

- In the **Export Business Process Archive** dialog, move on to the **Deployment** group. In the **Type** combobox, select **File**. Next, move on to the **Deployment location** textbox and enter the following into it: **C:\ActiveBPEL_Designer\Server\ActiveBPEL_Tomcat\bpr** and click **Finish**.

To make sure that the hello WS-BPEL process service has been deployed successfully, you can look at the Deployed Services page in the ActiveBPEL Administration Console. To do this, load the console by entering `http://localhost:8081/BpelAdmin` and then click the **Deployed Services link**. On the Deployed Services page, you should see the **helloService** within the list of the deployed services.

Testing the WS-BPEL Process Service

To test the hello WS-BPEL process service just deployed to the ActiveBPEL Server shipped with the ActiveBPEL Designer, you might use the following script:

```
<?php
 //File: SoapClient_hello.php
 $client = new SoapClient
   ("http://localhost:8081/active-bpel/services/helloService?wsdl");
 try {
  print($client->hello('Larry'));
 }
 catch (SoapFault $e) {
  print $e->getMessage();
 }
?>
```

The above script invokes the hello WS-BPEL process service discussed here and outputs the following hello message:

```
Hello, Larry!
```

Implementing Service-Oriented Orchestrations with ActiveBPEL Designer

Turning back to the example discussed in the *Implementing Service-Oriented Orchestrations* section in Chapter 5, let's look at how you might build the `poInfo` WS-BPEL process service that interacts with the two partner services: `poOrderDocService` and `poOrderStatusService`, using the ActiveBPEL Designer.

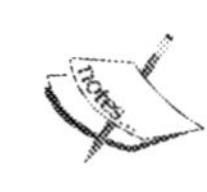

Just one reminder before you proceed further. The `poOrderDocService` and `poOrderStatusService` services are discussed in the *Building Fine-Grained Services* section in Chapter 4. It is assumed that you have them already created.

As you may recall from Chapter 5, the `poInfo` WS-BPEL process service discussed here is invoked upon receiving a request message containing two parameters: `pono` and `par`. The first one specifies the `pono` of the purchase order on which you need to get information, while the second one specifies what kind of information should be returned, meaning two possible choices: the entire document or the status of the document.

The following sections take you through the process of creating and deploying the `poInfo` WS-BPEL process service with ActiveBPEL Designer.

Creating the Project

To create the project for the `poInfo` WS-BPEL process service in the ActiveBPEL Designer, you can follow the steps below:

- In ActiveBPEL Designer, select **File->New->Project**.
- In the first screen of the Wizard, choose **Project** and click **Next**.
- In the next window of the Wizard, specify **poInfo_designer** as the name for the project and click **Finish**.

After you have performed the above steps, you should see the `poInfo_designer` folder in the Navigator view, containing the `.project` document.

Adding the WSDL Describing the WS-BPEL Process

Now that you have created the project for the `poInfo` WS-BPEL process, you can add a WSDL document describing this process service to the project. Of course, you might create this WSDL from the beginning. However, for simplicity's sake, you might use the `poInfo.wsdl` document discussed in the *Creating the WSDL Definition Describing the WS-BPEL Process* section in Chapter 5.

To start with, create a subfolder `wsdl,` within the `poInfo_designer` project folder in the Navigator view, as described at the beginning of the *Adding the WSDL Definition* section earlier in this chapter.

Now that you have created the `wsdl` folder in the root project folder, you can copy the `poInfo.wsdl` file to it. To do this, you should follow the steps below:

- Right-click the newly created **wsdl** folder in the **Navigator**.
- In the pop-up menu, choose **Import...**
- In the first Wizard window, choose **File System** and click **Next**.
- In the second Wizard window, click the **Browse...** button to the right of the **From directory:** box and select the **wsdl** directory of the **poInfo** project discussed in the *Implementing Service-Oriented Orchestrations* section in Chapter 5. In the right pane, select **poInfo.wsdl** and click **Finish**.

As a result, the `poInfo.wsdl` document should be in the `wsdl` folder, which is in the `poInfo_designer` root project folder.

The next step is to add the `poInfo.wsdl` document as a Web Reference. To do this, you need to move on to the Web References view, and perform the following steps:

- Right-click within the Web References view.
- In the pop-up menu, choose **Add Web Reference**.
- In the **Add Web Reference** dialog, click the **Browse Projects...** button and select **/poInfo_designer/wsdl/poInfo.wsdl**, and click **OK**.

As a result, the **poInfo.wsdl** node should appear in the Web References view.

Adding the WSDL Definitions Describing the Partner Services

If you recall, the `poInfo` WS-BPEL process service discussed here utilizes the two partner services, namely `poOrderDocService` and `poOrderStatusService` created as described in Chapter 4. This section discusses how to add WSDL documents describing these services as Web References.

First, let's add the `po_orderdoc.wsdl` located—if you recall from Chapter 4—at `http://localhost/WebServices/wsdl/po_orderdoc.wsdl`.

- Right-click within the Web References view.
- In the pop-up menu, choose **Add Web Reference**.
- In the **Add Web Reference** dialog, insert **http://localhost/WebServices/wsdl/po_orderdoc.wsdl** into the **WSDL or Schema URLs** textbox, and click **OK**.

As a result, the **po_orderdoc.wsdl** node should appear in the Web References view. Next, add the `po_orderstatus.wsdl` located at `http://localhost/WebServices/wsdl/po_orderstatus.wsdl`:

- Right-click within the Web References view.
- In the pop-up menu, choose **Add Web Reference**.
- In the **Add Web Reference** dialog, insert **http://localhost/WebServices/wsdl/po_orderstatus.wsdl** into the **WSDL or Schema URLs** textbox, and click **OK**.

As a result, the **po_orderstaus.wsdl** node should appear in the Web References view.

Creating the Process Definition

Now that you have added the `poInfo.wsdl` document to the project and added it, as well as the WSDL documents describing partner services, as Web References, it's time to build the WS-BPEL process definition for the `poInfo` service. To do this, you should follow the steps shown next:

- In the Navigator view, right-click the **poInfo_designer** folder and select **New->BPEL Process**.
- In the Wizard dialog, enter **poInfo.bpel** in the **File name** box and click **Finish**. As a result, **poInfo.bpel** should appear in the Navigator view within the **poInfo_designer** folder. The **poInfo.bpel** tab should also appear in the ActiveBPEL Process Editor.
- In the Web References view, expand the **poInfo.wsdl** node and then **poInfoPT**, which should contain the operation **getInfo**.
- Drag the **getInfo** operation from the Web References view to the **poInfo.bpel** canvas displayed within the ActiveBPEL Process Editor. As a result, the **Define Partner Link Type** dialog should appear.
- In the **Define Partner Link Type** dialog, click **Finish**. As a result, the **Operation:getInfo** dialog should appear.
- In the **Operation:getInfo** dialog, make sure that the **Receive-Reply** option is selected and click **Finish**. As a result, the **Receive** and **Reply** activities will be automatically added to the **poInfo.bpel** canvas.
- In the ActiveBPEL Process Editor, expand the **Palette** by putting the mouse cursor on its tab.
- In the **Palette**, choose **Sequence** from the **Container** section and put it on the canvas.

With the next steps, you just add all the required activities to the process definitions. Then, you will set up the properties of these activities.

- Drag the **Receive** activity located on the canvas to the **Sequence** container created in the preceding step, so that the **Receive** activity is within the container.
- Drag the **Reply** activity located on the canvas to the **Sequence** container, so that the **Reply** activity is within the container and under the **Receive** activity.
- In the Palette, choose **If** from the **Container** section and put it on the canvas, into the **Sequence** container between the **Receive** and **Reply** activities.
- In the Palette, choose **Sequence** from the **Container** section and put it into the **If** container added in the preceding step.

The **Sequence** container is required here because the **If** container will contain more than one activity.

- In the Web References view, expand the **po_orderdoc.wsdl** node and then **poOrderDocServicePortType**, which should contain the **getOrderDoc** operation.
- Drag the **getOrderDoc** operation from the Web References view to the **poInfo.bpel** canvas to the **Sequence** container located within the `If` container. As a result, the **Define Partner Link Type** dialog should appear.
- In the **Define Partner Link Type** dialog, click **Finish**. As a result, the **Operation:getOrderDoc** dialog should appear.
- In the **Operation:getOrderDoc** dialog, select the **invoke** option and click **Finish**. As a result, the **Invoke** activity will be automatically added to the **poInfo.bpel** canvas, in the **Sequence** container located within the **If** container.
- In the **Palette**, choose **Assign** from the **Activity** section and put it into the **Sequence** container just above the **Invoke** activity added in the preceding step.
- Add another **Assign** activity, putting it just under the **Invoke** activity within the **Sequence** container, which is within the **If** container.
- In the **Palette**, choose **If Condition** from the **Other** section and put it at the top of the **If** container added earlier. As a result, the **ElseIf** container should appear to the right of the **If** container.

When adding **If Condition** from the **Other** section to an **If** container, the ActiveBPEL Designer adds the **ElseIf** container. In this way, you can add as many **ElseIf** containers as needed. In this particular example, though, you need only one **ElseIf** block.

- In the **Palette**, choose **Sequence** from the **Container** section and put it into the **ElseIf** container added in the preceding step.
- In the Web References view, expand the **po_orderstatus.wsdl** node and then **poOrderStatusServicePortType**, which should contain the **getOrderStatus** operation.
- Drag the **getOrderStatus** operation from the Web References view to the **poInfo.bpel** canvas, to the **Sequence** container located within the **If** container. As a result, the **Define Partner Link Type** dialog should appear.
- In the **Define Partner Link Type** dialog, click **Finish**. As a result, the **Operation:getOrderStatus** dialog should appear.
- In the **Operation:getOrderStatus** dialog, select the **invoke** option and click **Finish**. As a result, the **Invoke** activity will be automatically added to the **poInfo.bpel** canvas, in the **Sequence** container located within the **ElseIf** container.

- In the **Palette**, choose **Assign** from the **Activity** section and put it into the **Sequence** container within the **ElseIf** container, just above the **Invoke** activity added in the preceding step.
- Add another **Assign** activity, putting it just under the **Invoke** activity within the **Sequence** container, which is within the **ElseIf** container.
- In the **Palette**, choose **Else** from the **Other** section and put it to the right of the **ElseIf** container added earlier. As a result, the **Else** container should appear to the right of the **ElseIf** container.
- In the **Palette**, choose **Assign** from the **Activity** section and put it into the **Else** container added in the preceding step.

Within the `Else` container used here, you don't use the `Sequence` container as you did when constructing the `If` and `ElseIf` blocks earlier in this example. This is because the `Else` container contains only one activity here.

The following figure shows what the `poInfo.bpel` canvas in the ActiveBPEL Process Editor should look like after you've completed the above steps.

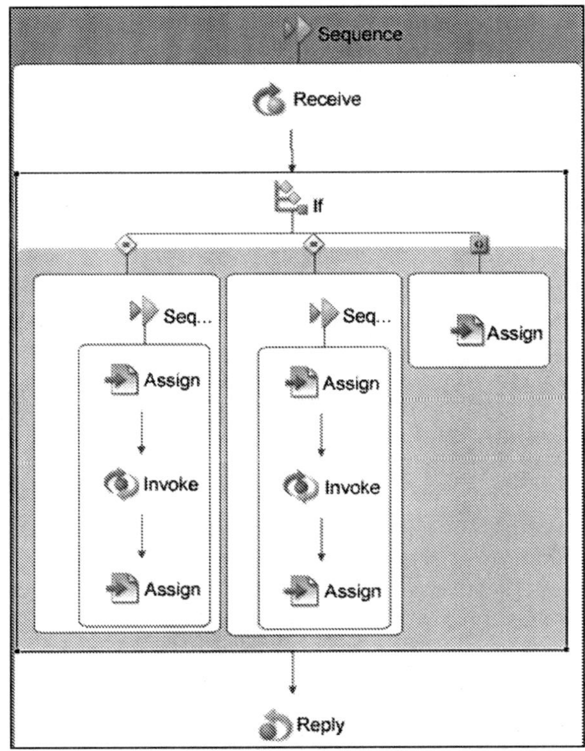

The next step in building the WS-BPEL process discussed here is to set up the properties of the activities composing the process to the appropriate values:

- On the canvas, select the **Receive** activity located within the **Sequence** container and open the Properties view by clicking the **Properties** tag located in the bottom part of the ActiveBPEL Designer perspective.
- In the Properties view, change the value of the **Create Instance** property to **Yes**.
- On the canvas, right-click the **If** container and select **Edit If Expression...** from the pop-up menu.
- In the **If Expression Builder** dialog, enter the following expression in the **If Expression** box: **$poInfoRequestMessage.payload/ns1:par = 'doc'** and click **OK**.
- On the canvas, right-click the **ElseIf** container and select **Edit If Expression...** from the pop-up menu.
- In the **If Expression Builder** dialog, enter the following expression in the **If Expression** box: **$poInfoRequestMessage.payload/ns1:par = 'status'** and click **OK**.
- On the canvas, select the **Assign** activity located at the top of the **Sequence** container within the **If** container and get back to the Properties view.
- In the Properties view, click to the **...** button to the right of the **value** field of the **Copy Operations** property. As a result, the **Copy Operations** dialog should appear.
- In the **Copy Operations** dialog, click the **New...** button. As a result, the **Copy Operation** dialog should appear.
- In the **Copy Operation** dialog, set up properties as follows. In the **From** group: **Type** to **Variable**, **Variable** to **poInfoRequestMessage**, **Part** to **payload**, **Query** to **ns1:pono**. In the **To** group, **Type** to **Variable**, **Variable** to **getOrderDocInput**, **Part** to **pono**. Then, click **OK**.
- In the **Copy Operations** dialog, click **OK**.

Looking through the visual representation of the WS-BPEL process discussed here, you may notice that it contains five `Assign` activities. The above five steps set up only one of the `Assign` activities used. Next, you set up the other four in a similar way.

- On the canvas, select the **Assign** activity located at the bottom of the **Sequence** container within the **If** container, and get back to the Properties view.

- In the Properties view, click to the **...** button to the right of the **value** field of the **Copy Operations** property. As a result, the **Copy Operations** dialog should appear.
- In the **Copy Operations** dialog, click the **New...** button. As a result, the **Copy Operation** dialog should appear.
- In the **Copy Operation** dialog, set up properties as follows. In the **From** group: **Type** to **Variable**, **Variable** to **getOrderDocOutput**, **Part** to **doc**. In the **To** group, **Type** to **Variable**, **Variable** to **poInfoResponseMessage**, **Part** to **payload**. Then, click **OK**.
- In the **Copy Operations** dialog, click **OK**.

You just finished setting up the `Assign` activities located within the `If` container. Next, you set up the `Assign` activities located within the `ElseIf` container.

- On the canvas, select the **Assign** activity located at the top of the **Sequence** container within the **ElseIf** container and get back to the Properties view.
- In the Properties view, click to the **...** button to the right of the **value** field of the **Copy Operations** property. As a result, the **Copy Operations** dialog should appear.
- In the **Copy Operations** dialog, click the **New...** button to invoke the **Copy Operation** dialog.
- In the **Copy Operation** dialog, set up properties as follows. In the **From** group: **Type** to **Variable**, **Variable** to **poInfoRequestMessage**, **Part** to **payload**, **Query** to **ns1:pono**. In the **To** group, **Type** to **Variable**, **Variable** to **getOrderStatusInput**, **Part** to **pono**. Then, click **OK**.
- In the **Copy Operations** dialog, click **OK**.
- On the canvas, select the **Assign** activity located at the bottom of the **Sequence** container within the **ElseIf** container and get back to the Properties view.
- In the Properties view, click to the **...** button to the right of the **value** field of the **Copy Operations** property. As a result, the **Copy Operations** dialog should appear.
- In the **Copy Operations** dialog, click the **New...** button to invoke the **Copy Operation** dialog.
- In the **Copy Operation** dialog, set up properties as follows. In the **From** group: **Type** to **Variable**, **Variable** to **getOrderStatusOutput**, **Part** to **status**. In the **To** group, **Type** to **Variable**, **Variable** to **poInfoResponseMessage**, **Part** to **payload**. Then, click **OK**.
- In the **Copy Operations** dialog, click **OK**.

The last `Assign` activity you need to set up is the one located within the `Else` container.

- On the canvas, select the **Assign** activity located at the bottom of the **Sequence** container within the **Else** container and get back to the Properties view.
- In the Properties view, click to the **...** button to the right of the **value** field of the **Copy Operations** property. As a result, the **Copy Operations** dialog should appear.
- In the **Copy Operations** dialog, click the **New...** button to invoke the **Copy Operation** dialog.
- In the **Copy Operation** dialog, set up properties as follows. In the **From** group: **Type** to **Literal, Literal Contents** to **Wrong input parameter. Should be either doc or status!.** In the **To** group, **Type** to **Variable, Variable** to **poInfoResponseMessage, Part** to **payload**. Then, click **OK**.

That is it. You just finished the `poInfo` WS-BPEL process definition. Now, select **File->Save** to save the process. Then, check out the Problems view; it should display no error.

Now if you click the **Source** tab in the ActiveBPEL Process Editor, assuming that the **poInfo.bpel** canvas is selected, you should see the following WS-BPEL code:

```
<?xml version="1.0" encoding="UTF-8"?>
<!--
BPEL Process Definition
Edited using ActiveBPEL(tm) Designer Version 3.0.0 (http://www.active-
endpoints.com)
-->
<bpel:process xmlns:bpel="http://docs.oasis-
  open.org/wsbpel/2.0/process/executable"
  xmlns:ns1="http://localhost:8081/active-bpel/services/poInfoService.
wsdl"
  xmlns:ns2="http://localhost/WebServices/wsdl/poOrderDoc"
  xmlns:ns3="http://localhost/WebServices/wsdl/poOrderStatus"
  xmlns:xsd="http://www.w3.org/2001/XMLSchema" name="poInfo"
  suppressJoinFailure="yes" targetNamespace="http://poInfo">
   <bpel:import importType="http://schemas.xmlsoap.org/wsdl/"
  location="wsdl/poInfo.wsdl"
  namespace="http://localhost:8081/active-
  bpel/services/poInfoService.wsdl"/>
   <bpel:import importType="http://schemas.xmlsoap.org/wsdl/"
  location="http://localhost/WebServices/wsdl/po_orderdoc.wsdl"
  namespace="http://localhost/WebServices/wsdl/poOrderDoc"/>
   <bpel:import importType="http://schemas.xmlsoap.org/wsdl/"
```

```
location="http://localhost/WebServices/wsdl/po_orderstatus.wsdl"
namespace="http://localhost/WebServices/wsdl/poOrderStatus"/>
 <bpel:partnerLinks>
    <bpel:partnerLink myRole="poInfoProviderRole" name="poInfoLT"
      partnerLinkType="ns1:poInfoLT"/>
    <bpel:partnerLink name="poDocLT" partnerLinkType="ns1:poDocLT"
      partnerRole="poDocProviderRole"/>
    <bpel:partnerLink name="poStatusLT"
      partnerLinkType="ns1:poStatusLT"
        partnerRole="poStatusProviderRole"/>
 </bpel:partnerLinks>
 <bpel:variables>
    <bpel:variable messageType="ns1:poInfoRequestMessage"
      name="poInfoRequestMessage"/>
    <bpel:variable messageType="ns1:poInfoResponseMessage"
      name="poInfoResponseMessage"/>
    <bpel:variable messageType="ns2:getOrderDocInput"
      name="getOrderDocInput"/>
    <bpel:variable messageType="ns2:getOrderDocOutput"
      name="getOrderDocOutput"/>
    <bpel:variable messageType="ns3:getOrderStatusInput"
      name="getOrderStatusInput"/>
    <bpel:variable messageType="ns3:getOrderStatusOutput"
      name="getOrderStatusOutput"/>
 </bpel:variables>
 <bpel:sequence>
    <bpel:receive createInstance="yes" operation="getInfo"
      partnerLink="poInfoLT" portType="ns1:poInfoPT"
      variable="poInfoRequestMessage"/>
    <bpel:if>
       <bpel:condition expressionLanguage=
                 "urn:oasis:names:tc:wsbpel:2.0:sublang:xpath1.0">$
                 poInfoRequestMessage.payload/ns1:par =
                'doc'</bpel:condition>
       <bpel:sequence>
          <bpel:assign>
             <bpel:copy>
                <bpel:from part="payload"
                  variable="poInfoRequestMessage">
                   <bpel:query>ns1:pono</bpel:query>
                </bpel:from>
                <bpel:to part="pono" variable="getOrderDocInput"/>
             </bpel:copy>
          </bpel:assign>
```

```
          <bpel:invoke inputVariable="getOrderDocInput"
            operation="getOrderDoc"
            outputVariable="getOrderDocOutput"
            partnerLink="poDocLT"
            portType="ns2:poOrderDocServicePortType"/>
          <bpel:assign>
             <bpel:copy>
                <bpel:from part="doc"
                  variable="getOrderDocOutput"/>
                <bpel:to part="payload"
                  variable="poInfoResponseMessage"/>
             </bpel:copy>
          </bpel:assign>
       </bpel:sequence>
       <bpel:elseif>
          <bpel:condition expressionLanguage=
            "urn:oasis:names:tc:wsbpel:2.0:sublang:xpath1.0">$
             poInfoRequestMessage.payload/ns1:par =
            'status'</bpel:condition>
          <bpel:sequence>
             <bpel:assign>
                <bpel:copy>
                   <bpel:from part="payload"
                      variable="poInfoRequestMessage">
                      <bpel:query>ns1:pono</bpel:query>
                   </bpel:from>
                   <bpel:to part="pono"
                     variable="getOrderStatusInput"/>
                </bpel:copy>
             </bpel:assign>
             <bpel:invoke inputVariable="getOrderStatusInput"
    operation="getOrderStatus" outputVariable="getOrderStatusOutput"
    partnerLink="poStatusLT"
    portType="ns3:poOrderStatusServicePortType"/>
             <bpel:assign>
                <bpel:copy>
                   <bpel:from part="status"
                     variable="getOrderStatusOutput"/>
                   <bpel:to part="payload"
                     variable="poInfoResponseMessage"/>
                </bpel:copy>
             </bpel:assign>
          </bpel:sequence>
       </bpel:elseif>
```

```
            <bpel:else>
               <bpel:assign>
                  <bpel:copy>
                     <bpel:from>
                        <bpel:literal>Wrong input parameter. Should be
                           either doc or status!</bpel:literal>
                     </bpel:from>
                     <bpel:to part="payload"
                       variable="poInfoResponseMessage"/>
                  </bpel:copy>
               </bpel:assign>
            </bpel:else>
         </bpel:if>
         <bpel:reply operation="getInfo" partnerLink="poInfoLT"
            portType="ns1:poInfoPT" variable="poInfoResponseMessage"/>
      </bpel:sequence>
   </bpel:process>
```

As you can see, the ActiveBPEL Designer generated all the required WS-BPEL code for you. Now you can move on to the deployment phase discussed in the next two sections.

Creating the Process Deployment Descriptor

Now that you have the WS-BPEL definition created, it's time to create the Process Deployment Descriptor document containing the deployment information. Following are the steps to create the `pdd` document for the `poInfo` WS-BPEL process service discussed here, with the ActiveBPEL Designer:

- In the Navigator view, right-click within the view to invoke the pop-up menu.
- In the pop-up menu, select **New->Deployment Descriptor** to open the **New Deployment Descriptor** dialog.
- In the **New Deployment Descriptor** dialog, open the **poInfo_designer** folder and select the **poInfo.bpel** document, so that it appears in the **Select BPEL Process file** textbox, and click **Next**.
- In the next screen of the **New Deployment Descriptor** dialog, make sure that the **Deployment Platform** field is set to **ActiveBPEL Engine** and click **Next**.
- In the next screen of the **New Deployment Descriptor** dialog, the **Partner Links** listbox should contain the following three items: **poDocLT**, **poInfoLT**, **poStatusLT**. Note that the status of **poDocLT** and **poStatusLT** is set to the following: **Missing a partner role endpoint reference type**.

- In the **Partner Links** listbox, select **poDocLT** and then move on to the **Partner Role** group. In the **Invoke Handler** combobox, select **address** and in the **Endpoint type** combobox, select **static**. As a result, the following code should appear in the **Endpoint Reference** box:

```
<wsa:EndpointReference
  xmlns:wsa="http://schemas.xmlsoap.org/ws/2003/03/addressing"
  xmlns:s="FILL_IN_NAMESPACE">
  <wsa:Address>FILL_IN_ADDRESS_URI</wsa:Address>
  <wsa:ServiceName PortName="FILL_IN_PORT_NAME">s:FILL_IN_SERVICE_
NAME</wsa:ServiceName>
</wsa:EndpointReference>
```

- In the **Endpoint Reference** box, replace the above code with the following:

```
<wsa:EndpointReference
  xmlns:s="http://localhost/WebServices/wsdl/poOrderDoc">
   <wsa:Address>http://localhost/WebServices/ch4
      /SoapServer_orderdoc.php</wsa:Address>
      <wsa:ServiceName
             PortName="poOrderDocServicePort">s:
             poOrderDocService</wsa:ServiceName>
           </wsa:EndpointReference>
```

- In the **Partner Links** listbox, select **poStatusLT**. In the **Invoke Handler** combobox, select **address**, and in the **Endpoint type** combobox, select **static**.
- In the **Endpoint Reference** box, replace the generated code with the following:

```
<wsa:EndpointReference xmlns:s=
                "http://localhost/WebServices/wsdl/poOrderStatus">
<wsa:Address>http://localhost/WebServices/ch4/
                          SoapServer_orderstatus.php</wsa:Address>
 <wsa:ServiceName PortName="poOrderStatusServicePort">
                          s:poOrderStatusService</wsa:ServiceName>
</wsa:EndpointReference>
```

- In **Partner Links** listbox, select **poInfoLT**.
- On the **MyRole** tab, set the properties as follows: **Binding** to **RPC Encoded**, **Service** to **poInfoService** and click **Finish**.

After you've performed the above steps, the newly created `poInfo.pdd` descriptor document should appear in the ActiveBPEL Process Editor and should look as follows:

```
<?xml version="1.0" encoding="UTF-8"?>
<process xmlns="http://schemas.active-endpoints.com/pdd/2006/08/pdd.
```

```
xsd" xmlns:bpelns="http://poInfo" xmlns:wsa="http://schemas.xmlsoap.
org/ws/2003/03/addressing" location="bpel/poInfo_designer/poInfo.bpel"
name="bpelns:poInfo">
   <partnerLinks>
      <partnerLink name="poDocLT">
         <partnerRole endpointReference="static"
             invokeHandler="default:Address">
            <wsa:EndpointReference
              xmlns:s="http://localhost/WebServices/wsdl/poOrderDoc">
             <wsa:Address>http://localhost/WebServices/ch4/SoapServer_
orderdoc.php</wsa:Address>
             <wsa:ServiceName
              PortName="poOrderDocServicePort">s:poOrderDocService
              </wsa:ServiceName>
            </wsa:EndpointReference>
         </partnerRole>
      </partnerLink>
      <partnerLink name="poInfoLT">
         <myRole allowedRoles="" binding="RPC"
           service="poInfoService"/>
      </partnerLink>
      <partnerLink name="poStatusLT">
         <partnerRole endpointReference="static"
           invokeHandler="default:Address">
            <wsa:EndpointReference
           xmlns:s="http://localhost/WebServices/wsdl/poOrderStatus">
              <wsa:Address>http://localhost/WebServices/ch4/
SoapServer_orderstatus.
    php</wsa:Address>
                <wsa:ServiceName
           PortName="poOrderStatusServicePort">s:poOrderStatusService
            </wsa:ServiceName>
            </wsa:EndpointReference>
         </partnerRole>
      </partnerLink>
   </partnerLinks>
   <references>
      <wsdl location="project:/poInfo_designer/wsdl/poInfo.wsdl"
        namespace="http://localhost:8081/active-
         bpel/services/poInfoService.wsdl"/>
      <wsdl
       location="http://localhost/WebServices/wsdl/po_orderdoc.wsdl"
       namespace="http://localhost/WebServices/wsdl/poOrderDoc"/>
      <wsdl
```

```
    location="http://localhost/WebServices/wsdl/po_orderstatus.wsdl"
    namespace="http://localhost/WebServices/wsdl/poOrderStatus"/>
  </references>
</process>
```

As you can see, the ActiveBPEL Designer can not only generate the WS-BPEL definitions but also `pdd` documents. The above document contains all the information required to deploy the `poInfo` WS-BPEL process service to an ActiveBPEL engine.

Deploying the WS-BPEL Process Service

Now that you have created all the required components for the `poInfo` WS-BPEL process service, you can deploy it.

To start with, let's create a separate folder in which you will save the deployment archive file:

- In the Navigator view, right-click the **poInfo_designer** folder.
- In the pop-up menu, select **New->Other...**
- In the first screen of the **New** wizard, select the node **Folder** in the box and click **Next**.
- In the next screen of the wizard, make sure that the **Enter or select the parent folder** editbox contains **poInfo_designer**. If so, enter **bpr** in the **Folder name** editbox, and click **Finish**.

As a result, the `bpr` folder should appear within the `poInfo_designer` folder in the Navigator. Now you can create the deployment archive for the `poInfo` WS-BPEL process service and deploy it to the ActiveBPEL Server by following the steps below:

- In the Navigator view, right-click the **poInfo_designer** folder.
- In the pop-up menu, select **Export...**
- In the **Export** dialog, make sure that **Business Process Archive File** under the **ActiveBPEL** node is selected and click **Next**.
- In the **Export Business Process Archive** dialog, make sure that the checkbox on the left to the **poInfo.pdd** node within the **poInfo_designer** folder is checked on.
- In the **Export Business Process Archive** dialog, move on to the **BPR file** textbox and enter the following into it: **C:\ActiveBPEL_Designer\Designer\eclipse\workspace\poInfo_designer\bpr\poInfo_designer.bpr**.

This example assumes that you have installed the ActiveBPEL Designer in the `C:\ActiveBPEL_Designer` folder. Actually, you may have another location.

- In the **Export Business Process Archive** dialog, move on to the **Deployment** group. In the **Type** combobox, select **File**. Next, move on to the **Deployment location** textbox and enter the following into it: **C:\ActiveBPEL_Designer\Server\ActiveBPEL_Tomcat\bpr**, and click **Finish**.

This example assumes that you are using the ActiveBPEL Server shipped with the ActiveBPEL Designer. So, you need to have this server running. For more details, you can go back to the *Deploying the WS-BPEL Service to the ActiveBPEL Server Shipped with ActiveBPEL Designer* section.

To check to see if the `poInfo` WS-BPEL process service has been deployed to the ActiveBPEL Server successfully, enter and then check out the following page generated by Axis:

`http://localhost:8081/active-bpel/services`

In this page, you should see, among others, the following nodes:

poInfoService (wsdl)

getInfo

The above indicates that the `poInfo` WS-BPEL process service discussed here has been deployed successfully.

Testing the WS-BPEL Process Service

To test the `poInfo` WS-BPEL process service just deployed to the ActiveBPEL Server shipped with the ActiveBPEL Designer, you might use the following script:

```
<?php
 //File: SoapClient_poInfo.php
 $client = new SoapClient("http://localhost:8081/active-
          bpel/services/poInfoService?wsdl");
 $xmldoc = '<wrapper><pono>108128476</pono><par>doc</par></wrapper>';
 $xmldoc = simplexml_load_string($xmldoc);
 try {
  print($client->getInfo($xmldoc));
 }
 catch (SoapFault $e) {
```

```
    print $e->getMessage();
  }
?>
```

The above script invokes the hello WS-BPEL process service discussed here, and outputs the entire `po` document whose `pono` is `108128476`.

When setting the `$xmldoc` variable in this script as shown below:

```
$xmldoc = '<wrapper><pono>108128476</pono><par>status</par></
wrapper>';
```

you should receive a short message: **shipped**, which indicates the status of the document.

Finally, if you specify neither `doc` nor `status` as the value of the par element, say, like this:

```
$xmldoc = '<wrapper><pono>108128476</pono><par>docum</par></wrapper>';
```

you should receive the following error message:

```
Wrong input parameter. Should be either doc or status!
```

Summary

As you no doubt have realized, the most important thing about the ActiveBPEL Designer is that it doesn't require you to manually code the WS-BPEL processes, providing a visual environment for creating and deploying WS-BPEL process services.

In this chapter, we looked at how the ActiveBPEL Designer can be used to quickly build all the required components of a WS-BPEL project, using a drag-and-drop user interface, and then deploy the WS-BPEL process service to either the ActiveBPEL Server shipped with ActiveBPEL Designer or a separate ActiveBPEL Server.

7 WS-BPEL Process Modeling

As you learned in the preceding two chapters, WS-BPEL is an efficient means when it comes to composing fine-grained services into composite service-oriented solutions supporting stateful interactions between partners. Although you've seen only simple examples of WS-BPEL orchestrations so far, WS-BPEL can actually be used to model complex service-oriented solutions.

While creating a complex WS-BPEL orchestration may require use of a set of different techniques and technologies together, the main emphasis of this chapter will be on how to implement parallel processing of activities within a WS-BPEL process. It also discusses asynchronous communication as an efficient way to call partner services without blocking the execution of the calling WS-BPEL process. In particular, in this chapter we will look at the following aspects:

- Parallel processing using the `Flow` container
- Parallel repetitive execution with the `forEach` activity
- Asynchronous interactions between WS-BPEL processes
- What to do if something goes wrong

Concurrency, Synchronization, and Asynchronous Communication in WS-BPEL

In the WS-BPEL examples discussed in the preceding chapters, you grouped activities within a WS-BPEL process with the `Sequence` container, thus instructing your BPEL engine to perform these activities sequentially.

This approach is appropriate if every subsequent activity within the container relies on the data returned by the preceding activity. In such cases, sequential processing is the only option for you. You have to organize the activities in the order in which they depend on each other.

However, often, you don't have to invoke the preceding activity to invoke the current one. If so, you may group several activities to be executed in parallel, since they don't depend on each other. To achieve this goal, you can group the activities within the `Flow` container.

Sometimes, you may want to model parallel repetitive execution. For example, when processing the purchase order items in a loop to submit requests to the concerned warehouses, you probably will not have to wait for completion of the current loop iteration to start the next one. In such cases, you can use the parallel form of the `forEach` activity.

The following sections discuss the above points in greater detail.

Parallel Processing versus Sequential Processing

It is important to understand that in practice partner services invoked from within a WS-BPEL process and that calling the WS-BPEL process are executed on different servers, which in turn may be running on different machines. This means that executing several partner services in parallel doesn't usually lead to increasing the load on a certain component in your system.

The following figure shows how sequential processing may result in run-time inefficiency, requiring a significant amount of time to get the job done.

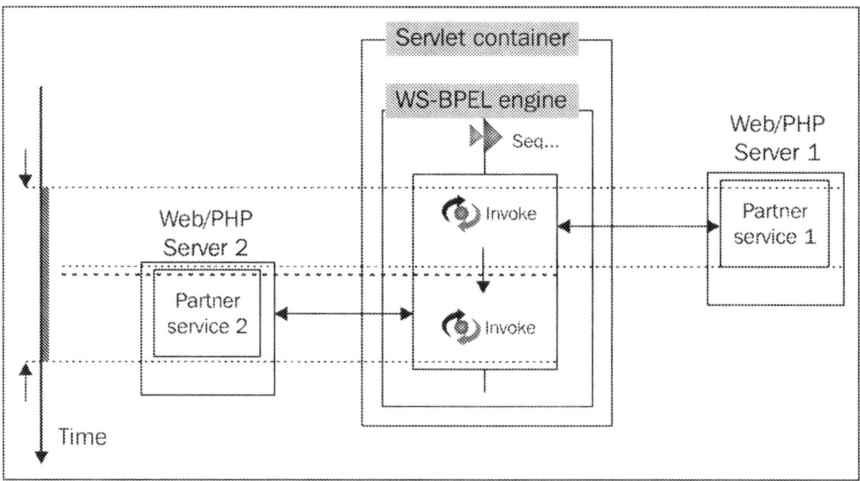

If in your WS-BPEL process you have several activities that might be started concurrently, it is often a good idea to do so rather than performing them sequentially. By doing this, you can significantly reduce the amount of time your WS-BPEL process takes to get the job done.

The following figure shows parallel processing efficiency in terms of time.

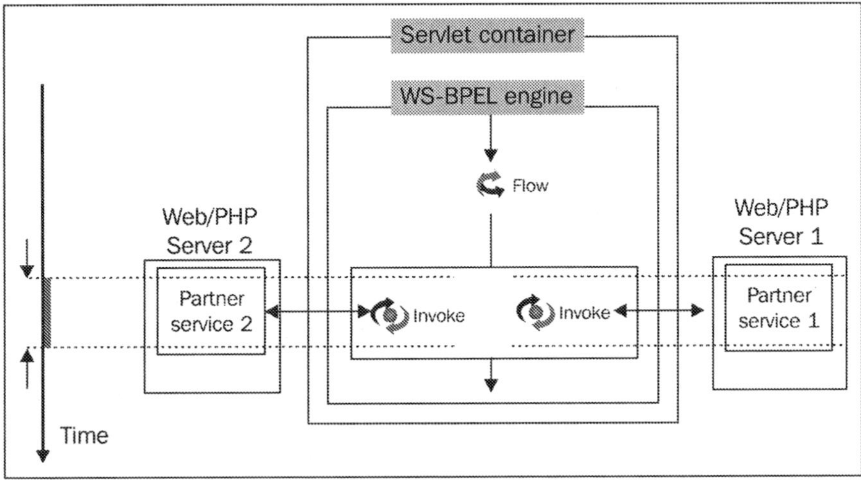

As you can see, the `Flow` activity actually lets you implement concurrent processing within a WS-BPEL process. You don't have to wait until **Partner service 1** is completed in order to invoke **Partner service 2**—they are invoked simultaneously. The `Flow` is completed when all the activities enclosed within it have been completed.

Parallel Processing in a Loop

WS-BPEL allows you to process activities in a parallel loop. To achieve this, you can use the `forEach` activity with the `parallel` attribute set to `yes`. In that case, every loop iteration will be executed concurrently rather than sequentially. A parallel loop can be useful when you need to process parts of the same document, for example, items of a purchase order.

[The section *Implementing a Parallel Loop*, later in this chapter, discusses how to implement parallel processing with WS-BPEL using the parallel form of the `forEach` activity.]

The following figure illustrates that a parallel loop can be much more efficient in terms of time than a sequential one. This is because the former performs all the iterations simultaneously, in parallel, rather than performing them sequentially.

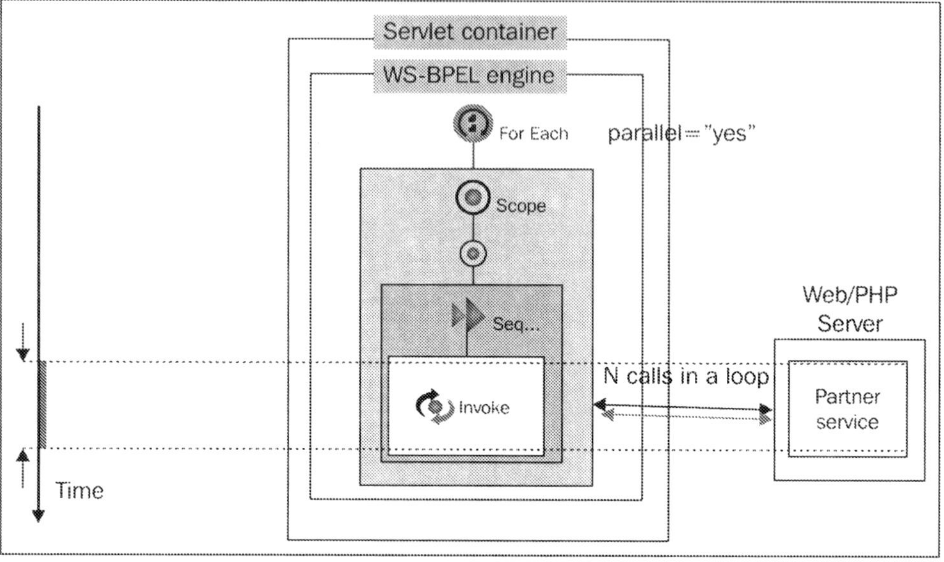

Note that the `forEach` container activity groups activities within the inner scope. As you will learn in the *Implementing a Parallel Loop* section later, if you invoke a partner service from within a loop, a parallel `forEach`, in order to perform parallel processing correctly, requires you to define and use the inner scope local variables being used for the invoke activity's messages.

Asynchronous Communication

Another interesting way to model efficient WS-BPEL processes is using asynchronous communication.

> The WS-BPEL examples discussed in the preceding chapters used the synchronous model, assuming that the WS-BPEL process service sends a message to its partner and waits for a response. This model can be useful when an immediate response is required and the partner service is supposed to generate that response quickly. However, in some situations your WS-BPEL process doesn't need to wait until the transaction is completed and can continue with some other processing. This is where asynchronous messaging comes into play.

The following figure shows an example of asynchronous conversation in action. In this example, two WS-BPEL process services running on the same server communicate asynchronously.

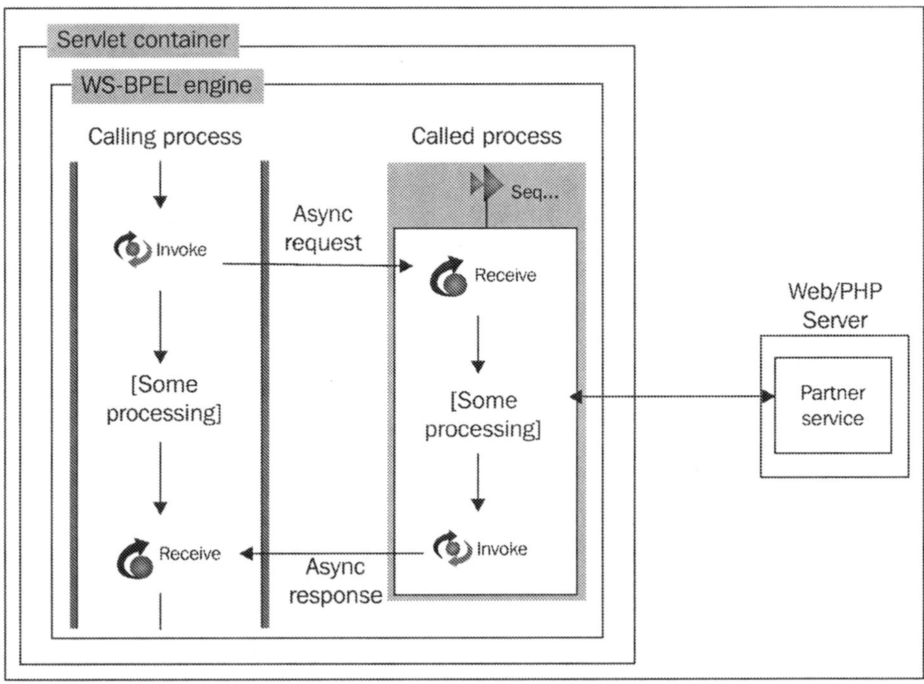

In the example depicted in the figure, the calling WS-BPEL process (left) sends an asynchronous request to the called process that is executed on the same WS-BPEL server. While the called process processes the request, say, makes a synchronous call to a partner service deployed to a Web/PHP server, the calling service can perform some other processing, rather than waiting for a response from the called service. Once the called service has completed its processing it sends the response back to the caller.

To correlate asynchronous responses with the correct process instances, the ActiveBPEL engine can either use correlation sets or engine-managed correlation. While the latter makes the ActiveBPEL engine automatically correlate inbound messages using WS-Addressing references in the SOAP header of a message, the approach based on correlation sets assumes that you explicitly define correlation properties in WSDL and WS-BPEL process definitions. We look at an example of using correlation sets when building an example discussed in the *Building an Asynchronous WS-BPEL Process Service* section later in this chapter.

Implementing Concurrency with the Flow Container

In the preceding examples, you looked at how you can implement sequential processing of activities in WS-BPEL using the `Sequence` container. In practice, though, you may have to organize parallel processing of activities used in your WS-BPEL process. The `Flow` container is specifically designed to address this problem.

The following sections walk you through creating a simple WS-BPEL process that uses parallel processing.

Defining Partner Services

Before we move on to create the WS-BPEL process, let's first build the partner services that will be invoked from it. For the sake of this example, two partner services will be enough. Since you are building a generic sample, the partner services being used might be called `thread1` and `thread2`. Each of these services should provide a time-consuming operation, so that you can see a noticeable difference between sequential and parallel processing performed by the WS-BPEL processes invoking these operations.

Let's start by creating the WSDL document describing the `thread1` service. Here is the `thread1.wsdl` document that you should save in the `WebServices\wsdl` directory:

```
<?xml version="1.0" encoding="utf-8"?>
<definitions name ="thread1Service"
             xmlns:http="http://schemas.xmlsoap.org/wsdl/http/"
             xmlns:soap="http://schemas.xmlsoap.org/wsdl/soap/"
             xmlns:xsd="http://www.w3.org/2001/XMLSchema"
             xmlns="http://schemas.xmlsoap.org/wsdl/"
             targetNamespace="http://localhost/WebServices/wsdl/
thread1"
             xmlns:tns="http://localhost/WebServices/wsdl/thread1">
    <message name="thread1Input">
        <part name="payload" type="xsd:string"/>
    </message>
    <portType name="thread1PortType">
        <operation name="startThread1">
           <input message="tns:thread1Input"/>
        </operation>
```

```
    </portType>
    <binding name="thread1ServiceBinding" type="tns:thread1PortType">
        <soap:binding style="rpc"
           transport="http://schemas.xmlsoap.org/soap/http"/>
        <operation name="startThread1">
           <soap:operation
             soapAction="http://localhost/WebServices/ch7/
startThread1"/>
           <input>
               <soap:body use="literal"/>
           </input>
        </operation>
    </binding>
    <service name="thread1Service">
        <port name="thread1ServicePort"
            binding="tns:thread1ServiceBinding">
           <soap:address
     location="http://localhost/WebServices/ch7/SOAPServer_thread1.
php"/>
        </port>
    </service>
</definitions>
```

As you can see, the operation defined in the above definition is a one-way operation assuming an inbound request only. This means that the service described by the above definition is not supposed to return anything to the consumer. That is OK for this particular example, since all you want from the partner service here is that it performs time-consuming processing when invoked by the WS-BPEL process service.

In the same way, you should create the `thread2.wsdl` document, replacing each occurrence of `thread1` with `thread2`. For example, the operation name `startThread1` should be replaced with `startThread2`. In all other respects, `thread2.wsdl` should be the same as `thread1.wsdl` shown in the above listing. Like `thread1.wsdl`, you should save the `thread2.wsdl` document in the `WebServices\wsdl` directory.

The `thread2.wsdl` document is not shown here to save space. As mentioned, `thread2.wsdl` should have the same structure as `thread1.wsdl` shown above.

The next step in creating the thread1 service is to create the PHP handler class for it. Here is the thread1.php handler class, which you should save in the WebServices\ch7 directory:

```
<?php
 //File thread1.php
 class thread1 {
   function startThread1($salutation) {
 sleep(15);
     ob_start();
     var_dump($salutation. ' thread1. Current time: '.date("H:i:s"));
     $buffer = ob_get_flush();
     file_put_contents('thread1.txt', $buffer);
     ob_end_clean();
   }
 }
?>
```

Note the use of the sleep function in the above PHP code. You use it here to simulate the time-consuming processing. By specifying 15 as the parameter of sleep, you instruct PHP to delay script execution for 15 seconds.

Similarly, you should create the thread2 handler class for the thread2 service, replacing each occurrence of thread1 with thread2. Like thread1.php, you should save thread2.php in the WebServices\ch7 directory.

The last step in creating the thread1 service is to create the SOAP server script. Here is the SoapServer_thread1.php script that you should save in the WebServices\ch7 directory:

```
<?php
//File: SoapServer_thread1.php
require_once "thread1.php";
$wsdl= "http://localhost/WebServices/wsdl/thread1.wsdl";
$srv= new SoapServer($wsdl);
$srv->setClass("thread1");
$srv->handle();
?>
```

In the same way, you should create the SoapServer_thread2.php script, replacing each occurrence of thread1 with thread2. Like SoapServer_thread1.php, you should save SoapServer_thread2.php in the WebServices\ch7 directory.

Creating the Project

Now that you have the partner services created and ready for use, you can move on and build the WS-BPEL process service that will invoke these services in parallel.

As usual, you start by creating the project for the WS-BPEL process service you are going to build. To do this in the ActiveBPEL Designer, you can follow the steps shown below:

- In the ActiveBPEL Designer, select **File->New->Project**.
- In the first screen of the Wizard, choose **Project** and click **Next**.
- In the next window of the Wizard, specify **check_concurrency** as the name for the project and click **Finish**.

After you have performed the above steps, you should see the **check_concurrency** folder in the Navigator view, containing the **.project** document.

Creating the WSDL Describing the WS-BPEL Process

Unlike the examples discussed in the preceding chapter where you made use of an already existing WSDL document for the WS-BPEL process service, you now create a WSDL document for the `check_concurrency` process service discussed here, from scratch.

Before you proceed to create the WSDL describing the `check_concurrency` process service, create the `wsdl` subfolder within the `check_concurrency` project folder. To do this, perform the following steps:

- Right-click the **check_concurrency** folder in the Navigator.
- In the pop-up menu, choose **New->Other...**
- In the first Wizard window, choose **Folder** and click **Next**.
- In the second Wizard window, type in **wsdl** as the name for the folder being created and click **Finish**.

The next step is to create the **checkconcur.wsdl** document in the **wsdl** folder created as discussed above. To do this, the following steps should be followed:

- Right-click the newly created **wsdl** folder in the **Navigator**.
- In the pop-up menu, choose **New->Other...**
- In the first Wizard window, choose **File** and click **Next**.

- In the second Wizard window, type in **checkconcur.wsdl** in the **File name:** textbox and click **Finish**. As a result, the **checkconcur.wsdl** document should appear in the **check_concurrency/wsdl** folder in the Navigator view.
- Right-click the newly created **checkconcur.wsdl** file in the Navigator view.
- In the pop-up menu, select **Open With\BPR Deployment Script Editor**. As a result, the empty **checkconcur.wsdl** document should appear in the ActiveBPEL Process Editor.
- In the **checkconcur.wsdl** canvas, insert the WSDL definition shown below:

```
<?xml version="1.0" encoding="UTF-8"?>
<definitions name="check_concur"
    targetNamespace="http://localhost:8081/active-
      bpel/services/check_concur.wsdl"
    xmlns:tns="http://localhost:8081/active-
      bpel/services/check_concur.wsdl"
    xmlns:plnk="http://schemas.xmlsoap.org/ws/2003/05/partner-link/"
    xmlns:xsd="http://www.w3.org/2001/XMLSchema"
    xmlns:ns2="http://localhost/WebServices/wsdl/thread1"
    xmlns:ns3="http://localhost/WebServices/wsdl/thread2"
    xmlns="http://schemas.xmlsoap.org/wsdl/">
  <import namespace="http://localhost/WebServices/wsdl/thread1"
        location="http://localhost/WebServices/wsdl/thread1.wsdl"/>
  <import namespace="http://localhost/WebServices/wsdl/thread2"
        location="http://localhost/WebServices/wsdl/thread2.wsdl"/>
  <message name="checkconcurResponseMessage">
    <part name="payload" type="xsd:string"/>
  </message>
  <message name="checkconcurRequestMessage">
    <part name="payload" type="xsd:string"/>
  </message>
  <portType name="checkconcurPT">
    <operation name="getRslt">
      <input message="tns:checkconcurRequestMessage"/>
      <output message="tns:checkconcurResponseMessage"/>
    </operation>
  </portType>
  <plnk:partnerLinkType name="checkconcurLT">
   <plnk:role name="checkconcurRole">
      <plnk:portType name="tns:checkconcurPT"/>
   </plnk:role>
  </plnk:partnerLinkType>
  <plnk:partnerLinkType name="thread1LT">
   <plnk:role name="thread1Role">
```

```
        <plnk:portType name="ns2:thread1PortType"/>
     </plnk:role>
   </plnk:partnerLinkType>
   <plnk:partnerLinkType name="thread2LT">
     <plnk:role name="thread2Role">
        <plnk:portType name="ns3:thread2PortType"/>
     </plnk:role>
   </plnk:partnerLinkType>
</definitions>
```

- Select **File->Save** to save the above WSDL document.

Now that you have created the `checkconcur.wsdl` document, the next step is to add this WSDL as a Web Reference. To do this, you need to move on to the Web References view, and perform the following steps:

- Right-click within Web References view.
- In the pop-up menu, choose **Add Web Reference**.
- In the **Add Web Reference** dialog, click the **Browse Projects...** button and select **/check_concurrency/wsdl/checkconcur.wsdl** and click **OK**.

As a result, the **checkconcur.wsdl** node should appear in the Web References view.

Adding Partner WSDL Definitions as Web References

The next step is to add the WSDL definitions describing the `thread1` and `thread2` services created as described in the *Defining Partner Services* section earlier, as Web References. To do this, you need to move on to the Web References view and perform the following steps:

- Right-click within Web References view.
- In the pop-up menu, choose **Add Web Reference**.
- In the **Add Web Reference** dialog, insert **http://localhost/WebServices/wsdl/thread1.wsdl** into the **WSDL or Schema URLs** textbox, and click **OK**.
- Repeat the above steps for the `thread2.wsdl`, inserting **http://localhost/WebServices/wsdl/thread2.wsdl** into the **WSDL or Schema URLs** textbox in the **Add Web Reference** dialog.

As a result, the `thread1.wsdl` and `thread2.wsdl` nodes should appear in the Web References view.

Creating the Process Definition

Now that you have added the `checkconcur.wsdl` document and the WSDL documents describing partner services as Web References to the project, it's time to build the WS-BPEL process definition for the `check_concurrency` service. To do this, you should follow the steps below:

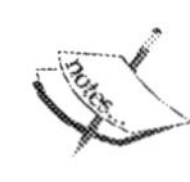

First you look at how to implement sequential processing of the invoke activities used to call the partner services. Then, by replacing the Sequence container enclosing the invoke activities with the Flow container, you move on to parallel processing of those invoke activities.

- In the Navigator view, right-click the **check_concurrency** folder and select **New->BPEL Process**.
- In the Wizard dialog, enter **checkconcur.bpel** in the **File name** box and click **Finish**. As a result, **checkconcur.bpel** should appear in the Navigator view within the **check_concurrency** folder. The **checkconcur.bpel** tab should also appear in the ActiveBPEL Process Editor.
- In the Web References view, expand the **checkconcur.wsdl** node and then **checkconcurPT**, which should contain the operation **getRslt**.
- Drag the **getRslt** operation from the Web References view to the **checkconcur.bpel** canvas displayed within the ActiveBPEL Process Editor. As a result, the **Define Partner Link Type** dialog should appear.
- In the **Define Partner Link Type** dialog, click **Finish**. As a result, the **Operation:getRslt** dialog should appear.
- In the **Operation:getRslt** dialog, make sure that the **Receive-Reply** option is selected, and click **Finish**. As a result, the **Receive** and **Reply** activities will be automatically added to the **checkconcur.bpel** canvas.
- In the ActiveBPEL Process Editor, expand the **Palette** by putting the mouse cursor on its tab.
- In the **Palette**, choose **Sequence** from the **Container** section and put it on the canvas.

The Sequence container added in the above step is used to enclose all the activities of the process. Later, you add another, inner Sequence container to enclose the invoke activities used to call the partner services.

- Drag the **Receive** activity located on the canvas to the **Sequence** container created in the preceding step, so that the **Receive** activity is within the container.

- Drag the **Reply** activity located on the canvas to the **Sequence** container, so that the **Reply** activity is within the container and under the **Receive** activity.

In the next step, you add the Sequence container that will then be used to enclose the `Invoke` activities calling the partner services. As mentioned, later you replace this **Sequence** container with `Flow`, thus moving from the sequential processing to parallel processing.

- In the **Palette**, choose **Sequence** from the **Container** section and put it on the canvas within the already existing **Sequence** between the **Receive** and **Reply** activities added above.

In the following four steps, you add the Invoke activity used to call the `thread1` partner service.

- In the Web References view, expand the **thread1.wsdl** node and then **thread1PortType**, which should contain the **startThread1** operation.
- Drag the **startThread1** operation from the Web References view to the **checkconcur.bpel** canvas, to the inner **Sequence** container. As a result, the **Define Partner Link Type** dialog should appear.
- In the **Define Partner Link Type** dialog, click **Finish**. As a result, the **Operation:startThread1** dialog should appear.
- In the **Operation:startThread1** dialog, select the **invoke** option and click **Finish**. As a result, the **Invoke** activity will be automatically added to the **checkconcur.bpel** canvas, within the inner **Sequence** container.
- Repeat the above four steps for the **thread2.wsdl** node located in the Web References view. As a result, you should have two **Invoke** activities within the inner **Sequence** container.

Next, you need to add three `Assign` activities as described in the following steps.

- In the Palette, choose **Assign** from the **Activity** section and put it into the outer **Sequence** container between the **Receive** activity and the inner **Sequence** container.
- Add another **Assign** activity, putting it just under the **Assign** activity added in the preceding step.
- Finally, put another **Assign** between the inner **Sequence** and **Reply** activity.

The following figure shows a fragment of the `check_concurrency` WS-BPEL process visual representation, representing the inner `Sequence` container.

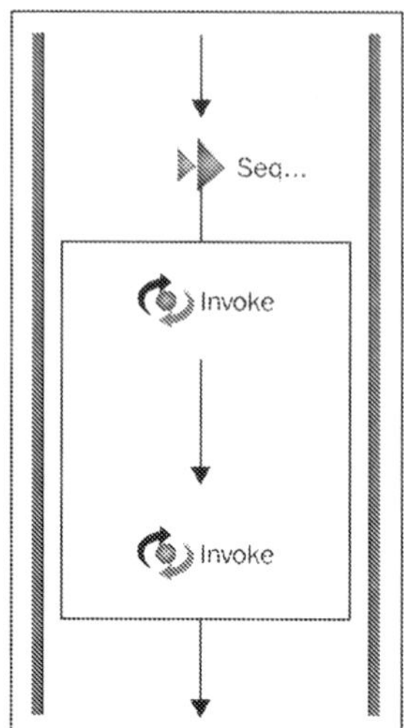

The next step in building the `check_concurrency` WS-BPEL process service discussed here is to set up the properties of the activities composing the process to the appropriate values. To do this, follow the steps below:

- On the canvas, select the **Receive** activity located within the outer **Sequence** container and open the Properties view by clicking the **Properties** tag located in the bottom part of the ActiveBPEL Designer perspective.
- In the Properties view, change the value of the **Create Instance** property to **Yes**.
- On the canvas, select the upper **Assign** activity within the outer **Sequence** container and get back to the Properties view.
- In the Properties view, click to the **...** button to the right of the **Value** field of the **Copy Operations** property. As a result, the **Copy Operations** dialog should appear.
- In the **Copy Operations** dialog, click the **New...** button. As a result, the **Copy Operation** dialog should appear.
- In the **Copy Operation** dialog, set up properties as follows. In the **From** group: **Type** to **Variable, Variable** to **checkconcurRequestMessage, Part** to **payload**; in the **To** group, **Type** to **Variable, Variable** to **thread1Input, Part** to **payload**. Then, click **OK**.
- In the **Copy Operations** dialog, click **OK**.

- On the canvas, select the **Assign** activity located below the **Assign** whose properties were set as described in the previous steps and get back to the Properties view. Then, repeat the previous four steps, setting the properties in the **Copy Operation** dialog as follows: In the **From** group: **Type** to **Variable, Variable** to **checkconcurRequestMessage, Part** to **payload**; in the **To** group: **Type** to **Variable, Variable** to **thread2Input, Part** to **payload.**
- On the canvas, select the *lowest* **Assign** activity located above the **Reply** activity and get back to the Properties view. Then, repeat the four steps as above, setting the properties in the **Copy Operation** dialog as follows: In the **From** group: **Type** to **Literal, Literal Contents** to **Two threads completed successfully!**; in the **To** group: **Type** to **Variable, Variable** to **checkconcurResponseMessage, Part** to **payload.**

You have just finished the **check_concurrency** WS-BPEL process definition. All that's left is to select **File->Save** to save the definition. Then, check out the Problems view to make sure that it displays no errors.

Creating the Process Deployment Descriptor

Now that you have the WS-BPEL definition created, it's time to create the Process Deployment Descriptor document containing the deployment information. The following steps create the **pdd** document for the **check_concurrency** WS-BPEL process service discussed here, with the ActiveBPEL Designer:

- In the Navigator view, right-click within the view to invoke the pop-up menu.
- In the pop-up menu, select **New->Deployment Descriptor** to open the **New Deployment Descriptor** dialog.
- In the **New Deployment Descriptor** dialog, open the **check_concurrency** folder and select the **checkconcur.bpel** document, so that it appears in the **Select BPEL Process file** textbox, and click **Next.**
- In the next screen of the **New Deployment Descriptor** dialog, make sure that the **Deployment Platform** field is set to **ActiveBPEL Engine** and click **Next.**
- In the next screen of the **New Deployment Descriptor** dialog, the **Partner Links** listbox should contain the following three items: **checkconcurLT, thread1LT**, and **thread2LT.** Note that the status of the last two is set to the following: **Missing a partner role endpoint reference type.**
- In the **Partner Links** listbox, select **thread1LT** and then move on to the **Partner Role** group. In the **Invoke Handler** combobox, select **address**, and in the **Endpoint type** combobox, select **static.** As a result, the following code should appear in the **Endpoint Reference** box:

```
<wsa:EndpointReference
  xmlns:wsa="http://schemas.xmlsoap.org/ws/2003/03/addressing"
  xmlns:s="FILL_IN_NAMESPACE">
    <wsa:Address>FILL_IN_ADDRESS_URI</wsa:Address>
    <wsa:ServiceName
      PortName="FILL_IN_PORT_NAME">s:FILL_IN_SERVICE_NAME
        </wsa:ServiceName>
 </wsa:EndpointReference>
```

- In the **Endpoint Reference** box, replace the above code with the following:

```
<wsa:EndpointReference
  xmlns:s="http://localhost/WebServices/wsdl/thread1">

<wsa:Address>http://localhost/WebServices/ch7/SoapServer_thread1.
php
 </wsa:Address>
   <wsa:ServiceName
   PortName="thread1ServicePort">s:thread1Service</wsa:
ServiceName>
    </wsa:EndpointReference>
```

- In the **Partner Links** listbox, select **thread2LT**. In the **Invoke Handler** combobox, select **address**, and in the **Endpoint type** combobox, select **static**.
- In the **Endpoint Reference** box, replace the generated code with the following:

```
<wsa:EndpointReference
  xmlns:s="http://localhost/WebServices/wsdl/thread2">

<wsa:Address>
      http://localhost/WebServices/ch7/SoapServer_thread2.php
  </wsa:Address>
  <wsa:ServiceName
  PortName=
      "thread2ServicePort">s:thread2Service</wsa:ServiceName>
    </wsa:EndpointReference>
```

- In the **Partner Links** listbox, select **checkconcurLT**.
- On the **MyRole** tab, set the properties as follows: **Binding** to **RPC Encoded**, **Service** to **checkconcurService**, and click **Finish**.

As a result, the **checkconcur.pdd** descriptor document should appear in the **check_concurrency** folder in the Navigator, and in the ActiveBPEL Process Editor, where you may review it.

Deploying the Process Service

Now that you have created all the required components for the **check_concurrency** WS-BPEL process service, you can deploy it.

Before proceeding further, you might want to create a separate folder within the **check_concurrency** folder, to which you will save the deployment archive file. To do this, perform the following steps:

- In the Navigator view, right-click the **check_concurrency** folder.
- In the pop-up menu, select **New->Other...**
- In the first screen of the **New** Wizard, select the node **Folder** in the box, and click **Next**.
- In the next screen of the Wizard, make sure that the **Enter or select the parent folder** editbox contains **check_concurrency**. If so, enter **bpr** in the **Folder name** editbox and click **Finish**.

After you've performed the above steps, the `bpr` folder should appear within the `check_concurrency` folder in the Navigator. Now you can create the deployment archive for the `check_concurrency` WS-BPEL process service and deploy it to the ActiveBPEL Server by following the steps below:

- In the Navigator view, right-click the **check_concurrency** folder.
- In the pop-up menu, select **Export...**
- In the **Export** dialog, make sure that **Business Process Archive File** under the **ActiveBPEL** node is selected and click Next.
- In the **Export Business Process Archive** dialog, make sure that the checkbox on the left of the **checkconcur.pdd** node within the **check_concurrency** folder is checked on.
- In the **Export Business Process Archive** dialog, move on to the **BPR file** textbox and enter the following into it: **C:\ActiveBPEL_Designer\Designer\eclipse\workspace\check_concurrency\bpr\checkconcur.bpr**.
- In the **Export Business Process Archive** dialog, move on to the **Deployment** group. In the **Type** combobox, select **File**. Next, move on to the **Deployment location** textbox and enter the following into it: **C:\ActiveBPEL_Designer\Server\ActiveBPEL_Tomcat\bpr**, and click **Finish**.

In this example, you are using the ActiveBPEL Server shipped with your ActiveBPEL Designer, assuming you have this server running. For more details, you can refer to the *Deploying the WS-BPELService to the ActiveBPEL Server Shipped with ActiveBPEL Designer* section in Chapter 6.

Once you've done all that, you should have the `check_concurrency` WS-BPEL process service deployed to the ActiveBPEL Server and ready for use. The simplest way to check to see if the WS-BPEL process service has been deployed successfully is to enter and then check out the following page generated by Axis:

```
http://localhost:8081/active-bpel/services
```

In this page, you should see the following nodes among others:

checkconcurService (wsdl)

getRslt

If so, the `check_concurrency` WS-BPEL process service discussed here has been deployed successfully.

Testing the Sequential Version of the WS-BPEL Process

Now that you have the sequential version of the `check_concurrency` WS-BPEL process service, it's time to test it. For that, you might use the `checkConcurClient.php` SOAP client script shown below:

```
<?php
 //File: checkConcurClient.php
 $client = new SoapClient("http://localhost:8081/active-
         bpel/services/checkconcurService?wsdl");
 $sol = 'Hello,';
 try {
  print($client->getRslt($sol));
 }
 catch (SoapFault $e) {
  print $e->getMessage();
 }
?>
```

When executed, the above script invokes the `check_concurrency` WS-BPEL process service created and deployed as discussed in the preceding sections, passing the `Hello` string as the payload in the request message. The above script should produce the following output:

```
Two threads completed successfully!
```

Execution should take at least 30 seconds, because each partner service invoked by the WS-BPEL process is executed for at least 15 seconds, and they are executed sequentially. Now if you check the `WebServices\ch7` directory in which you saved the `checkConcurClient.php` script discussed here, you should notice the `thread1.txt` and `thread2.txt` files. If you open the `thread1.txt` file, it might contain the following contents:

```
string(38) "Hello, thread1. Current time: 22:33:00"
```

The `thread2.txt` might contain the following:

```
string(38) "Hello, thread2. Current time: 22:33:15"
```

As you might have guessed, the `thread2.txt` file was created 15 seconds after the `thread1.txt file`. This is because the `thread1` and `thread2` services were invoked by the `check_concurrency` WS-BPEL process service in sequential order.

Replacing Sequence with Flow

Now that you've seen how the sequential version of the `check_concurrency` WS-BPEL process works, let's move on and modify this WS-BPEL process so that it invokes the `thread1` and `thread2` partner services in parallel. To achieve this goal, you should accomplish the following general steps:

- In the `check_concurrency` WS-BPEL process definition, replace the inner `Sequence` container with a `Flow` container.
- Re-deploy the `check_concurrency` WS-BPEL process service.

To implement the first task, you should perform the following steps:

- In the ActiveBPEL Process Editor, click the **checkconcur.bpel** tab to move on to the visual representation of the **checkconcur.bpel** process definition.
- On the canvas, drag the **Invoke** activities from within the inner **Sequence** container to any other area on the canvas.
- On the canvas, select the inner **Sequence** container and hit *Delete* on your keyboard in order to delete the container.
- In the Palette, choose **Flow** from the **Container** section and put it between the second and third **Assign** activities on the canvas, where the inner **Sequence** container was located before deletion.

- Drag the **Invoke** activities earlier located within the inner **Sequence** container to the **Flow** container created in the previous step. As a result, the fragment of the diagram representing the **Flow** container on the canvas should look like the following figure:

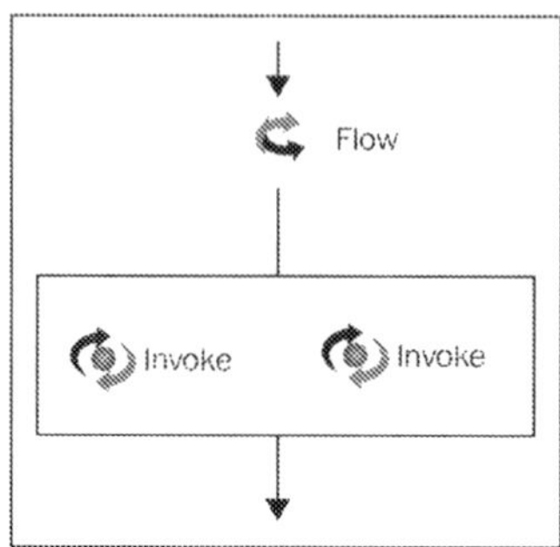

After you've performed the above steps, select **File | Save** to save the changes made. Then, to make sure that everything is OK, check to see that the Problems view displays no errors.

The next step is to re-deploy the `check_concurrency` WS-BPEL process service. To do this, you should use the Export Wizard as discussed in detail in the *Deploying the Process Service* section earlier. As a result, the `check_concurrency` WS-BPEL process service will be re-deployed to the ActiveBPEL Server shipped with your ActiveBPEL Designer.

Testing the WS-BPEL Process Using a Parallel Flow to Handle Partner Services

To test the `check_concurrency` WS-BPEL process service modified as discussed in the preceding section, you can use the `checkConcurClient.php` script discussed in the *Testing the Sequential Version of the WS-BPEL Process* section earlier. This time, though, the `checkConcurClient.php` script, when executed, will behave a little differently in that it is executed for about 15 seconds rather than the 30 seconds it took when you tested the sequential version of the `check_concurrency` WS-BPEL process. Now if you open the `thread1.txt` file, it should contain contents like the following:

```
string(38) "Hello, thread1. Current time: 21:54:44"
```

The `thread2.txt` file's contents might look as follows:

```
string(38) "Hello, thread2. Current time: 21:54:44"
```

As you can see, both these files were created at the same time. This means that both the thread1 and thread2 services were invoked at the same time rather than at the 15 second interval you had in the case of the sequential version of the check_concurrency WS-BPEL process.

Implementing a Parallel Loop

As you learned in the *Parallel Processing in a Loop* section previously, performing all the loop iterations simultaneously is usually more efficient in terms of time than performing them sequentially.

> It is important to realize, though, that there are some situations in which you cannot use a parallel loop. For example, if every subsequent loop iteration depends on the preceding one, of course you cannot take advantage of a parallel loop.

The following sections take you through the process of creating a WS-BPEL process service that calls a partner service in a loop, processing items of a purchase order. First, you build a WS-BPEL process that uses a sequential forEach loop to get the job done. Then, you move on to the parallel form of the forEach loop.

Defining the Partner Service Being Called from within the Loop

First, you need to build the partner service, say, orderProcessing that will be invoked from within the loop in the WS-BPEL process, processing items of a purchase order.

As usual, let's start by creating the WSDL document describing the orderProcessing partner service. Here is the orderProcessing.wsdl document that you should save in the WebServices\wsdl directory:

```
<?xml version="1.0" encoding="utf-8"?>
<definitions name ="orderProcessingService"
             xmlns:http="http://schemas.xmlsoap.org/wsdl/http/"
             xmlns:soap="http://schemas.xmlsoap.org/wsdl/soap/"
             xmlns:xsd="http://www.w3.org/2001/XMLSchema"
             xmlns="http://schemas.xmlsoap.org/wsdl/"
             targetNamespace="http://localhost/WebServices/wsdl/
orderProcessing"
             xmlns:tns="http://localhost/WebServices/wsdl/
orderProcessing">
    <message name="orderProcessingInput">
```

```
        <part name="partId" type="xsd:int"/>
        <part name="quantity" type="xsd:decimal"/>
        </message>
        <portType name="orderProcessingPortType">
        <operation name="startProcessing">
           <input message="tns:orderProcessingInput"/>
        </operation>
        </portType>
        <binding name="orderProcessingServiceBinding" type="tns:
    orderProcessingPortType">
            <soap:binding style="rpc" transport="http://schemas.xmlsoap.
    org/soap/http"/>
            <operation name="startProcessing">
               <soap:operation soapAction="http://localhost/WebServices/
    ch7/startProcessing"/>
               <input>
                   <soap:body use="literal"/>
               </input>
            </operation>
        </binding>
        <service name="orderProcessingService">
            <port name="orderProcessingServicePort" binding="tns:
    orderProcessingServiceBinding">
               <soap:address location=
          "http://localhost/WebServices/ch7/SOAPServer_orderProcessing.
    php"/>
            </port>
        </service>
    </definitions>
```

As you can see, the `orderProcessing` service described by the above WSDL definition offers the `startProcessing` operation, which is a one-way operation since it includes only an input message. This means that the WS-BPEL process service will send only request messages to this service, receiving nothing in response. With request messages, the WS-BPEL service will send data for processing. In this particular example, a request message is supposed to contain the `partId` and `quantity` of a purchase order item being processed.

Next, let's create the PHP handler class for the service. For that, you might create the `orderProcessing` class in the `orderProcessing.php` script as show below. You should save `orderProcessing.php` in the `WebServices\ch7 directory`.

```
<?php
 //File orderProcessing.php
 class orderProcessing {
```

```
    function startProcessing($partId, $quantity) {
     sleep(5);
     $item = "Part id: ".$partId. " Quantity: ".$quantity.
             " Current time: ".date("H:i:s")."\n";
     $handle = fopen('orderProcessingLog.txt', 'a');
     fwrite($handle, $item);
     fclose($handle);
    }
  }
?>
```

As you can see, the above code doesn't perform actual processing. Instead, it simply delays execution for 5 seconds and then logs the information about the purchase order item being processed along with the current time to the `orderProcessingLog.txt` text file.

> Later, looking through the `orderProcessingLog.txt` log file, you can easily determine the way in which the request messages arrive and, therefore, understand why parallel processing is more efficient than sequential.

Finally, you should create the SOAP server script. Here is the `SoapServer_orderProcessing.php` script that you should also save in the `WebServices\ch7` directory:

```
<?php
//File: SoapServer_orderProcessing.php
require_once "orderProcessing.php";
$wsdl= "http://localhost/WebServices/wsdl/orderProcessing.wsdl";
$srv= new SoapServer($wsdl);
$srv->setClass("orderProcessing");
$srv->handle();
?>
```

Creating the Project

Now that you have the `orderProcessing` partner service created and ready for use, you can switch your focus to building the WS-BPEL process service that will invoke this service from within the loop when processing a purchase order.

As usual, let's start by creating the project for the WS-BPEL process service. To do this in ActiveBPEL Designer, you can follow the steps below:

- In ActiveBPEL Designer, select **File->New->Project**.
- In the first screen of the Wizard, choose **Project** and click **Next**.
- In the next window of the Wizard, specify **parallel_loop** as the name for the project and click **Finish**.

After you have performed the above steps, you should see the **parallel_loop** folder in the Navigator view, containing the **.project** document.

Creating the WSDL Describing the WS-BPEL Process

Before you can create the WSDL describing the `parallel_loop` WS-BPEL process service, you should create the subfolder `wsdl` within the `parallel_loop` project folder. To do this, perform the following steps:

- Right-click the **parallel_loop** folder in the Navigator.
- In the pop-up menu, choose **New->Other...**
- In the first Wizard window, choose **Folder** and click **Next**.
- In the second Wizard window, type in **wsdl** as the name for the folder being created and click **Finish**.

The next step is to create the `parallelloop.wsdl` document in the `wsdl` folder created as discussed above. To do this, you should follow the steps below:

- Right-click the newly created **wsdl** folder in the Navigator.
- In the popup menu, choose **New->Other...**
- In the first Wizard window, choose **File** and click **Next**.
- In the second Wizard window, type in **parallelloop.wsdl** in the **File name:** textbox and click **Finish**. As a result, the **parallelloop.wsdl** document should appear in the **parallel_loop/wsdl** folder in the Navigator view.
- Right-click the newly created **parallelloop.wsdl** file in the Navigator view.
- In the pop-up menu, select **Open With\BPR Deployment Script Editor**. As a result, the empty **parallelloop.wsdl** document should appear in the ActiveBPEL Process Editor.

- In the **parallelloop.wsdl** canvas, insert the WSDL definition shown below:

```
<?xml version="1.0" encoding="UTF-8"?>
<definitions name="parallel_loop"
    targetNamespace="http://localhost:8081/active-
      bpel/services/parallel_loop"
     xmlns:tns="http://localhost:8081/active-
      bpel/services/parallel_loop"
    xmlns:plnk="http://schemas.xmlsoap.org/ws/2003/05/
                                                    partner-link/"
    xmlns:xsd="http://www.w3.org/2001/XMLSchema"
    xmlns:xsd1="http://localhost/XSD/po/"
    xmlns:ns2=
            "http://localhost/WebServices/wsdl/orderProcessing"
    xmlns="http://schemas.xmlsoap.org/wsdl/">
  <import namespace=
        "http://localhost/WebServices/wsdl/orderProcessing"

location=
      "http://localhost/WebServices/wsdl/orderProcessing.wsdl"/>
    <types>
     <schema elementFormDefault="qualified"
       targetNamespace="http://localhost/XSD/po/"
        xmlns="http://www.w3.org/2001/XMLSchema">
       <element name="purchaseOrder">
        <complexType>
         <sequence>
          <element name="pono" type="xsd:string" />
          <element name="shipTo" type="xsd1:AddressType" />
          <element name="billTo" type="xsd1:AddressType"/>
          <element name="items" type="xsd1:LineItemsType"/>
         </sequence>
        </complexType>
       </element>
       <complexType name="AddressType">
        <sequence>
         <element name="name" type="xsd:string"/>
         <element name="street" type="xsd:string"/>
         <element name="city" type="xsd:string"/>
         <element name="state" type="xsd:string"/>
         <element name="zip" type="xsd:int"/>
         <element name="country" type="xsd:NMTOKEN" />
        </sequence>
       </complexType>
       <complexType name="LineItemsType">
```

```
        <sequence>
         <element minOccurs=
                         "1" maxOccurs="unbounded" name="item"
           type="xsd1:LineItemType" />
        </sequence>
       </complexType>
       <complexType name="LineItemType">
        <sequence>
         <element name="partId" type="xsd:int"/>
         <element name="quantity" type="xsd:decimal"/>
         <element name="price" type="xsd:decimal"/>
        </sequence>
       </complexType>
     </schema >
    </types>
  <message name="loopProcessResponseMessage">
    <part name="payload" type="xsd:string"/>
  </message>
  <message name="loopProcessRequestMessage">
    <part name="order" element="xsd1:purchaseOrder"/>
  </message>
  <portType name="loopProcessPT">
    <operation name="processOrder">
      <input message="tns:loopProcessRequestMessage"/>
      <output message="tns:loopProcessResponseMessage"/>
    </operation>
  </portType>
  <plnk:partnerLinkType name="loopProcessLT">
   <plnk:role name="loopProcessRole">
      <plnk:portType name="tns:loopProcessPT"/>
   </plnk:role>
  </plnk:partnerLinkType>
  <plnk:partnerLinkType name="orderProcessingLT">
   <plnk:role name="orderProcessingRole">
      <plnk:portType name="ns2:orderProcessingPortType"/>
   </plnk:role>
  </plnk:partnerLinkType>
</definitions>
```

- Finally, select **File** | **Save** to save the above wsdl document.

As you can see, this WSDL document contains the `types` construct in which the `purchaseOrder` complex element is described. The highlighted line is the `item` element of the `LineItemType` type, describing a line item of a purchase order document being processed.

Adding WSDL Definitions as Web References

Once you have the `parallelloop.wsdl` document created as discussed in the preceding section, the next step is to add this WSDL as a Web Reference. To do this, you need to switch to the Web References view, and perform the following steps:

- Right-click within the Web References view.
- In the pop-up menu choose **Add Web Reference**.
- In the **Add Web Reference** dialog, click the **Browse Projects...** button and select **/parallel_loop/wsdl/parallelloop.wsdl** and click **OK**.

As a result, the **parallelloop.wsdl** node should appear in the Web References view.

The next step is to add the WSDL definition describing the `orderProcessing` partner service created as described in the *Defining the Partner Service Being Called from within the Loop* section earlier, as a Web Reference. To do this, you need to move on to the Web References view and perform the following steps:

- Right-click within the Web References view.
- In the pop-up menu choose **Add Web Reference**.
- In the **Add Web Reference** dialog insert **http://localhost/WebServices/wsdl/orderProcessing.wsdl** into the **WSDL or Schema URLs** textbox and click **OK**.

As a result, the **orderProcessing.wsdl** nodes should appear in the Web References view.

Creating the Process Definition

Now you are ready to build the WS-BPEL process definition for the `parallel_loop` service. To do this, you should follow the steps shown below:

> As mentioned, you first build a sequential version of the `parallel_loop` WS-BPEL process service, meaning you are using a sequential `forEach` loop. Then, you modify the process to use a parallel `forEach` loop.

- In the Navigator view right-click the **parallel_loop** folder and select **New->BPEL Process**.
- In the Wizard dialog, enter **parallelloop.bpel** in the **File name** box and click **Finish**. As a result, **parallelloop.bpel** should appear in the Navigator view within the **parallel_loop** folder. The **parallelloop.bpel** tab should also appear in the ActiveBPEL Process Editor.

- In the Web References view expand the **parallelloop.wsdl** node and then **loopProcessPT**, which should contain the operation **processOrder**.
- Drag the **processOrder** operation from the Web References view to the **parallelloop.bpel** canvas displayed within the ActiveBPEL Process Editor. As a result, the **Define Partner Link Type** dialog should appear.
- In the **Define Partner Link Type** dialog click **Finish**. As a result, the **Operation:processOrder** dialog should appear.
- In the **Operation:processOrder** dialog make sure that the **Receive-Reply** option is selected and click **Finish**. As a result, the **Receive** and **Reply** activities will be automatically added to the **parallelloop.bpel** canvas.
- In the ActiveBPEL Process Editor expand the Palette by putting the mouse cursor on its tab.
- In the Palette choose **Sequence** from the **Container** section and put it on the canvas.
- Drag the **Receive** activity located on the canvas to the **Sequence** container created in the preceding step, so that the **Receive** activity is within the container.
- Drag the **Reply** activity located on the canvas to the **Sequence** container, so that the **Reply** activity is within the container and under the **Receive** activity.

Next, you add the `forEach` container, defining a loop in the process.

- In the Palette, choose **forEach** from the **Container** section and put it on the canvas within the already existing **Sequence** between the **Receive** and **Reply** activities added above.
- In the Palette, choose **Sequence** from the **Container** section and put it on the canvas within the **Scope** of the **forEach** activity added in the preceding step.

In the following four steps, you add the `Invoke` activity used to call the `orderProcessing` partner service.

- In the Web References view expand the **orderProcessing.wsdl** node and then **orderProcessingPortType**, which should contain the **startProcessing** operation.
- Drag the **startProcessing** operation from the Web References view to the **parallelloop.bpel** canvas, to the **Sequence** container within the **Scope** within the **forEach** container. As a result, the **Define Partner Link Type** dialog should appear.
- In the **Define Partner Link Type** dialog, click **Finish**. As a result, the **Operation:startProcessing** dialog should appear.

- In the **Operation:startProcessing** dialog, select the **invoke** option, and click **Finish**. As a result, the **Invoke** activity will be automatically added to the **parallelloop.bpel** canvas, within the **Sequence** container that is in turn within the **forEach** container.

Next, you need to add two Assign activities as described in the following steps.

- In the Palette, choose **Assign** from the **Activity** section and put it into the **Sequence** within the **forEach** scope in the area just above the **Invoke** activity added into this scope earlier.
- Then, put another **Assign** between the **forEach** and the **Reply** activity.

The following figure shows a fragment of the `parallel_loop` WS-BPEL process visual representation, representing the `forEach` container.

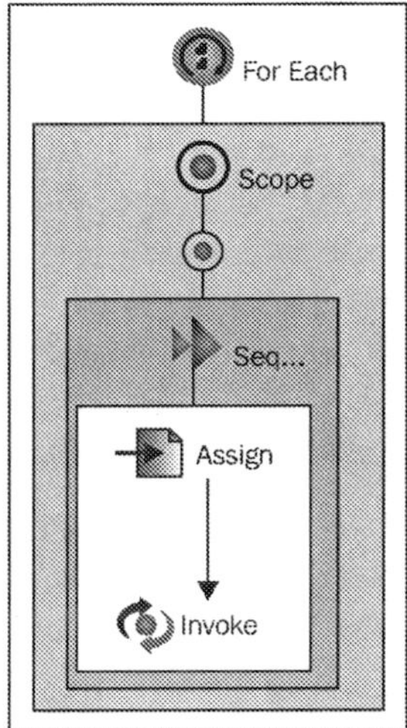

Now that you have placed all the required activities on the `parallelloop.bpel` canvas, it's time to set up their properties to the appropriate values. To do this, follow the steps shown below:

- On the canvas select the **Receive** activity located within the outer **Sequence** container, and open the Properties view by clicking the **Properties** tag located at the bottom part of the ActiveBPEL Designer perspective.
- In the Properties view, change the value of the **Create Instance** property to **Yes**.
- On the canvas select the **forEach** activity and get back to the Properties view.

- In the Properties view, set the properties of the **forEach** activity as follows: **Counter Name** to **mycounter**, **Final Counter Value** to **count($loopProcessRequestMessage.order/ns:items/ns:item)**, **Start Counter Value** to **'1'**.
- On the canvas select the **Assign** activity within the **Sequence** container located within the **forEach** scope and get back to the Properties view.
- In the Properties view, click to the **...** button to the right of the **Value** field of the **Copy Operations** property. As a result, the **Copy Operations** dialog should appear.
- In the **Copy Operations** dialog, click the **New...** button. As a result, the **Copy Operation** dialog should appear.
- In the **Copy Operation** dialog, set up properties as follows: in the **From** group: **Type** to **Variable**, **Variable** to **loopProcessRequestMessage**, **Part** to **order**, **Query** to **ns:items/ns:item[$mycounter]/ns:partId**; in the **To** group: **Type** to **Variable**, **Variable** to **orderProcessingInput**, **Part** to **partId**. Then, click **OK**.
- In the **Copy Operations** dialog, click the **New...** button. As a result, the **Copy Operation** dialog should appear again.
- In the **Copy Operation** dialog, set up properties as follows: in the **From** group: **Type** to **Variable**, **Variable** to **loopProcessRequestMessage**, **Part** to **order**, **Query** to **ns:items/ns:item[$mycounter]/ns:quantity**; in the **To** group: **Type** to **Variable**, **Variable** to **orderProcessingInput**, **Part** to **quantity**. Then, click **OK**.
- In the **Copy Operations** dialog, click **OK**.
- On the canvas, select the **Assign** activity located between the **forEach** and the **Reply** activity, and get back to the Properties view. Then, create a new operation as described above, setting the properties in the **Copy Operation** dialog as follows: in the **From** group: **Type** to **Literal**, **Literal Contents** to **Order processing completed successfully!**; in the **To** group, **Type** to **Variable**, **Variable** to **loopProcessResponseMessage**, **Part** to **payload.**

You have just finished the `parallel_loop` WS-BPEL process definition. Now you have to select **File->Save** to save the definition. Then, check out the Problems view to make sure that it displays no errors.

Creating the PDD Descriptor

The next step in building the `parallel_loop` WS-BPEL process service is to create the Process Deployment Descriptor document containing the deployment information. To do this, follow the as steps shown:

- In the Navigator view, right-click within the view to invoke the pop-up menu.
- In the pop-up menu, select **New->Deployment Descriptor** to open the **New Deployment Descriptor** dialog.
- In the **New Deployment Descriptor** dialog, open the **parallel_loop** folder and select the **parallelloop.bpel** document, so that it appears in the **Select BPEL Process file** textbox, and click **Next**.
- In the next screen of the **New Deployment Descriptor** dialog, make sure that the **Deployment Platform** field is set to **ActiveBPEL Engine** and click **Next**.
- In the next screen of the **New Deployment Descriptor** dialog, the **Partner Links** listbox should contain the following two items: **loopProcessLT**, and **orderProcessingLT**. Note that the status of the latter is set to the following: **Missing a partner role endpoint reference type**.
- In the **Partner Links** listbox, select **orderProcessingLT** and then move on to the **Partner Role** group. In the **Invoke Handler** combobox, select **address**, and in the **Endpoint type** combobox, select **static**. As a result, the following code should appear in the **Endpoint Reference** box:

```
<wsa:EndpointReference
  xmlns:wsa="http://schemas.xmlsoap.org/ws/2003/03/addressing"
  xmlns:s="FILL_IN_NAMESPACE">
  <wsa:Address>FILL_IN_ADDRESS_URI</wsa:Address>
  <wsa:ServiceName
    PortName="FILL_IN_PORT_NAME">s:FILL_IN_SERVICE_NAME
                              </wsa:ServiceName>
</wsa:EndpointReference>
```

- In the **Endpoint Reference** box, replace the above code with the following:

```
<wsa:EndpointReference
  xmlns:s="http://localhost/WebServices/wsdl/orderProcessing">
      <wsa:Address>
 http://localhost/WebServices/ch7/SoapServer_orderProcessing.php
       </wsa:Address>
      <wsa:ServiceName
     PortName="orderProcessingServicePort">s:
                         orderProcessingService</wsa:ServiceName>
</wsa:EndpointReference>
```

- In the **Partner Links** listbox, select **loopProcessLT**.
- On the **MyRole** tab, set the properties as follows: **Binding** to **RPC Encoded**, **Service** to **loopProcessService**, and click **Finish**.

As a result, the `parallelloop.pdd` descriptor document should appear in the `parallel_loop` folder in the Navigator and in the ActiveBPEL Process Editor, where you may review it.

Deploying the WS-BPEL Process Service

Now that you have created the `pdd` descriptor for the `parallel_loop` WS-BPEL process service, you are ready to deploy it.

Let's start by creating a separate folder within the `parallel_loop` folder, in which you will save the deployment archive file. To do this, perform the steps shown below:

- In the Navigator view right-click the **parallel_loop** folder.
- In the pop-up menu, select **New->Other...**
- In the first screen of the **New** wizard, select the node **Folder** in the box, and click Next.
- In the next screen of the wizard, make sure that the **Enter or select the parent folder** editbox contains **parallel_loop**. If so, enter **bpr** in the **Folder name** editbox and click **Finish**.

After you've performed the above steps, the **bpr** folder should appear within the **parallel_loop** folder in the Navigator.

To create the deployment archive for the `parallel_loop` WS-BPEL process service and deploy it to the ActiveBPEL Server, follow the steps shown below:

- In the Navigator view, right-click the **parallel_loop** folder.
- In the pop-up menu, select **Export...**
- In the **Export** dialog, make sure that **Business Process Archive File** under **ActiveBPEL** node is selected, and click **Next**.
- In the **Export Business Process Archive** dialog, make sure that the checkbox on the left to the **parallelloop.pdd** node within the **parallel_loop** folder is checked on.
- In the **Export Business Process Archive** dialog, move on to the **BPR file** textbox and enter the following into it: **C:\ActiveBPEL_Designer\Designer\eclipse\workspace\parallel_loop\bpr\parallelloop.bpr.**
- In the **Export Business Process Archive** dialog, move on to the **Deployment** group. In the **Type** combobox, select **File**. Next, move on to the **Deployment location** textbox and enter the following into it: **C:\ActiveBPEL_Designer\Server\ActiveBPEL_Tomcat\bpr** and click **Finish**.

This example assumes that you are using the ActiveBPEL Server shipped with your ActiveBPEL Designer. For more details, you can refer to the *Deploying the WS-BPELService to the ActiveBPEL Server Shipped with ActiveBPEL Designer* section in Chapter 6.

Once you've done all that, you should have the `parallel_loop` WS-BPEL process service deployed to the ActiveBPEL Server and ready for use. Before proceeding further, you might want to check to see if the WS-BPEL process service has been deployed to the ActiveBPEL engine successfully. For that, enter and then check out the following page generated by Axis:

`http://localhost:8081/active-bpel/services`

In this page, you should see the following nodes among others:

loopProcessService (wsdl)

processOrder

If you can see the above, the `parallel_loop` WS-BPEL process service discussed here has been deployed successfully.

It's important to understand that although the WS-BPEL process discussed here is called `parallel_loop`, the loop used in the process is still sequential. In the *Moving to a Parallel forEach* section later, you will see how to modify the `parallel_loop` WS-BPEL process to use the parallel form of the `forEach` activity.

Testing the Sequential Form of the forEach Activity

To test the `parallel_loop` WS-BPEL process service created and deployed as discussed in the preceding sections, you might use the `SoapClient_loopTest.php` SOAP client script shown below:

```
<?php
 //File: SoapClient_loopTest.php
 require_once "obj2Arr.php";
 $wsdl = "http://localhost:8081/active-
  bpel/services/loopProcessService?wsdl";
 $xmldoc = simplexml_load_file('purchaseOrder.xml');
 $xmlarr = obj2Arr($xmldoc);
 $client = new SoapClient($wsdl);
```

```
 try {
  print $result=$client->processOrder($xmlarr);
 }
 catch (SoapFault $exp) {
  print $exp->getMessage();
 }
?>
```

Note that this script uses the `obj2Arr` function defined in the `obj2Arr.php` script and discussed in the *Structuring Complex Data for Sending* section in Chapter 2. So, before you can run the above script, you should copy the `obj2Arr.php` script from the `WebServices/ch2` to the `WebServices/ch7` directory. Another requirement is a `purchaseOrder.xml` file. You might use the one discussed in the *Building the Service Requestor* section in Chapter 2. Again, it's assumed that you copy this file from the `WebServices/ch2` to the `WebServices/ch7` directory.

When executed, the above script invokes the `parallel_loop` WS-BPEL process service discussed here, passing the `purchaseOrder` XML document stored in the `purchaseOrder.xml` file as the payload in the request message.

The script should produce the following output:

```
Order processing completed successfully!
```

If you've used the `purchaseOrder` XML document representing a purchase order with two line items, as discussed in the *Building the Service Requestor* section in Chapter 2, then the execution of the above script should take at least 10 seconds, because in this case the `orderProcessing` partner service will be invoked twice in a sequential loop and each invocation will take at least 5 seconds.

If you recall from the *Defining the Partner Service Being Called from within the Loop* section, the `startProcessing` method in the `orderProcessing.php` PHP handler class uses the `sleep` function with `5` as the argument to delay the execution for 5 seconds.

After the execution of the `SoapClient_loopTest.php` script is completed, the `orderProcessingLog.txt` file should appear in the `WebServices\ch7` directory. At the moment, this file should contain two lines that might look like this:

```
Part id: 743 Quantity: 4 Current time: 22:08:04
Part id: 235 Quantity: 7 Current time: 22:08:09
```

As you can see, the first line appeared in the file 5 seconds before the second line. This is because the `forEach` loop used in the WS-BPEL process is performed in the sequential mode.

After each execution, another two lines similar to these ones should appear in the file.

Moving to a Parallel forEach

Now that you've seen the sequential form of the `forEach` activity in action, it's time to move on and modify the `parallel_loop` WS-BPEL process so that it invokes the `orderProcessing` partner services from within a parallel `forEach` activity. To achieve this goal, you should accomplish the following general steps:

- In the `parallel_loop` WS-BPEL process definition, set the **Parallel Execution Flag** property of the **forEach** activity to **Yes**.
- Remove the **orderProcessingInput** variable holding a message of **ns2: orderProcessingInput** from the global scope of the process and put it inside the **forEach** inner scope.
- Re-deploy the **parallel_loop** WS-BPEL process service.

To implement the first task from the above list, you should perform the following steps:

- In the ActiveBPEL Process Editor, click the **parallelloop.bpel** tab to move on to the visual representation of the **parallelloop.bpel** process definition.
- On the **parallelloop.bpel** canvas, select the **forEach** container and get to the Properties view.
- In the Properties view, set the **Parallel Execution Flag** property to **Yes**.
- To save the changes made, select **File->Save**.

To implement the second task, you should perform the following steps:

- In the ActiveBPEL Process Editor, click the **parallelloop.bpel** tab.
- In the Outline view, expand the following node: **parallelloop/Variables** and right-click the **orderProcessingInput** variable.
- In the pop-up menu, select **Cut**. As a result, the **orderProcessingInput** variable should disappear from the **Variables** node.
- In the Outline view, right-click the **parallelloop/Process Activities/ Sequence/For Each/Scope/Variables** node.

- In the pop-up menu, select **Paste**. As a result, the **orderProcessingInput** variable should appear in the **parallelloop/Process Activities/ Sequence/For Each/Scope/Variables** node. After you have pasted the **orderProcessingInput** variable, the Outline view might look like the following figure:

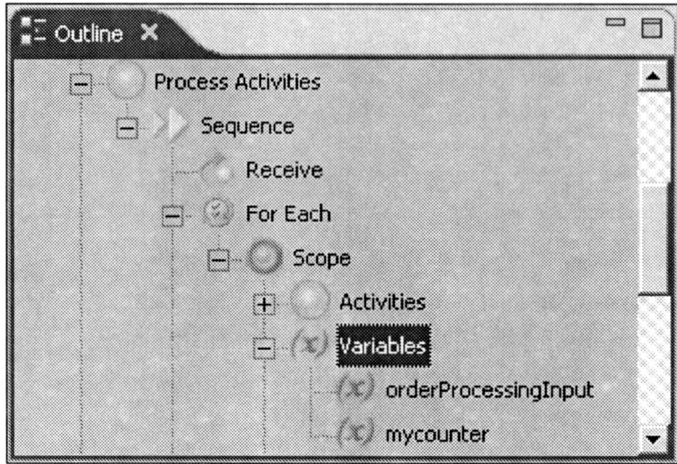

- To save the changes made, select **File->Save**.

Finally, to re-deploy the `parallel_loop` WS-BPEL process service, you should use the Export wizard as discussed in the *Deploying the WS-BPEL Process Service* section earlier.

Testing the Parallel forEach

To test the `parallel_loop` WS-BPEL process service updated as discussed in the preceding section, you can use the `SoapClient_loopTest.php` script discussed in the *Testing the Sequential Form of the forEach Activity* section earlier.

Now if you execute `SoapClient_loopTest.php`, it should take only 5 seconds to complete and not 10 seconds as before. This is because this time the `orderProcessing` service is invoked from within a parallel `forEach` activity, meaning loop iterations are performed in parallel and not sequentially.

When the execution is completed, two new lines should appear in the `orderProcessingLog.txt` file. They might look like the following:

```
Part id: 743 Quantity: 4 Current time: 22:15:24
Part id: 235 Quantity: 7 Current time: 22:15:24
```

As you can see, this time both of these lines were created at the same time. This just confirms that the `parallel_loop` WS-BPEL process invoked the `orderProcessing` service concurrently and not sequentially.

Building an Asynchronous WS-BPEL Process Service

The following sections take you through the process of building a kind of asynchronous echo example consisting of two WS-BPEL processes, where the first process makes an asynchronous call to the second one.

The example built as discussed in the next sections differs from the one depicted in the figure shown in the *Asynchronous Communication* section earlier in this chapter only in that the WS-BPEL process called asynchronously here doesn't make a synchronous call to a partner service built with PHP. This is done purely for the sake of simplicity.

Creating the Project

As usual, let's start by creating the project for the sample discussed here. To do this in ActiveBPEL Designer, you can follow the steps shown below:

- In ActiveBPEL Designer, select **File->New->Project**.
- In the first screen of the Wizard, choose **Project** and click **Next**.
- In the next window of the Wizard, specify **asyncSample** as the name for the project and click **Finish**.

After you have performed the above steps, you should see the `asyncSample` folder in the Navigator view, containing the `.project` document.

Unlike the examples discussed previously, this project will contain two WS-BPEL process definitions describing the process service called asynchronously and the process service making an asynchronous call. So, the project will contain two deployment descriptors.

Creating the WSDL Describing the Asynchronous WS-BPEL Process

The next step is to create the `async_called_service.wsdl` document. To do this, you should follow the steps shown below:

- Right-click the **asyncSample** folder in the Navigator.
- In the pop-up menu choose **New->Other...**
- In the first Wizard window choose **File** and click **Next**.
- In the second Wizard window, type in **async_called_service.wsdl** in the **File name:** textbox and click **Finish**. As a result, the **async_called_service.wsdl** document should appear in the **asyncSampl**e folder in the Navigator view.
- Right-click the newly created **async_called_service.wsdl** file in the Navigator view.
- On the pop-up menu, select **Open With\BPR Deployment Script Editor**. As a result, the empty **async_called_service.wsdl** document should appear in the ActiveBPEL Process Editor.
- In the **async_called_service.wsdl** canvas, insert the WSDL definition shown below:

```
<?xml version="1.0" encoding="UTF-8"?>
<wsdl:definitions targetNamespace="http://localhost:8081/active-
   bpel/services/async_called_service.wsdl"
  xmlns:impl="http://localhost:8081/active-
    bpel/services/async_called_service.wsdl"
  xmlns:wsdl="http://schemas.xmlsoap.org/wsdl/"
  xmlns:wsdlsoap="http://schemas.xmlsoap.org/wsdl/soap/"
  xmlns:xsd="http://www.w3.org/2001/XMLSchema">

   <wsdl:message name="initiateRequestMessage">
      <wsdl:part name="payload" type="xsd:string"/>
   </wsdl:message>

   <wsdl:portType name="AsyncCalledServicePT">
      <wsdl:operation name="initiateAsync">
         <wsdl:input message="impl:initiateRequestMessage"
            name="initiateRequestMessage"/>
      </wsdl:operation>
   </wsdl:portType>
   <wsdl:binding name="AsyncCalledServiceBinding"
      type="impl:AsyncCalledServicePT">
      <wsdlsoap:binding style="rpc"
```

```
            transport="http://schemas.xmlsoap.org/soap/http"/>
         <wsdl:operation name="initiateAsync">
            <wsdlsoap:operation soapAction=""/>
            <wsdl:input name="initiateRequestMessage">
               <wsdlsoap:body
             encodingStyle=
                         "http://schemas.xmlsoap.org/soap/encoding/"
              namespace="http://localhost:8081/active-
              bpel/services/async_called_service.wsdl"
                                         use="encoded"/>
            </wsdl:input>
         </wsdl:operation>
      </wsdl:binding>
      <wsdl:service name="AsyncCalledServiceService">
         <wsdl:port binding="impl:AsyncCalledServiceBinding"
            name="AsyncCalledServicePort">
            <wsdlsoap:address location=
               "http://localhost:8081/active-
               bpel/services/AsyncCalledService"/>
         </wsdl:port>
      </wsdl:service>
   </wsdl:definitions>
```

- Select **File->Save** to save the above `wsdl` document.

Note that this document contains binding information that will be used by the WS-BPEL process making an asynchronous call to this process. Including binding information in the WSDL document will allow you to call this process service much like any other partner service.

Creating the WSDL Describing the WS-BPEL Process Calling the Asynchronous WS-BPEL Process

In the same way as described in the preceding section, you should create the `async_ service.wsdl` document in the `asyncSample` project folder and fill it with the following code:

```
<?xml version="1.0" encoding="UTF-8"?>
<definitions name="async_service"
targetNamespace="http://localhost:8081/active-
  bpel/services/async_service.wsdl"
 xmlns:tns="http://localhost:8081/active-
```

```
    bpel/services/async_service.wsdl"
   xmlns:bpws="http://schemas.xmlsoap.org/ws/2003/03/business-process/"
   xmlns:plnk="http://schemas.xmlsoap.org/ws/2003/05/partner-link/"
   xmlns:xsd="http://www.w3.org/2001/XMLSchema"
   xmlns:ns2="http://localhost:8081/active-
    bpel/services/async_called_service.wsdl"
   xmlns="http://schemas.xmlsoap.org/wsdl/">
    <import namespace="http://localhost:8081/active-
    bpel/services/async_called_service.wsdl" location="project:/
  asyncSample/async_called_service.wsdl"/>

    <message name="asyncResponseMessage">
      <part name="payload" type="xsd:string"/>
    </message>
    <message name="asyncRequestMessage">
      <part name="payload" type="xsd:string"/>
    </message>
    <portType name="asyncCallbackPT">
      <operation name="onResult">
        <input message="tns:asyncResponseMessage"/>
      </operation>
    </portType>
    <portType name="AsyncCallerPT">
      <operation name="echo">
        <input message="tns:asyncRequestMessage"/>
        <output message="tns:asyncResponseMessage"/>
      </operation>
    </portType>

       <binding name="asyncRequesterServiceBinding"
          type="tns:asyncCallbackPT">
        <soap:binding style="rpc"
           transport="http://schemas.xmlsoap.org/soap/http"
            xmlns:soap="http://schemas.xmlsoap.org/wsdl/soap/"/>
        <operation name="onResult">
         <soap:operation soapAction="" style="rpc"
           xmlns:soap="http://schemas.xmlsoap.org/wsdl/soap/"/>
           <input>
          <soap:body encodingStyle=
            "http://schemas.xmlsoap.org/soap/encoding/" use="encoded"
             xmlns:soap="http://schemas.xmlsoap.org/wsdl/soap/"/>
           </input>
        </operation>
     </binding>
```

```
    <service name="asyncRequesterService">
        <port binding="tns:asyncRequesterServiceBinding"
          name="asyncRequesterServicePort">
         <soap:address location="http://localhost:8081/active-
           bpel/services/asyncRequesterService"
           xmlns:soap="http://schemas.xmlsoap.org/wsdl/soap/"/>
        </port>
    </service>
  <bpws:property name="asyncCorrelationData" type="xsd:string"/>
    <plnk:partnerLinkType name="AsyncCallerPLT">
     <plnk:role name="AsyncCallerRole">
        <plnk:portType name="tns:AsyncCallerPT"/>
     </plnk:role>
    </plnk:partnerLinkType>
    <plnk:partnerLinkType name="asyncRequester">
     <plnk:role name="asyncProvider">
        <plnk:portType name="ns2:AsyncCalledServicePT"/>
     </plnk:role>
     <plnk:role name="asyncReplyReceiver">
        <plnk:portType name="tns:asyncCallbackPT"/>
     </plnk:role>
    </plnk:partnerLinkType>
  <bpws:propertyAlias messageType="ns2:initiateRequestMessage"
     part="payload" propertyName="tns:asyncCorrelationData"/>
  <bpws:propertyAlias messageType="tns:asyncResponseMessage"
    part="payload" propertyName="tns:asyncCorrelationData" />
   </definitions>
```

Note that this WSDL definition contains binding information describing the `asyncRequesterService` service exposing the `on Result` operation. This operation will be used by the called process to make an asynchronous callback. This is the simplest way in which you can provide information about the calling process to be used by the called service for the callback to be made.

Also note that the above definition doesn't contain binding information for the `AsyncCallerPT` port type providing the `echo` operation that will be used by a client consuming the calling WS-BPEL process. As you learned in the preceding examples, this information will be automatically generated during run time.

In the above definition, the highlighted lines are the ones in which you define the property to be used for message correlation, and the property aliases. Later, when defining the WS-BPEL definition for the calling process, you will define the correlation set based on the correlation property defined here.

Now that you have the `async_service.wsdl` and `async_called_service.wsdl` documents created, you should add them as Web References in the same way as described in the *Adding WSDL Definitions as Web References* section earlier in this chapter.

Creating the Process Definition for the Calling Process

Now you are ready to build the WS-BPEL process definition for the `async_service` process service that will be invoked by a client and then asynchronously call the `async_called_service` process service created as discussed in the *Creating the Process Definition for the Called Process* section later. To do this, you should perform the following steps:

- In the Navigator view, right-click the **asyncSample** folder and select **New->BPEL Process**.
- In the Wizard dialog, enter **async_service.bpel** in the **File name** box and click **Finish**. As a result, **async_service.bpel** should appear in the Navigator view within the **asyncSample** folder. The **async_service.bpel** tab should also appear in the ActiveBPEL Process Editor.
- In the ActiveBPEL Process Editor, expand the Palette by putting the mouse cursor on its tab.
- In the Palette, choose **Sequence** from the **Container** section and put it on the **async_service.bpel** canvas.

First, you create the `Receive/Reply` activity pair that is required to synchronously communicate with a client consuming the WS-BPEL process created here.

- In the Web References view, expand the **async_service.wsdl** node and then **AsyncCallerPT**, which should contain the **echo** operation.
- Drag the **echo** operation from the Web References view to the **async_service.bpel** canvas displayed within the ActiveBPEL Process Editor, putting it into the **Sequence** container placed on the canvas earlier. As a result, the **Define Partner Link Type** dialog should appear.
- In the **Define Partner Link Type** dialog, click **Finish**. As a result, the **Operation:echo** dialog should appear.
- In the **Operation:echo** dialog, make sure that the **Receive-Reply** option is selected and click **Finish**. As a result, the **Receive** and **Reply** activities will be automatically added to the **async_service.bpel** canvas, into the **Sequence** container added earlier.

Next, you need to add the **Assign** activity whose **Copy** operation, added as discussed later in this section, will be used to initialize the message variable to be asynchronously sent to the called WS-BPEL process discussed in the next section.

- In the Palette, choose **Assign** from the **Activity** section and put it into the **Sequence** container between the **Receive** and **Reply** activities added earlier.

Then, you have to add the **Invoke** activity required to make an asynchronous call to the called WS-BPEL process created as discussed in the next section.

- In the Web References view, expand the **async_called_service.wsdl** node and then **AsyncCalledServicePT**, which should contain the operation **initiateAsync**.
- Drag the **initiateAsync** operation from the Web References view to the **async_service.bpel** canvas displayed within the ActiveBPEL Process Editor, putting it into the **Sequence** container between the **Assign** and **Reply** activities. As a result, the **Define Partner Link Type** dialog should appear.
- In the **Define Partner Link Type** dialog, click **Finish**. As a result, the **Operation:initiateAsync** dialog should appear.
- In the **Operation:initiateAsync** dialog, select the **Invoke** option, and click **Finish**. As a result, the **Invoke** activity should appear in the **async_service.bpel** canvas within the **Sequence** container between the **Assign** and **Reply** activities.

Next, you need to add the `Receive` activity that will be used to receive the asynchronous call sent back by the called WS-BPEL process.

- In the Web References view, expand the **async_service.wsdl** node and then **asyncCallbackPT**, which should contain the operation **onResult**.
- Drag the **onResult** operation from the Web References view to the **async_service.bpel** canvas displayed within the ActiveBPEL Process Editor, putting it into the **Sequence** container between the **Invoke** and **Reply** activities. As a result, the **Define Partner Link Type** dialog should appear.
- In the **Define Partner Link Type** dialog, click **Finish**. As a result, the **Operation:onResult** dialog should appear.
- In the **Operation:onResult** dialog, make sure that the **Receive** option is selected and click **Finish**. As a result, the `Receive` activity should appear in the **async_service.bpel** canvas within the **Sequence** container between the **Invoke** and **Reply** activities.

The next step in building the `async_service` WS-BPEL process service discussed here is to set up the properties of the activities added to the `async_service.bpel` canvas as discussed above. To do this, perform the following steps:

- On the **async_service.bpel** canvas, select the upper **Receive** activity and move on to the Properties view.
- In the Properties view, change the value of the **Create Instance** property to **Yes**.
- On the canvas, double-click the **Assign** activity. As a result, the **Copy Operations** dialog should appear.
- In the **Copy Operations** dialog, click the **New...** button. As a result, the **Copy Operation** dialog should appear.
- In the **Copy Operation** dialog, set up properties as follows: in the **From** group: **Type** to **Variable**, **Variable** to **asyncRequestMessage**, **Part** to **payload**; in the **To** group, **Type** to **Variable**, **Variable** to **initiateRequestMessage**, **Part** to **payload**. Then, click **OK**.
- In the **Copy Operations** dialog, click **OK**.
- Select **File->Save** to save the changes made and to make sure that everything is OK so far, check out the Problems view; it should display no errors.

Next, you need to set up the correlation set that will be used to correlate asynchronous responses arriving from the called WS-BPEL process.

- In the ActiveBPEL Process Editor, make sure that the **async_service.bpel** canvas is selected.
- Move on to the Outline view.
- In the Outline view, right-click the **Correlation Sets** node.
- In the pop-up menu, select **Add->Declaration->Correlation Set**. As a result, the Correlation Set Properties dialog should appear.
- In the Correlation Set Properties dialog, select the **ns1:asyncCorrelationData** item in the Available Properties box and click the **>>** button to move **ns1: asyncCorrelationData** to the **Selected Correlation Set Properties** box. Then, click **OK**. As a result, **CS1** should appear in the Correlations Sets in the Outline view.
- On the **async_service.bpel** canvas, click the **Invoke** activity and get to the Properties view.
- In the Properties view, click the **...** button to the right of the **Value** field of the **Correlations** property. As a result the Correlation Sets dialog should appear.

- In the Correlation Sets dialog, click the **Add** button. As a result, a new correlation set containing **none** in each field should appear.
- In the newly created record in the Correlation Sets dialog, double-click the **Correlation Set** field and then select **CS1** from the list. Then, in the **Initiate** field select **Yes**. Finally, select **Request** in the **Pattern** field and click **OK**. As a result, the **Correlation Set** property should be set to **(CS1, Yes, Request).**
- On the **async_service.bpel** canvas, click the **Receive** activity located under the **Invoke** activity and get back to the Properties view.
- In the Properties view, click the **...** button to the right of the **Value** field of the **Correlations** property. As a result the Correlation Sets dialog should appear.
- In the Correlation Sets dialog, click the **Add** button. As a result, a new correlation set containing **none** in each field should appear.
- In the newly created record in the Correlation Sets dialog, double-click the **Correlation Set** field and then select **CS1** from the list. Then, in the **Initiate** field, select **No** and click **OK**. As a result, the **Correlation Set** property should be set to **(CS1, No).**
- Select **File->Save** to save the changes made. Make sure that the Problems view displays no errors.

You have just finished the WS-BPEL process definition `async_service` for the process that will make an asynchronous call to the `async_called_service` WS-BPEL process created as discussed in the next section.

Creating the Process Definition for the Called Process

Now let's build the WS-BPEL process definition for the `async_called_service` process service that will be asynchronously called by the `async_service` process service created as discussed in the preceding section later. To do this, perform the following steps:

- In the Navigator view, right-click the **asyncSample** folder and select **New->BPEL Process**.
- In the Wizard dialog, enter **async_called_server.bpel** in the **File name** box and click **Finish**. As a result, **async_called_server.bpel** should appear in the Navigator view within the `asyncSample` folder. The **async_called_server.bpel** tab should also appear in the ActiveBPEL Process Editor.
- In the ActiveBPEL Process Editor, expand the Palette, choose **Sequence** from the **Container** section, and put it on the **async_called_service.bpel** canvas.

- In the Web References view, expand the **async_called_server.wsdl** node and then **AsyncCalledServicePT**, which should contain the operation **initiateAsync**.
- Drag the **initiateAsync** operation from the Web References view to the **async_called_server.bpel** canvas, putting it into the **Sequence** container created earlier. As a result, the **Define Partner Link Type** dialog should appear.
- In the **Define Partner Link Type** dialog, click **Finish**. As a result, the **Operation:initiateAsync** dialog should appear.
- In the **Operation:initiateAsync** dialog, make sure that the **Receive** option is selected, and click **Finish**. As a result, the **Receive** activity will be automatically added to the **async_called_server.bpel** canvas within the **Sequence** container.
- In the Palette, choose **Assign** from the **Activity** section and put it into the **Sequence** container under the **Receive** activity.
- In the ActiveBPEL Process Editor, expand the Palette, choose **Wait** from the **Activity** section and put it on the canvas into the **Sequence** container just under the **Assign** activity added in the preceding step.
- In the Web References view, expand the **async_server.wsdl** node and then **asyncCallbackPT**, which should contain the operation **onResult**.
- Drag the **onResult** operation from the Web References view to the **async_called_server.bpel** canvas, putting it into the **Sequence** container under the **Wait** activity. As a result, the **Define Partner Link Type** dialog should appear.
- In the **Define Partner Link Type** dialog, click **Finish**. As a result, the **Operation:onResult** dialog should appear.
- In the **Operation:onResult** dialog, make sure that the **Invoke** option is selected and click **Finish**. As a result, the **Invoke** activity will be automatically added to the **async_called_server.bpel** canvas within the **Sequence** container.

Now that you have placed all the required activities on the `async_called_service.bpel` canvas, you have to set up the properties of these activities. To do this, follow the steps below:

- On the **async_called_service.bpel** canvas, select the **Receive** activity, and move on to the Properties view.
- In the Properties view, change the value of the **Create Instance** property to **Yes**.

- On the canvas, double-click the **Assign** activity. As a result, the **Copy Operations** dialog should appear.
- In the **Copy Operations** dialog, click the **New...** button. As a result, the **Copy Operation** dialog should appear.
- In the **Copy Operation** dialog, set up properties as follows: in the **From** group: **Type** to **Variable**, **Variable** to **initiateRequestMessage**, **Part** to **payload**; in the **To** group, **Type** to **Variable**, **Variable** to **asyncResponseMessage**, **Part** to **payload**. Then, click **OK**.
- In the **Copy Operations** dialog, click **OK**.
- On the canvas, select the **Wait** activity and get to the Properties view.
- In the Properties view, set the **Wait Type** property to **Duration**, and **Wait Expression** to **'PT5S'**.
- Select **File | Save** to save the changes made and to make sure that everything is OK. check out the Problems view; it should display no errors.

Creating the PDD Descriptor for the Calling Process

The next step in building the example is to create the Process Deployment Descriptor document containing the deployment information for the `async_service` WS-BPEL process service created as discussed in the *Creating the Process Definition for the Calling Process* section earlier. To do this, perform the following steps:

- In the Navigator view, right-click within the view to invoke the pop-up menu.
- In the pop-up menu, select **New->Deployment Descriptor** to open the **New Deployment Descriptor** dialog.
- In the **New Deployment Descriptor** dialog, open the **asyncSample** folder and select the **async_service.bpel** document, so that it appears in the **Select BPEL Process file** textbox, and click **Next**.
- In the next screen of the **New Deployment Descriptor** dialog, make sure that the **Deployment Platform** field is set to **ActiveBPEL Engine** and click **Next**.
- In the next screen of the **New Deployment Descriptor** dialog, the **Partner Links** listbox should contain the following two items: **AsyncCallerPLT** and **asyncRequester**. Note that the status of the latter is set to the following: **Missing a partner role endpoint reference type**.
- In the **Partner Links** listbox, select the **AsyncCallerPLT**.
- On the **MyRole** tab, set the properties as follows: **Binding** to **RPC Encoded**, **Service** to **AsyncCallerService**.

- In the **Partner Links** listbox, select the **asyncRequester** and then move on to the **Partner Role** group. In the **Invoke Handler** combobox, select **address**, and in the **Endpoint type** combobox, select **static**. As a result, the following code should appear in the **Endpoint Reference** box:

```
<wsa:EndpointReference
  xmlns:wsa="http://schemas.xmlsoap.org/ws/2003/03/addressing"
  xmlns:s="FILL_IN_NAMESPACE">
  <wsa:Address>FILL_IN_ADDRESS_URI</wsa:Address>
  <wsa:ServiceName
    PortName="FILL_IN_PORT_NAME">s:FILL_IN_SERVICE_NAME
        </wsa:ServiceName>
</wsa:EndpointReference>
```

- In the **Endpoint Reference** box, replace the above code with the following:

```
<wsa:EndpointReference xmlns:cs="http://localhost:8081/active-
   bpel/services/async_called_service.wsdl"
   xmlns:wsa="http://schemas.xmlsoap.org/ws/2003/03/addressing">
       <wsa:Address>http://localhost:8081/active-
         bpel/services/AsyncCalledServiceService</wsa:Address>
       <wsa:ServiceName
     PortName="AsyncCalledServicePort">cs:
AsyncCalledServiceService
          </wsa:ServiceName>
             <wsa:ReferenceProperties>
                     <wsa:ReplyTo>
                        <wsa:ServiceName
                           xmlns:s="http://localhost:8081/active-
                           bpel/services/async_service.wsdl"
                           PortName="asyncRequesterServicePort"
                           >s:asyncRequesterService
                           </wsa:ServiceName>
               <wsa:Address>http://localhost:8081/active-
                 bpel/services/asyncRequesterService</wsa:Address>
                    </wsa:ReplyTo>
             </wsa:ReferenceProperties>
</wsa:EndpointReference>
```

- On the **MyRole** tab, set the properties as follows: **Binding** to **RPC Encoded**, **Service** to **asyncRequesterService**, and click **Finish**.

As a result, the `async_service.pdd` descriptor document should appear in the `asyncSample` folder in the Navigator, and in the ActiveBPEL Process Editor, where you may review it. If you click the `async_service.pdd` document in the Navigator, you should see the following code in the ActiveBPEL Process Editor:

```
<?xml version="1.0" encoding="UTF-8"?>
<process xmlns="http://schemas.active-endpoints.com/pdd/2006/08/pdd.
xsd" xmlns:bpelns="http://async_service" xmlns:wsa="http://schemas.
xmlsoap.org/ws/2003/03/addressing"
  location="asyncSample/async_service.bpel" name="bpelns:async_
service">
   <partnerLinks>
      <partnerLink name="AsyncCallerPLT">
         <myRole allowedRoles="" binding="RPC"
           service="AsyncCallerService"/>
      </partnerLink>
      <partnerLink name="asyncRequester">
         <partnerRole endpointReference="static"
           invokeHandler="default:Address">
            <wsa:EndpointReference
              xmlns:cs="http://localhost:8081/active-
              bpel/services/async_called_service.wsdl"
            xmlns:wsa="http://schemas.xmlsoap.org/ws/2003/03/
addressing">
       <wsa:Address>http://localhost:8081/active-
         bpel/services/AsyncCalledServiceService</wsa:Address>
       <wsa:ServiceName
         PortName="AsyncCalledServicePort">cs:
AsyncCalledServiceService
           </wsa:ServiceName>
      <wsa:ReferenceProperties>
               <wsa:ReplyTo>
                  <wsa:ServiceName
                    xmlns:s="http://localhost:8081/active-
                    bpel/services/async_service.wsdl"
                    PortName="asyncRequesterServicePort"
                    >s:asyncRequesterService</wsa:ServiceName>
        <wsa:Address>http://localhost:8081/active-
          bpel/services/asyncRequesterService</wsa:Address>
              </wsa:ReplyTo>
      </wsa:ReferenceProperties>
</wsa:EndpointReference>
         </partnerRole>
         <myRole allowedRoles="" binding="RPC"
           service="asyncRequesterService"/>
      </partnerLink>
   </partnerLinks>
   <references>
      <wsdl location="project:/asyncSample/async_service.wsdl"
        namespace="http://localhost:8081/active-
```

```
            bpel/services/async_service.wsdl"/>
        <wsdl location="project:/asyncSample/async_called_service.wsdl"
           namespace="http://localhost:8081/active-
             bpel/services/async_called_service.wsdl"/>
    </references>
</process>
```

In this deployment descriptor, note the use of the `<wsa:ReferenceProperties>` element (highlighted) within the `<wsa:EndpointReference>` element describing the `asyncRequester` partner link. The `<wsa:ReplyTo>` used within `<wsa:ReferenceProperties>` contains information about the service to which the process service called asynchronously should send a response. In this example, you specify that the service called asynchronously should send a response back to the calling service, in particular, to the `asyncRequesterService` service.

Creating the PDD Descriptor for the Called Process

The next step in building the sample is to create the Process Deployment Descriptor document containing the deployment information for the `async_called_service` WS-BPEL process service created as discussed in the *Creating the Process Definition for the Called Process* section earlier. To do this, perform the following steps:

- In the Navigator view, right-click within the view to invoke the pop-up menu.
- In the pop-up menu, select **New->Deployment Descriptor** to open the **New Deployment Descriptor** dialog.
- In the **New Deployment Descriptor** dialog, open the **asyncSample** folder and select the **async_called_service.bpel** document, so that it appears in the **Select BPEL Process file** textbox, and click **Next**.
- In the next screen of the **New Deployment Descriptor** dialog, make sure that the **Deployment Platform** field is set to **ActiveBPEL Engine**, and click **Next**.
- In the next screen of the **New Deployment Descriptor** dialog, the **Partner Links** listbox should contain only the item **asyncRequester**. Note that the status of this partner link is set to the following: **Missing a partner role endpoint reference type**.
- In the **Partner Links** listbox, select **asyncRequester** and then move on to the **Partner Role** group. In the **Invoke Handler** combobox, select **(System Default)** and in the **Endpoint type** combobox, select **invoke**.
- On the **MyRole** tab, set the properties as follows: **Binding** to **RPC Encoded**, **Service** to **AsyncCalledServiceService**, and click **Finish**.

As a result, the `async_called_service.pdd` descriptor document should appear in the `asyncSample` folder in the Navigator. Now if you click `async_called_service.pdd` in the Navigator, you should see the following code in the ActiveBPEL Process Editor:

```
<?xml version="1.0" encoding="UTF-8"?>
<process xmlns="http://schemas.active-endpoints.com/pdd/2006/08/pdd.
xsd" xmlns:bpelns="http://async_called_service" xmlns:wsa="http://
schemas.xmlsoap.org/ws/2003/03/addressing"
  location="asyncSample/async_called_service.bpel"
  name="bpelns:async_called_service">
   <partnerLinks>
      <partnerLink name="asyncRequester">
         <partnerRole endpointReference="invoker"/>
         <myRole allowedRoles="" binding="RPC" service="AsyncCalledSer
viceService"/>
      </partnerLink>
   </partnerLinks>
   <references>
      <wsdl location="project:/asyncSample/async_service.wsdl"
        namespace="http://localhost:8081/active-
          bpel/services/async_service.wsdl"/>
      <wsdl location="project:/asyncSample/async_called_service.wsdl"
        namespace="http://localhost:8081/active-
        bpel/services/async_called_service.wsdl"/>
   </references>
</process>
```

Deploying the Example

Now that you have created the deployment descriptors for the WS-BPEL processes discussed here, you can deploy the example. To do this, perform the following steps:

- In the Navigator view, right-click the **asyncSample** folder.
- In the pop-up menu, select **New->Other...**
- In the first screen of the **New** Wizard, select the **Folder** node in the box and click **Next**.
- In the next screen of the Wizard, make sure that the **Enter or select the parent folder** editbox contains **asyncSample**. If so, enter **bpr** in the **Folder name** editbox and click **Finish**.
- In the Navigator view, right-click the **asyncSample** folder.
- In the pop-up menu, select **Export...**

- In the **Export** dialog, make sure that **Business Process Archive File** under the **ActiveBPEL** node is selected and click **Next**.
- In the **Export Business Process Archive** dialog, make sure that both the **async_service.pdd** and **async_called_service.pdd** nodes within the **asyncSample** folder are checked on.
- In the **Export Business Process Archive** dialog, move on to the **BPR file** textbox and enter the following into it: **C:\ActiveBPEL_Designer\Designer\eclipse\workspace\asyncSample\bpr\asyncSample.bpr**.
- In the **Export Business Process Archive** dialog, move on to the **Deployment** group. In the **Type** combobox, select **File**. Next, move on to the **Deployment location** textbox and enter the following into it: **C:\ActiveBPEL_Designer\Server\ActiveBPEL_Tomcat\bpr** and click **Finish**.

This example assumes that you are using the ActiveBPEL Server shipped with your ActiveBPEL Designer. For more details, you can refer to the *Deploying the WS-BPEL Service to the ActiveBPEL Server Shipped with ActiveBPEL Designer* section in Chapter 6.

Now if you open the ActiveBPEL Admin:

```
http://localhost:8081/BpelAdmin
```

and then click the **Deployment Log** link in the ActiveBPEL Admin page, you should see the log regarding the preceding deployment, which might look as follows:

```
06/27/2007 11:15:11:406 [asyncSample.bpr] [async_service.wsdl] Added resource mapped to location hint: project:/asyncSample/async_service.wsdl
06/27/2007 11:15:11:406 [asyncSample.bpr] [async_called_service.wsdl] Added resource mapped to location hint: project:/asyncSample/async_called_service.wsdl
06/27/2007 11:15:11:453 [asyncSample.bpr] [async_called_service.pdd] Successfully deployed.
06/27/2007 11:15:11:484 [asyncSample.bpr] [async_service.pdd] Successfully deployed.
```

Testing the Asynchronous Example

To test the example built and deployed as discussed in preceding sections, you might create and then execute the following PHP script:

```
<?php
 //File: SoapClient_asyncSample.php
 $wsdl = "http://localhost:8081/active-
```

```
  bpel/services/AsyncCallerService?wsdl";
 $client = new SoapClient($wsdl);
 try {
  print $result=$client->echo('Hello!');
 }
 catch (SoapFault $exp) {
  print $exp->getMessage();
 }
?>
```

When executed, the above script should produce the following output after about a 5 second delay:

```
Hello!
```

The amount of delay depends on the value of the `Wait Expression` property of the `Wait` activity used in the `async_called_service` WS-BPEL process created as discussed in the *Creating the Process Definition for the Called Process* section.

If Something Goes Wrong

As you no doubt have realized, the task of building a WS-BPEL application using asynchronous communication may be a challenge. What if your asynchronous application doesn't work as expected and you cannot understand what the problem is?

Let's turn back to the example discussed in the preceding sections and try to simulate a problem. For example, you might remove the `<wsa:ReferenceProperties>` element from the `async_service.pdd` descriptor discussed in the *Creating the PDD Descriptor for the Calling Process* section earlier. The code to be removed is highlighted in the listing of `async_service.pdd` provided in that section. Then, re-deploy the sample as discussed in the *Deploying the Example* section. You should have no problem with deployment. However, when you run the `SoapClient_asyncSample.php` script discussed in the preceding section, it hangs and eventually times out.

In this particular case, you know what the problem is—the calling process doesn't provide information about where to send a callback anymore and therefore, the called process cannot make a response. However, let's try to figure out the problem using the ActiveBPEL Admin tool installed by the default during the ActiveBPEL engine installation, and discussed in the *Deploying the WS-BPEL Process Service* section in Chapter 5.

First, you should load the ActiveBPEL Admin. The address you enter might look as follows, assuming that you have installed your Tomcat server at `http://localhost:8081`:

```
http://localhost:8081/BpelAdmin
```

Once it has been loaded, click the **Configuration** link. Then, on the Configuration page, set **Logging Level** to **Full** and click the **Update** button.

Assuming you have run the `SoapClient_asyncSample.php` script, click the **Active Processes** link in the ActiveBPEL Admin. As a result, you should see the Active Processes page, which might look like the following figure:

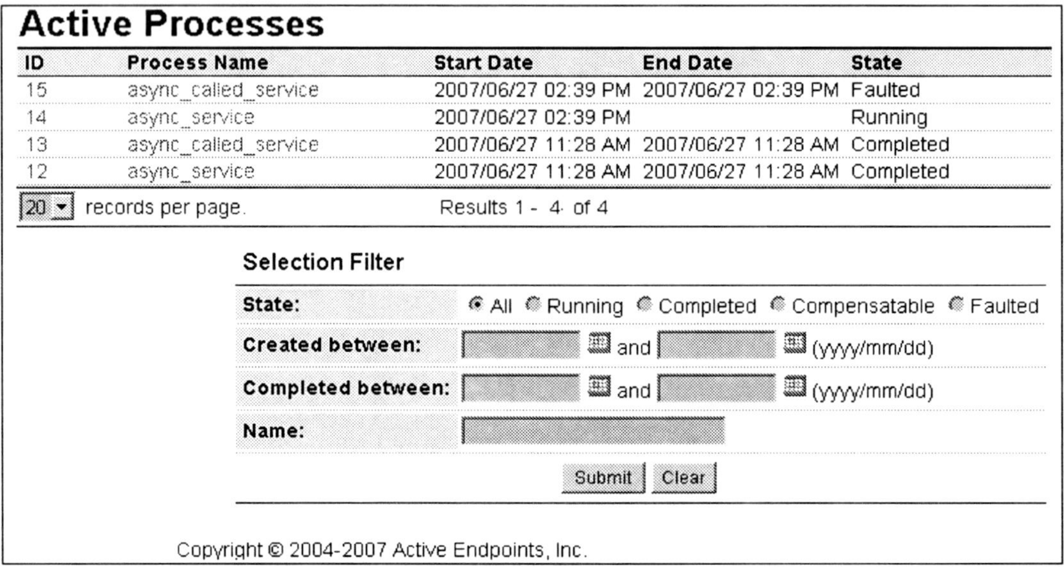

Now, on the Active Processes page, if you click the **async_called_service** link whose state is **Faulted**, you should see the page shown in the following figure:

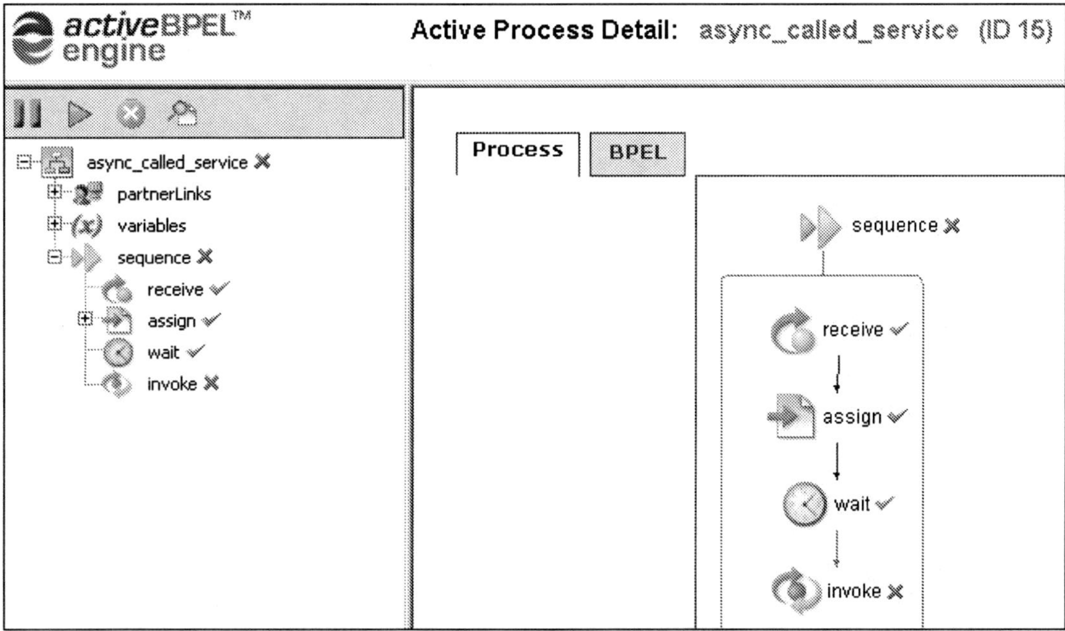

As you can see in the figure, the problem occurred during processing the `Invoke` activity of the `async_called_service` process.

Now that you know where in the process the problem occurs, you might want to get more detailed information. To do this, you can select the **Invoke** activity on the Active Process Detail page and then click the **View Process Log** button that can be found in the panel located at the top-left corner of the page. As a result, the Process Details page should appear, providing the log information that might look as follows:

```
[15][2007-06-27 14:39:03.734] : Executing [/process]
[15][2007-06-27 14:39:03.734] : Executing [/process/sequence]
[15][2007-06-27 14:39:03.734] : Executing [/process/sequence/receive]
[15][2007-06-27 14:39:03.750] : Completed normally [/process/
                                 sequence/receive]
[15][2007-06-27 14:39:03.750] : Executing [/process/sequence/assign]
[15][2007-06-27 14:39:03.750] : Completed normally [/process/
                                 sequence/assign]
[15][2007-06-27 14:39:03.750] : Executing [/process/sequence/wait]
[15][2007-06-27 14:39:03.750] Wait :  = Wed Jun 27 14:39:08 PDT 2007
                                       [/process/sequence/wait]
```

```
    [15][2007-06-27 14:39:08.750] : Completed normally [/process/sequence/
    wait]
    [15][2007-06-27 14:39:08.750] : Executing [/process/sequence/invoke]
[15][2007-06-27 14:39:08.765] : Completed with fault: systemError (Error
calling invoke: No service name for endpoint reference.) :  [/process/
sequence/invoke] [f]
    [15][2007-06-27 14:39:08.781] : Completed with fault: systemError
    (...) :  [/process/sequence] [f]
    [15][2007-06-27 14:39:08.781] : Executing [/process_
    ImplicitFaultHandler]
    [15][2007-06-27 14:39:08.781] : Executing [/process_
    ImplicitFaultHandler_ImplicitCompensateActivity]
    [15][2007-06-27 14:39:08.781] : Completed normally [/process_
    ImplicitFaultHandler_ImplicitCompensateActivity]
    [15][2007-06-27 14:39:08.781] : Completed normally [/process_
    ImplicitFaultHandler]
    [15][2007-06-27 14:39:08.781] : Completed with fault: systemError
    (...) :  [/process] [f]
```

As you can see in the above log, the `Invoke` activity failed because of `No service name for endpoint reference`. To make the sample work again, you should go back to the `async_service.pdd` deployment descriptor and replace the `<wsa:ReferenceProperties>` element and then re-deploy the sample as discussed earlier.

Summary

In this chapter, we looked at concurrency, synchronization, and asynchronous communication in WS-BPEL. With the help of simple examples, you learned why parallel processing is more efficient than sequential processing, and how to organize parallel repetitive execution in a loop. Then, we moved to asynchronous communication, looking at how two WS_BPEL processes may interact asynchronously. At the end, you learned how the ActiveBPEL Admin tool installed by default with the ActiveBPEL engine might be used for finding problems that arise during execution of WS-BPEL processes.

A
Setting Up Your Work Environment

To follow the examples provided in this book, you need to have a few pieces of software installed and working properly in your system. In particular, you have to install the following software components:

- A Web/PHP server with the PHP SOAP extension enabled
- Oracle Database XE or MySQL server
- Apache Tomcat 5.x
- ActiveBPEL engine
- ActiveBPEL Designer

It's important to note that all the above software can be downloaded and used for free. This appendix takes you through the steps needed to install and configure the above software components.

Installing Apache HTTP Server

Before you can install PHP, you must have a Web server installed and working in your system. Although PHP has support for most of the Web servers worth mentioning, Apache/PHP remains the most popular combination among developers.

The Apache HTTP server is distributed under the Apache License, a free software/open-source license whose current version can be found on the **Licenses** page of the Apache website at: `http://www.apache.org/licenses/`.

You can download the Apache HTTP server from the download page of the Apache website at: `http://httpd.apache.org/download.cgi`.

Installing Apache is a very easy process. On Windows, if you have downloaded the version of Apache for Windows with the `.msi` extension (the recommended way), you just run the Apache `.msi` file and then follow the Wizard. On Unix-like systems, once you have downloaded a source version of the Apache HTTP server, you perform the standard operations that you normally deal with when it comes to installing new software from sources: extract, configure, compile, and install.

Once you have Apache installed and configured, you can start it. On Windows, Apache is normally run as a service. You can configure the service startup by choosing `Automatic`, `Manual`, or `Disabled`. On Unix-like systems, Apache, the `httpd` program, is run as a demon. It is recommended that you use the `apachectl` control script to invoke the `httpd` executable:

```
# /usr/local/apache2/bin/apachectl start
```

To make sure that your Web server is up and running on your machine, open your Web browser to the URL: `http://localhost/`.

The following figure shows the default page of Apache Web server.

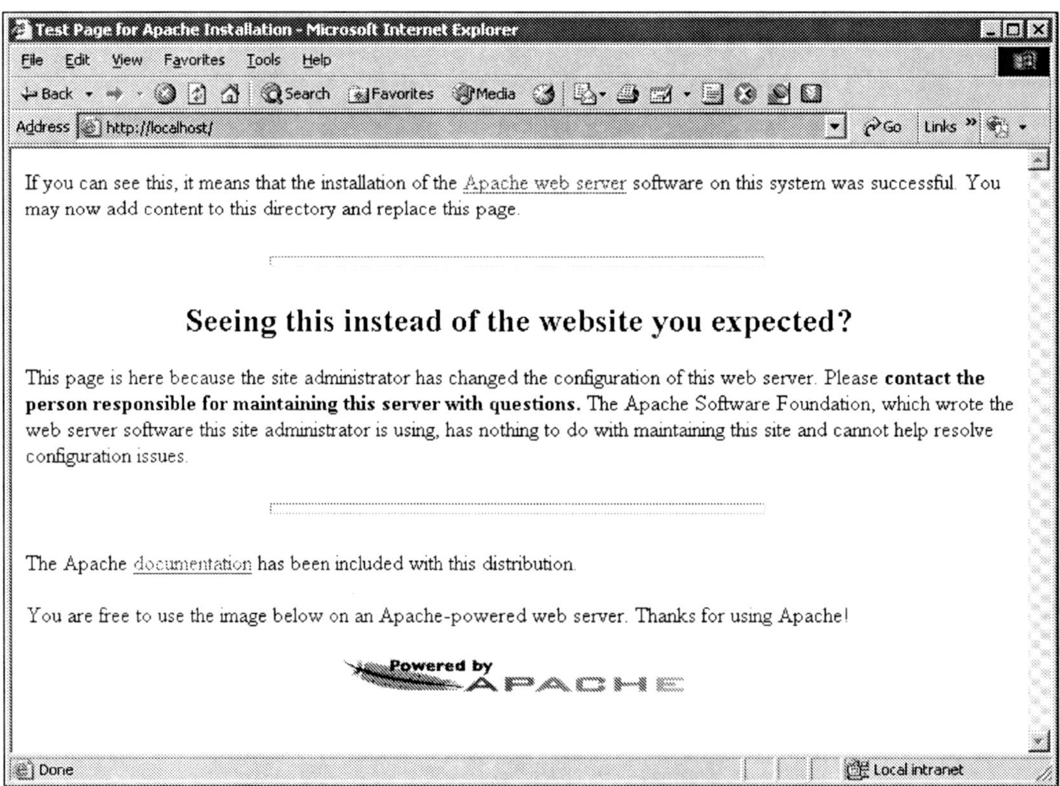

Now that you have your Web server up and running, you can move on to the next step, obtaining and installing PHP.

Installing PHP

The current recommended releases of PHP are available for download from the downloads page of the php.net site at:

```
http://www.php.net/downloads.php
```

From this page, you can download the latest stable release of PHP 5 and then follow the steps shown below to install PHP in your system. For further assistance along the way, you may consult the *Installation and Configuration* manual available on the php.net website at: `http://www.php.net/manual/install.php`. Alternatively, you might read the `install.txt` file that is shipped with PHP.

Installing PHP on Windows

Here are the basic installation steps for PHP 5 on Windows:

- Extract the distribution file into the `c:\php` directory.
- Add the `C:\php` directory to the PATH to make `php5ts.dll` available to the Web server modules.
- Rename `php.ini-recommended` to `php.ini`.
- In `php.ini`, set the `doc_root` to your Apache `htdocs` directory. For example:

  ```
  doc_root = c:\Program Files\Apache Group\Apache2\htdocs
  ```

- In `php.ini`, uncomment the SOAP extension line in the `Windows Extensions` section:

  ```
  extension=php_soap.dll
  ```

- In `php.ini`, uncomment the OCI8 extension line:

  ```
  extension=php_oci8.dll
  ```

It is assumed here that you will be using an Oracle database when following the book examples. If you're going to use MySQL, you need to uncomment the `extension=php_mysql.dll` and `extension=php_mysqli.dll` lines in `php.ini` instead.

- In `php.ini`, set the `extension_dir` directive to the directory in which the extention DLLs reside:

  ```
  extension_dir= c:\php\ext
  ```

- In the Apache `httpd.conf` configuration file, to install PHP as an Apache module, insert two lines that lookslike this:

  ```
  LoadModule php5_module "c:/php/php5apache2.dll"
  AddType application/x-httpd-php .php
  ```

- In the Apache `httpd.conf` configuration file, configure the path to `php.ini`:

  ```
  PHPIniDir "C:/php"
  ```

- Restart Apache.

As an alternative to the above manual installation, you might use the Windows PHP installer that is also available from the downloads page of the php.net website.

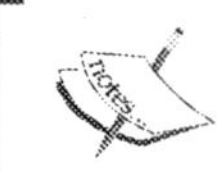

> Although the Windows PHP installer is the fastest way to make PHP work, it doesn't allow you to set every option as you might want to. So, using the installer isn't the recommended method for installing PHP.

Once you have PHP installed on your Windows system, you might want to set some extensions for added functionality. It is important to note that many extensions are built into the Windows version of PHP. To use these extensions, you just uncomment them in the `php.ini` configuration file—no additional DLLs are required. However, some of the extensions require extra DLLs to work. For example, the PHP OCI8 extension needs the Oracle Client libraries if you have your Oracle database and Web server running on different machines. The above steps assume that you have both the database and Web server installed on the same computer. In this case, you already have all the required Oracle components, and no Instant Client is required.

Installing PHP on Unix-Like Systems

Here are basic installation steps for PHP 5 on Unix-like systems:

- Extract the distribution file:

  ```
  # gunzip php-5xx.tar.gz
  # tar -xvf php-5xx.tar
  ```

- Change dir to the directory containing the PHP sources:

  ```
  # cd php-5xx
  ```

- Set the `ORACLE_HOME` environment variable:

```
# export
ORACLE_HOME=/usr/lib/oracle/xe/app/oracle/product/10.2.0/server
```

- Configure your PHP installation:

```
# ./configure \
--with-oci8=$ORACLE_HOME \
--with-apxs2=/usr/local/apache2/bin/apxs \
--with-config-file-path=/usr/local/apache2/conf \
--enable-sigchild
--enable-soap
```

It is assumed here that you will be using an Oracle database XE when following the book examples. However, if you're going to use MySQL, you must use `--with-mysql` and `--with-mysqli=mysql_config_path/mysql_config` configuration options, where `mysql_config_path` is the path to the `mysql_config` program that comes with MySQL.

- Compile and then install PHP:

```
# make
# make install
```

- Set up `php.ini`:

```
# cp php.ini-dist /usr/local/lib/php.ini
```

- Edit the `httpd.conf` Apache configuration file to load the PHP module into Apache:

```
LoadModule php5_module modules/libphp5.so
```

- In `httpd.conf`, add handlers for files with the `.php` and `.phps` extensions:

```
AddType application/x-httpd-php .php
AddType application/x-httpd-php-source .phps
```

- Restart Apache:

```
# usr/local/apache2/bin/apachectl start
```

By now you should have a working Apache/PHP Web server.

Installing MySQL

Installing MySQL is a very straightforward process. The following sections explain how to install MySQL on Windows and Linux.

Installing MySQL on Windows

Here are the basic steps to install MySQL on Windows:

- Download the MySQL distribution from `http://dev.mysql.com/downloads/mysql/5.1.html`, picking up the `Windows Essentials` file from the **Windows downloads** section on the page. This file contains the minimum set of files needed to install MySQL, including the Configuration Wizard. If you want to download the package containing all the MySQL components, consider the **Complete Package** available on the same page and packed within a ZIP archive: `mysql-5.1.xx-beta-win32.zip`.

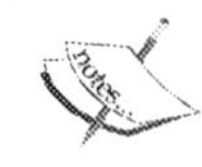

The above URL assumes that you download MySQL 5.1. At the time of this writing, though, MySQL 6.0 is available. You can download MySQL 6.0 from `http://dev.mysql.com/downloads/mysql/6.0.html`.

- Execute the downloaded `mysql-essential-5.1.xx-beta-win32.msi` or `Setup.exe` extracted from `mysql-5.1.xx-beta-win32.zip`, in order to install MySQL.
- In the **Setup Type** page of the MySQL Installation Wizard, you have to choose **Typical**, **Complete**, or **Custom**. To be able to follow the book examples, you might choose the **Typical** installation type.
- In the **Confirmation** dialog, click the **Install** button to start the installation.
- After the installation is completed, on the final screen of the installer, make sure that the **Configure the MySQL Server now** checkbox is checked, and click **Finish**. As a result, the MySQL Configuration Wizard will be launched.
- In the **Configuration Type** dialog of the Configuration Wizard, choose the **Standard Configuration** option if you want to get started with MySQL quickly.

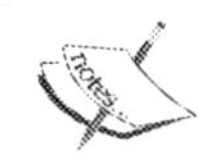

The following steps assume that you choose the **Standard Configuration** option in the preceding step.

- In the next dialog, make sure that the **Install As Windows Service** option is selected.
- In the next dialog, you have to set the root password.
- In the final dialog on the MySQL Configuration Wizard, click the **Execute** button to start the configuration process.

Once you've completed these steps, you should have the MySQL server up and running on your machine.

Installing MySQL on Linux

Here are basic installation steps for MySQL on Linux:

- Download the MySQL distribution from `http://dev.mysql.com/downloads/mysql/5.1.html`, picking up RPMs for `Server` and `Client` from the appropriate section. These packages are required for a standard minimal installation.

Using the RPM packages is the recommended way to install MySQL on Linux. The following steps assume that your Linux supports RPMs.

- Perform the following commands to install the above RPMs:

```
# rpm -i MySQL-server-VERSION.i386.rpm
# rpm -i MySQL-client-VERSION.i386.rpm
```

By default, the server RPM creates and adds the entries to `/etc/init.d/`, which are required to start the `mysqld` server automatically at boot time.

- After the installation, it is highly recommended that you assign a password to the anonymous accounts:

```
# mysql -u root
mysql> SET PASSWORD FOR ''@'localhost' = PASSWORD('new_pswd');
mysql> SET PASSWORD FOR ''@'your_hostname' = PASSWORD('new_pswd');
```

Once you've completed these steps, you should have the MySQL server up and running on your machine.

Installing Oracle Database Express Edition (XE)

If you want to use a free edition of Oracle database, consider Oracle Database Express Edition—a lightweight Oracle database that is free to develop, deploy, and distribute. The following sections describe the basic installation steps for this Oracle Database edition on Windows and on Linux.

Once you have completed the following installation steps, you will have an Oracle Database XE Server (including an Oracle database), Oracle Database XE Client, and SQL*Plus installed on your computer.

Installing Oracle Database XE on Windows

Here are the installation steps for Oracle Database 10g Express Edition on Windows:

- Log in to Windows as a user of the Administrators group.
- Make sure that the `ORACLE_HOME` environment variable is not set in your system. Otherwise delete it. This can be done from the `System Properties` dialog, which can be invoked from **Control Panel/System**.
- Double-click the Oracle Database XE installation executable downloaded from OTN to run Oracle Database XE Server installer.

The following figure shows the screen of the Oracle Database XE Server installer after you run it.

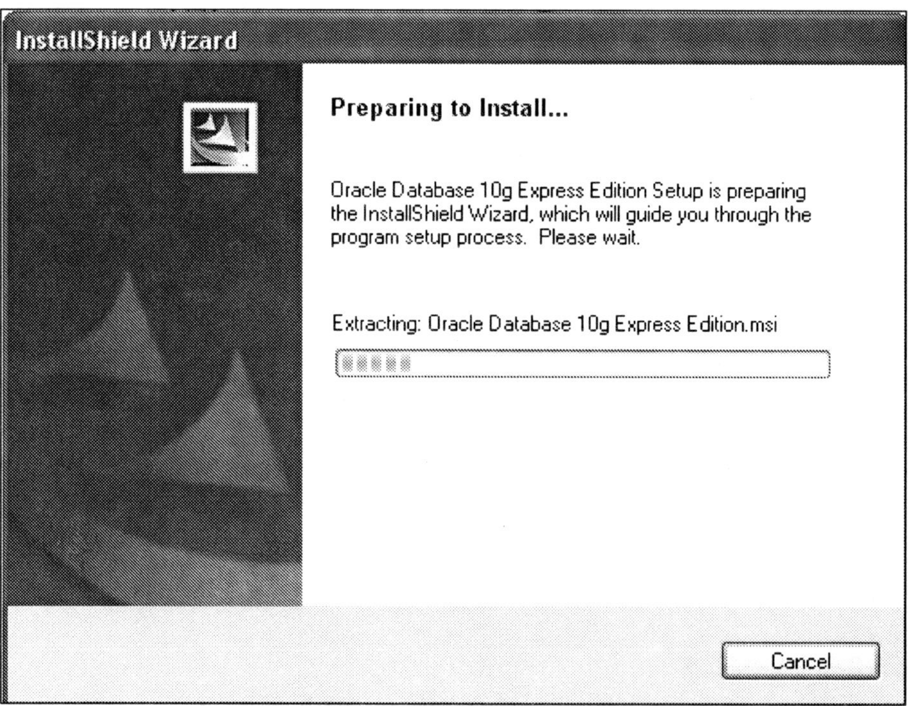

- In the Welcome window of the Wizard, click **Next**.
- In the **License Agreement window**, click **I accept** and then click **Next**.

- In the **Choose Destination Location** window, choose the directory for installation and click **Next**.
- If at least one of the port numbers 1521, 2030, and 8080 is already in use in your system, you will be prompted to enter an available port number. Otherwise, the above numbers will be used automatically.
- In the **Specify Database Passwords** window, enter the passwords for the **SYS** and **SYSTEM** database accounts and click **Next**.
- In the **Summary** window, click **Install** to proceed to installation, or **Back** to turn back and modify the settings.
- After the installation is complete, click **Finish**.

That is it. Your database is up and ready for use now.

Installing Oracle Database XE on Linux

Here are the installation steps for Oracle Database 10g Express Edition on Linux:

- Log in to your computer as root.
- Change directory to the one in which you downloaded the Oracle Database XE `oracle-xe-10.2.0.1-1.0.i386.rpm` installation executable and install the RPM: `$ rpm -ivh oracle-xe-10.2.0.1-1.0.i386.rpm`.
- When prompted, run the following command to configure the database: `$ /etc/init.d/oracle-xe configure`.
- When entering configuration information, accept the default port numbers for the Oracle Database XE graphical user interface and Oracle database listener: **8080** and **1521** respectively. Also, enter and confirm the passwords for the `SYS` and `SYSTEM` default user accounts.

If, when configuring the database, you select **Yes** when asked whether you want the database to automatically start along with the computer, then the database is up and ready for use now. Otherwise you have to start it manually as follows: `$ /etc/init.d/oracle-xe start`.

Installing Apache Tomcat 5.5

Before you can install ActiveBPEL engine, you need to install a servlet container. According to the documentation, ActiveBPEL engine has been tested with Apache Tomcat 5.x. The following sections discuss how to install Apache Tomcat 5.5 on Windows and on Linux.

For details concerning installing Apache Tomcat 5.5 for running on different platforms, you can refer to `http://tomcat.apache.org/tomcat-5.5-doc/setup.html`.

Installing Apache Tomcat 5.5 on Windows

Here are the steps for installing Tomcat 5.5 on Windows:

- Download Apache Tomcat 5.5 from `http://tomcat.apache.org/download-55.cgi`, picking up the `apache-tomcat-5.5.xx.exe` file from the **Binary Distribution/Core** section.
- Run the downloaded `apache-tomcat-5.5.xx.exe` to launch the Installation Wizard.
- In the **Choose Components** dialog, make sure that the **Normal** installation option is selected, and click **Next**.
- In the **Configuration** dialog, you may need to change the value of the **HTTP 1.1/Connector Port**, set by default to **8080**. For example, if you have an Oracle database installed on your machine, Oracle XML DB HTTP server may already use port 8080. So, you may choose 8081 for the Tomcat server port. In this page, also make sure to specify the password for the Administrator user.
- In the next dialog, you have to specify the path to the J2SE 5 JRE installed on your computer, and click **Install**.

After the above steps are completed, you will have the Tomcat server installed in your system as a Windows service.

Installing Apache Tomcat 5.5 on Linux

Here are the steps for installing Tomcat 5.5 on Linux:

- Get the binary distribution of Apache Tomcat 5.5 from `http://tomcat.apache.org/download-55.cgi`. In particular, you will need the `Core tar.gz` package.
- Unzip the package as follows:

```
# tar -xzf apache-tomcat-5.5.xx.tar.gz
```

- Create a simlink to the Tomcat directory:

```
# ln -s apache-tomcat-5.5.xx tomcat
```

Before you can run Tomcat, you should have the `CATALINA_HOME` environment variable set to the directory in which you installed Tomcat, say, `/opt/tomcat`, and `JAVA_HOME` set to the base path of the JDK installed in your system.

- If you need to change the Tomcat port set by default to `8080`, open the `CATALINA_HOME/conf/server.xml` configuration file and set the `port` attribute of the `Connector` element to an appropriate value, say `8081`.
- To start Tomcat, you should run the following script:

```
# $CATALINA_HOME/bin/startup.sh
```

After performing these steps, you should have the Tomcat 5.5 servlet container installed and configured on your machine.

Installing the ActiveBPEL Engine

As mentioned, you need to have a servlet container installed and properly configured before you can install the ActiveBPEL engine. The next steps assume that you have installed and configured Tomcat 5.x as discussed in the preceding sections.

For detailed information on how to install the ActiveBPEL engine, you can refer to `http://www.active-endpoints.com/installation-guide.htm`.

- To download the ActiveBPEL engine, you can start with the home page of the Active Endpoints website at `http://www.active-endpoints.com/`. In this page, click the **ActiveBPEL Open Source Engine** link under the **free downloads** section. As a result, you will be taken to the Download Terms and Conditions page, where you should examine **Terms of Use**. If you select **Accept** and then click the **Submit** button, you will be directed to the ActiveBPEL Engine Download page, on which you can select the latest version of the ActiveBPEL engine and download the ZIP archive.
- Extract the distribution from the downloaded archive, putting the files in any directory.

- Change the current directory to the one containing the ActiveBPEL engine files extracted in the preceding step, and run the `install.bat` script on Windows or `install.sh` on Linux. This might look like the following on Windows:

```
Command Prompt
C:\activebpel3>
C:\activebpel3>
C:\activebpel3>install.bat


Creating BPR Directory
Copying Libraries...
Copying Configuration files...
Deploying Web-Applications...
Deploying Remote Debugging BPR...


Congratulations, you have just installed ActiveBPEL.
Access http://localhost:8080/BpelAdmin to test and administer your installation.


C:\activebpel3>
C:\activebpel3>_
```

- Restart Apache:

```
# usr/local/apache2/bin/apachectl start
```

These steps complete the ActiveBPEL engine installation. The ActiveBPEL engine will automatically start with the servlet container.

The install script executed in the penultimate step creates the `$CATALINA_HOME/bpr` directory to which you will deploy your ActiveBPEL projects as `bpr` archives, as discussed in Chapter 5.

Installing ActiveBPEL Designer

Here are the general steps to install ActiveBPEL Designer:

- To download ActiveBPEL Designer, you can start with the home page of the Active Endpoints website at `http://www.active-endpoints.com/`. In this page, click the **ActiveBPEL Designer** link under the **free downloads** section. As a result, you will be taken to the **Product Download Form** page, where you should select the **ActiveBPEL Designer x.x** checkbox and fill out the form below and then click the **Submit** button. As a result, you will be directed to the **Thank you** page.

- The **Thank you** page informs you that your submission has been received and, upon approval, the product download and installation instructions will be sent to the email address submitted.
- To complete the installation, follow the steps in the email received.

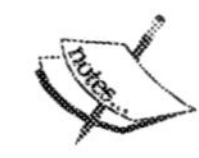

Note that the ActiveBPEL Designer ships with the Tomcat/ActiveBPEL Server. So, if you've installed ActiveBPEL Designer, you don't need to have a separate Tomcat/ActiveBPEL Server installation.

By now, you should have installed all the software components required to follow the examples provided in the book.

Index

A

C

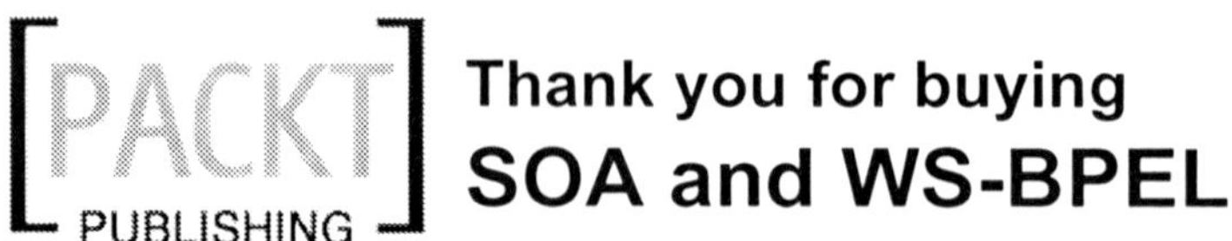

Thank you for buying
SOA and WS-BPEL

Packt Open Source Project Royalties

When we sell a book written on an Open Source project, we pay a royalty directly to that project. Therefore by purchasing SOA and WS-BPEL, Packt will have given some of the money received to Active Endpoints, the company behind the open source ActiveBPEL server, whose examples are used throughout this book.

In the long term, we see ourselves and you—customers and readers of our books—as part of the Open Source ecosystem, providing sustainable revenue for the projects we publish on. Our aim at Packt is to establish publishing royalties as an essential part of the service and support a business model that sustains Open Source.

If you're working with an Open Source project that you would like us to publish on, and subsequently pay royalties to, please get in touch with us.

Writing for Packt

We welcome all inquiries from people who are interested in authoring. Book proposals should be sent to `authors@packtpub.com`. If your book idea is still at an early stage and you would like to discuss it first before writing a formal book proposal, contact us; one of our commissioning editors will get in touch with you.

We're not just looking for published authors; if you have strong technical skills but no writing experience, our experienced editors can help you develop a writing career, or simply get some additional reward for your expertise.

About Packt Publishing

Packt, pronounced 'packed', published its first book "Mastering phpMyAdmin for Effective MySQL Management" in April 2004 and subsequently continued to specialize in publishing highly focused books on specific technologies and solutions.

Our books and publications share the experiences of your fellow IT professionals in adapting and customizing today's systems, applications, and frameworks. Our solution-based books give you the knowledge and power to customize the software and technologies you're using to get the job done. Packt books are more specific and less general than the IT books you have seen in the past. Our unique business model allows us to bring you more focused information, giving you more of what you need to know, and less of what you don't.

Packt is a modern, yet unique publishing company, which focuses on producing quality, cutting-edge books for communities of developers, administrators, and newbies alike. For more information, please visit our website: `www.PacktPub.com`.

Business Process Execution Language for Web Services 2nd Edition

ISBN: 1-904811-81-7 Paperback: 350 pages

An Architects and Developers Guide to BPEL and BPEL4WS

1. Architecture, syntax, development and composition of Business Processes and Services using BPEL
2. Advanced BPEL features such as compensation, concurrency, links, scopes, events, dynamic partner links, and correlations
3. Oracle BPEL Process Manager and BPEL Designer Microsoft BizTalk Server as a BPEL server

---

BPEL Cookbook: Best Practices for SOA-based integration and composite applications development

ISBN: 1-904811-33-7 Paperback: 188 pages

Ten practical real-world case studies combining business process management and web services orchestration

1. Real-world BPEL recipes for SOA integration and Composite Application development
2. Combining business process management and web services orchestration
3. Techniques and best practices with downloadable code samples from ten real-world case studies

Please check **www.PacktPub.com** for information on our titles

Printed in the United Kingdom
by Lightning Source UK Ltd.
131862UK00001B/249/A

9 781847 192707